C#

Your visual blueprint for building .NET applications

by Eric Butow and Tommy Ryan

Visual

From

maranGraphics®

&

Hungry Minds™

Best-Selling Books • Digital Downloads • e-Books • Answer Networks • e-Newsletters • Branded Web Sites • e-Learning

New York, NY • Cleveland, OH • Indianapolis, IN

C#: Your visual blueprint for building .NET applications

Published by
Hungry Minds, Inc.
909 Third Avenue
New York, NY 10022

maranGraphics, Inc.
5755 Coopers Avenue
Mississauga, Ontario, Canada
L4Z 1R9

Library of Congress Control Number: 2001089361
ISBN: 0-7645-3601-X
Printed in the United States of America

10 9 8 7 6 5 4 3 2

1V/QW/RR/QR/IN

Distributed in the United States by Hungry Minds, Inc.

Distributed by CDG Books Canada Inc. for Canada; by Transworld Publishers Limited in the United Kingdom; by IDG Norge Books for Norway; by IDG Sweden Books for Sweden; by IDG Books Australia Publishing Corporation Pty. Ltd. for Australia and New Zealand; by TransQuest Publishers Pte Ltd. for Singapore, Malaysia, Thailand, Indonesia, and Hong Kong; by Gotop Information Inc. for Taiwan; by ICG Muse, Inc. for Japan; by Intersoft for South Africa; by Eyrolles for France; by International Thomson Publishing for Germany, Austria and Switzerland; by Distribuidora Cuspide for Argentina; by LR International for Brazil; by Galileo Libros for Chile; by Ediciones ZETA S.C.R. Ltda. for Peru; by WS Computer Publishing Corporation, Inc., for the Philippines; by Contemporanea de Ediciones for Venezuela; by Express Computer Distributors for the Caribbean and West Indies; by Micronesia Media Distributor, Inc. for Micronesia; by Chips Computadoras S.A. de C.V. for Mexico; by Editorial Norma de Panama S.A. for Panama; by American Bookshops for Finland.

For U.S. corporate orders, please call maranGraphics at 800-469-6616 or fax 905-890-9434.

For general information on Hungry Minds' products and services please contact our Customer Care Department within the U.S. at 800-762-2974, outside the U.S. at 317-572-3993 or fax 317-572-4002.

For sales inquiries and reseller information, including discounts, premium and bulk quantity sales, and foreign-language translations, please contact our Customer Care Department at 800-434-3422, fax 317-572-4002, or write to Hungry Minds, Inc., Attn: Customer Care Department, 10475 Crosspoint Boulevard, Indianapolis, IN 46256.

For information on licensing foreign or domestic rights, please contact our Sub-Rights Customer Care Department at 212-884-5000.

For information on using Hungry Minds' products and services in the classroom or for ordering examination copies, please contact our Educational Sales Department at 800-434-2086 or fax 317-572-4005.

For press review copies, author interviews, or other publicity information, please contact our Public Relations department at 317-572-3168 or fax 317-572-4168.

For authorization to photocopy items for corporate, personal, or educational use, please contact Copyright Clearance Center, 222 Rosewood Drive, Danvers, MA 01923, or fax 978-750-4470.

Screen shots displayed in this book are based on pre-released software and are subject to change.

Trademark Acknowledgments

Permissions

maranGraphics

 is a trademark of Hungry Minds, Inc.

U.S. Corporate Sales	U.S. Trade Sales
Contact maranGraphics at (800) 469-6616 or fax (905) 890-9434.	Contact Hungry Minds at (800) 434-3422 or (317) 572-4002.

C#

Your visual blueprint for building .NET applications

maranGraphics is a family-run business located near Toronto, Canada.

At **maranGraphics**, we believe in producing great computer books — one book at a time.

maranGraphics has been producing high-technology products for over 25 years, which enables us to offer the computer book community a unique communication process.

Our computer books use an integrated communication process, which is very different from the approach used in other computer books. Each spread is, in essence, a flow chart — the text and screen shots are totally incorporated into the layout of the spread. Introductory text and helpful tips complete the learning experience.

maranGraphics' approach encourages the left and right sides of the brain to work together — resulting in faster orientation and greater memory retention.

Above all, we are very proud of the handcrafted nature of our books. Our carefully-chosen writers are experts in their fields, and spend countless hours researching and organizing the content for each topic. Our artists rebuild every screen shot to provide the best clarity possible, making our screen shots the most precise and easiest to read in the industry. We strive for perfection, and believe that the time spent handcrafting each element results in the best computer books money can buy.

Thank you for purchasing this book. We hope you enjoy it!

Sincerely,

Robert Maran

President

maranGraphics

Rob@maran.com

www.maran.com

www.hungryminds.com/visual

CREDITS

Acquisitions, Editorial, and Media Development

Project Editor
Jade L. Williams

Acquisitions Editor
Jen Dorsey

Product Development Supervisor
Lindsay Sandman

Copy Editor
Timothy Borek

Technical Editor
Namir Shammas

Editorial Manager
Rev Mengle

Media Development Manager
Laura Carpenter

Permissions Editor
Carmen Krikorian

Media Development Specialist
Megan Decraene

Media Development Coordinator
Marisa E. Pearman

Production

Book Design
maranGraphics®

Production Coordinator
Nancee Reeves

Layout
LeAndra Johnson, Adam Mancilla,
Kristin Pickett, Jill Piscitelli

Screen Artists
Ronda David-Burroughs,
David E. Gregory, Mark Harris,
Jill A. Proll

Cover Illustration
Russ Marini

Proofreader
Laura Albert, Laura L. Bowman,
John Greenough,
Andy Hollandbeck, Carl Pierce,
Dwight Ramsey

Indexer
TECHBOOKS Production Services

Special Help
Microsoft Corporation,
Richard Graves

ACKNOWLEDGMENTS

Hungry Minds Technology Publishing Group: Richard Swadley, Senior Vice President and Publisher; Mary Bednarek, Vice President and Publisher, Networking; Joseph Wikert, Vice President and Publisher, Web Development Group; Mary C. Corder, Editorial Director, Dummies Technology; Andy Cummings, Publishing Director, Dummies Technology; Barry Pruett, Publishing Director, Visual/Graphic Design

Hungry Minds Manufacturing: Ivor Parker, Vice President, Manufacturing

Hungry Minds Marketing: John Helmus, Assistant Vice President, Director of Marketing

Hungry Minds Production for Branded Press: Debbie Stailey, Production Director

Hungry Minds Sales: Michael Violano, Vice President, International Sales and Sub Rights

ABOUT THE AUTHORS

Eric Butow

Eric Butow is the president and CEO of E.E. Butow Communications LLC (www.eebutow.com), a technical communications firm based in Roseville, California. Butow is also the author of several other Hungry Minds books including *Master Visually Windows 2000 Server* and *FrontPage 2002 Weekend Crash Course*.

Tommy Ryan

Tommy graduated from Clemson University with a degree in Chemical Engineering. Tommy has over twelve years of technical project experience and over four years of pure software consulting experience. Tommy's area of focus is consulting for Microsoft Internet technologies, including Microsoft ASP.NET, C#, SQL Server 2000, BizTalk Server 2000, and Commerce Server 2000. Tommy has used several processes for software development, including variants of the Rational Unified Process, and the Microsoft Solutions Framework. On projects, Tommy normally plays the role of Technical Lead. His certifications include MCSE, MCSD, MCT, and MCP + Internet. Tommy is a recent instructor of MSF Design, Microsoft Site Server 3.0, Interdev 6.0, and several of the Visual Basic 6.0 classes. Tommy is the co-author of *"ASP.NET: Your visual blueprint for creating Web applications on the .NET framework."* You can contact Tommy at tryan@threewill.com and learn more about him at http://www.threewill.com/people/tryan.

AUTHORS' ACKNOWLEDGMENTS

Eric Butow

I would like to acknowledge all the people at Hungry Minds for their support and assistance in making this book possible, especially my editors, Jade Williams and Jennifer Dorsey.

Tommy Ryan

I would like to thank all of the hardworking people at Hungry Minds for helping produce this book – especially Jennifer Dorsey, Jade Williams, and other editors. Jennifer made sure that I was paid (very important) and Jade did an great job of explaining how to write with style.

To the clients that I have worked with during the past couple of years for challenging me to be a better consultant, including Nick Callivas, Brian Blinco, Jay Dalke, Bob Hughes, and Harwell Thrasher.

To my previous employer, Extreme Logic, and all of the exceptional people that helped me mature as a consultant and an educator. This company has taught me some valuable lessons.

To my colleagues at W.L. Gore and Associates that helped me start my professional career, including John Reaney, Mark Fundakowsi, Diccon Bancroft, John Pysczynski, Pamela Perdue, Erik Nightwine, Debra Raup, Ray Edmanson, Bob McCleary, Lawrence Anderson, Wolfgang Holma and Line 10 Production Team; the WinCC Team at Siemens that helped me in my transition to being a Microsoft geek, including Emilio Matt, Rob Bohm, Bob Meads, Rich Miceli, Charlie Moore, Jörg Allmendinger, and Rene Wolf; and my extended family and friends for the support in the things outside of work, including Joe and Rosemarie Markiewicz, Robert and Donna Philips, Joe and Jan Markiewicz, and Chuck and Mary Hanson, Rob and Gretchen Pfeiffer, and Reverend Joe Ciccone CSP.

A special thanks goes out to my brother, Danny Ryan. Without Danny, I would not have taken or completed my contribution to this book or the ASP.NET book. Danny is an excellent partner and I look forward to the great things that we will accomplish in our new endeavors.

Eric Butow

To my grandmother, who instilled her Midwestern sensibilities in me.

Tommy Ryan

To my eternal partner, Linda.

TABLE OF CONTENTS

4) PROGRAMMING C# BUILDING BLOCKS

5) WORKING WITH TYPES AND INTERFACES

6) PROGRAMMING METHODS AND EVENTS

TABLE OF CONTENTS

7) USING ARRAYS

8) WORKING WITH STRINGS

9) ACCESSING PROPERTIES

10) BUILDING FORMS

11) PROGRAMMING WEB APPLICATIONS

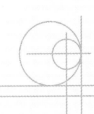
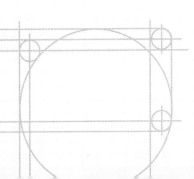

TABLE OF CONTENTS

15) WORKING WITH ERRORS

APPENDIX A) C# QUICK REFERENCE

APPENDIX B) ABOUT THE CD-ROM

INDEX

HOW TO USE THIS BOOK

C#: Your visual blueprint for building .NET applications uses simple, straightforward examples to teach you how to create powerful and dynamic programs.

To get the most out of this book, you should read each chapter in order, from beginning to end. Each chapter introduces new ideas and builds on the knowledge learned in previous chapters. Once you become familiar with *C#: Your visual blueprint for building .NET applications*, this book can be used as an informative desktop reference.

Who This Book Is For

If you are interested in writing programs for the new Microsoft C# programming language, then *C#: Your visual blueprint for building .NET applications* is the book for you.

This book will take you through the basics of using the Visual Studio Microsoft Development Environment (MDE) window and familiarize you with the essentials of C# programming. The book even covers advanced topics including creating forms, macros, and Web applications.

No prior experience with programming is required, but familiarity with the Microsoft Windows operating system installed on your computer is an asset.

What You Need To Use This Book

To perform the tasks in this book, you need a computer with Microsoft Windows NT 4.0 or 2000 installed as well as Microsoft Visual Studio.NET. You do not require any special development tools since all the tools are contained within Visual Studio .NET. However, you do need a Web browser such as Microsoft Internet Explorer.

The Conventions In This Book

A number of typographic and layout styles have been used throughout *C#: Your visual blueprint for building .NET applications* to distinguish different types of information.

Courier Font

Indicates the use of C# code such as tags or attributes, scripting language code such as statements, operators or functions and ASP code such as objects, methods or properties.

Bold

Indicates information that must be typed by you.

Italics

Indicates a new term being introduced.

Apply It

An Apply It section usually contains a segment of code that takes the lesson you just learned one step further. Apply It sections offer inside information and pointers that can be used to enhance the functionality of your code.

Extra

An Extra section provides additional information about the task you just accomplished. Extra sections often contain interesting tips and useful tricks to make working with C# easier and more efficient.

The Organization Of This Book

C#: Your visual blueprint for building .NET applications contains 15 chapters and two appendixes.

The first chapter, Getting Started with C#, introduces you to C#, how to start Visual Studio .NET and open a new C# project, how to learn about C# online and how you can run C# with Web pages and Java.

Chapter 2, Exploring the C# Interface, shows you how to navigate and work with the Visual Studio .NET MDE window and receive online help. This chapter helps you use the power of the MDE window to your greatest advantage when you create C# programs.

Chapter 3, Working wiht Visual C# Basics, introduces you to the essentials of C#. This chapter also covers some C# programming fundamentals that enable you to use the material in the following chapters to create your own C# programs.

The fourth chapter, Programming C# Building Blocks, gets you started with programming C# modules and their two main building blocks, classes and structures.

Chapters 5 through 9 explore how you can add different C# elements to your program — types and interfaces, methods and events, arrays, strings, and properties. You are shown in detail how to access and utilize each of these fundamental elements of C#.

Chapter 10, Building Forms, shows you how to build forms in C# so users can interact with your program.

Chapter 11, Programming Web Applications, shows you how you can integrate forms, buttons, controls, and other Web features into your program for distribution and use on the Web.

Chapter 12, Accessing DATA with C# and ADO.NET, shows you how you can design C# and XML components and create and run C# macros.

Chapter 13, Using the XML Framework Class, shows you how to distribute your program on one computer, on the network, and on the Web. You will also learn how to manage program changes and distribute those changes.

Chapter 14, Creating and Deploying Distributed Applications, shows you how to check the performance of your program, manage the debugger

Chapter 15, Working with Errors, shows you how to review common C# errors that you should avoid.

The first appendix contains a reference section. Once you are familiar with the contents of this book, you can use the C# references to obtain at-a-glance information for some of the most commonly used C# statements.

What Is On The CD-ROM

The CD-ROM disc included in this book contains the sample code from each of the two-page lessons. This saves you from having to type the code and helps you quickly get started creating C# code. The CD-ROM disc also contains several shareware and evaluation versions of programs that can be used to work with *C#: Your visual blueprint for building .NET applications*. An e-version of the book is also available on the disc.

INTRODUCTION TO C#

C# is a new programming language created by Microsoft and introduced with the release of Visual Studio .NET (also known as Visual Studio .NET 7.0).

C# lets you write programs that enable you to manipulate the computer to perform certain tasks.

The Birth of C#

As a recent birth in the programming language family, C# has two programming language parents: C++ and Java. C# contains many C++ features but also adds the object-oriented features from Java.

C# contains many different components, including:

- Versioning support, so that your base and derived classes — templates that define how an object performs — remain compatible as you develop them

- Events, so that your program can notify clients of a class about something that has happened to an object

- Type safety and verification that increases reliability and ensures code security

- Garbage collection, so that your program can identify objects that your program can no longer reach

- Unsafe mode, where you can use pointers to manipulate memory outside the garbage collector's control, including methods and properties

Close Relations with C and C++

C# is built on the C++ language, so it behaves much like the language. Like C++, C# lets you write enterprise applications, and C# contains many C++ features, including statements and operators. C# also provides access to common Application Program Interface (API) styles including Component Object Model (COM) and C-style APIs.

Security

Computer networks let programmers share Visual Studio .NET code including C# programs across the network. This collaborative effort lets you and your programming team create C# programs much more quickly than one person alone. The problem with collaborating over a network is that unauthorized users from within or outside your network may try to gain access to your C# program code.

Visual Studio .NET provides built-in security features so you or the leader of your programming team can determine who on your network gets access to your C# program code and resources. You can also set different levels of security for different people in case you want only certain people to have access to certain program code.

Integration

The primary advantage of using Visual Studio .NET is that all of the programming languages have been designed to work together from the start. When you write a new C# program, Visual Studio .NET gives you tools that you can use to program links from your C# program into another program written in another Visual Studio .NET language.

For example, you can create a database in Visual FoxPro and then create a C# program that links into the Visual FoxPro database. If you have written or acquired completed programs in a Visual Studio language such as Visual C++ or Visual Basic, you can include links from your C# program into those programs. The end result is seamless integrated functionality between programs.

Differences Between C# and C++

Microsoft includes Visual C++ and C# in Visual Studio .NET. On the surface, C# has few differences from Visual C++. When you look carefully and start programming, you will notice that C# differs in several important respects from Visual C++:

- C# has an alternate method of accessing the C++ initialization list when constructing the base class.

- A class can inherit implementation from only one base class.

- You can call overridden base class members from derived classes.

- C# has a different syntax for declaring C# arrays.

- There are differences in several different types including `bool`, `struct`, and `delegate`.

- The `Main` method is declared differently.

- Support of the new `ref` and `out` method parameters that are used instead of pointers for passing parameters by reference.

- New keywords including `extern` and `static`.

- New statements including `switch` and `finally`.

- New operators including `is` and `typeof`.

- Different functionality for some operators and for overloading operators.

DLLs

The advent of Windows brought *dynamic link libraries* (DLLs) to programmers. DLLs are small, independent programs that contain executable routines that programs can use to produce a certain result in Windows. For example, if a program needs to open a file, you can write your C# program that uses the code in the DLL to open the file. Using DLLs frees up your time to work on your program without having to reprogram the same code in your C# program over and over again.

You can access DLLs from your C# program, and create DLLs in C# for your C# program to refer to when necessary. C# has full COM/Platform support, so you can integrate C# code with any programming language that can produce COM DLLs such as Visual C++.

XML

Extensible Markup Language (XML) is a more powerful version of HyperText Markup Language (HTML), the standard Web page language. Visual Studio .NET and C# let you document your program using XML and then extract the XML code into a separate file.

Visual Studio .NET supports XML so that you can integrate your C# programs with the World Wide Web. You can document your C# code using XML and then use XML for creating Web Services and Web controls that let you and your code interact with a Web site. For example, you may have an inventory system written in C# that interacts with the order-taking page on your company's Web site.

COMPARE C#, VISUAL C++, AND JAVA

Many of the simple programming procedures that you use in C# are similar in both parent languages — Visual C++ and Java — and in some cases the procedures are identical. The following are examples of simple programming procedures that illustrate the similarities and differences between C#, Visual C++, and Java.

Declaring Variables

C#:	Visual C++:	Java:
`int x;`	`int x;`	`int x;`
`int x=3;`	`int x=3;`	`int x=3;`

FOR Loops

C#:
```
for (int i = 1; i <= 10; i++)
    Console.WriteLine("The number is {0}", i);
```

Visual C++:
```
for (int i = 1; i < 11; i++)
    printf("%d\n", i);
```

Java:
```
for (int i = 1; i < 11; i++)
    System.out.println("The number is " + i);
```

Assignments

C#:	Visual C++:	Java:
`xValue=7;`	`xValue=7;`	`xValue=7;`

WHILE Loops

C#:
```
while (x < 100);
    x++;
```

Visual C++:
```
while (x < 100);
    x++;
```

Java:
```
while (x < 100);
    x++;
```

If-Else Statements

C#:
```
if (nCount < nMax)
{
  nTotal += nCount;
  nCount++;
}
else {
  nTotal += nCount;
  nCount —;
}
```

Visual C++:
```
if (nCount < nMax) {
  nTotal += nCount;
  nCount++;
}
else {
  nTotal += nCount;
  nCount —;
};
```

Java:
```
if (nCount < nMax) {
  nTotal += nCount;
  nCount++;
}
else {
  nTotal += nCount;
  nCount —;
}
```

START VISUAL STUDIO .NET

Visual Studio .NET contains a graphical programming environment called the Microsoft Development Environment (MDE). The MDE enables you to create programs in Visual C# and other Visual Studio .NET languages.

When you start Visual Studio .NET, the MDE window appears with several windows within the MDE window. In the largest area of the MDE window, which is called the parent window, the Visual Studio Start page appears. The Start page lists any recent projects and provides two buttons so that you can open a project file or create a new project.

The Start page lets you log into the Microsoft Developers Network (MSDN) Web site directly from the MDE, so you can receive the latest information from Microsoft about Visual Studio, get technical help from fellow Visual Studio users at Microsoft's online forum, and search for information online.

Visual Studio .NET also lets you create and change your profile so that you can view windows, enter keyboard commands, and receive help for the programming language in which you are working. For example, if you have used an older version of Visual Studio in the past and you prefer to use the old windows and keyboard commands, Visual Studio lets you use Visual Basic and C++ windows and menus.

START VISUAL STUDIO .NET

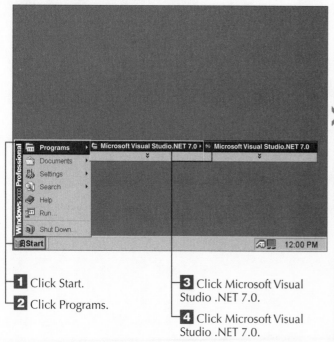

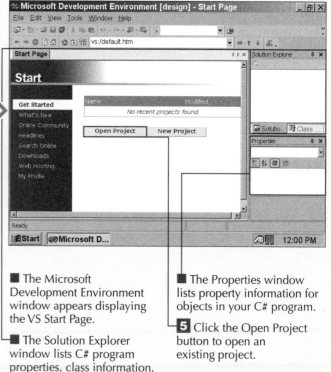

1 Click Start.

2 Click Programs.

3 Click Microsoft Visual Studio .NET 7.0.

4 Click Microsoft Visual Studio .NET 7.0.

■ The Microsoft Development Environment window appears displaying the VS Start Page.

■ The Solution Explorer window lists C# program properties, class information, and help topics.

■ The Properties window lists property information for objects in your C# program.

5 Click the Open Project button to open an existing project.

Extra

You can change what appears on the MDE when you start up — it does not have to be the Start page. You can start in an empty environment without the Start page by clicking the My Profile option and then clicking Show Empty Environment from the At Startup drop-down list box. The next time you start Visual Studio .NET, the parent window will have nothing in it — it will display your default Windows background color.

If you want to start Visual Studio .NET from your desktop, you can create a shortcut that opens the MDE window when you double-click the desktop icon. Consult your Windows documentation for information about how to create a shortcut. No matter what parent directory you installed Visual Studio into, the MDE program appears in the `\Common7\IDE\` subdirectory with the devenv.exe filename. For example, if you installed Visual Studio .NET in its default location on your primary hard drive, the path would be `C:\Program Files\Visual Studio .NET\Common7\ IDE\devenv.exe`.

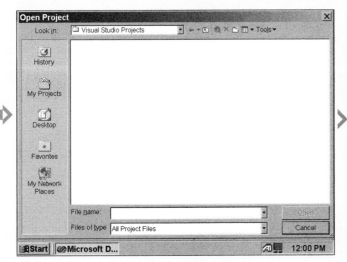

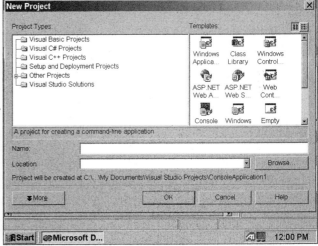

■ The Open Project window appears so you can open an existing C# project.

6 Click the New Project button in step 5.

■ The New Project window appears so you can open a new C# project.

OPEN A NEW C# PROJECT

After you start the MDE window, you can open a new project. A project contains all the files related to your C# program. After you determine the type of C# program you want to write, Visual Studio creates all of the project files you need to start programming. Visual Studio contains project templates that let you create different types of programs. The MDE window lets you create eight different projects so you can tailor your C# program to the needs of your program users.

You can create three different application types, each with a different user interface. First, you can create a Windows application that has a graphical, form-based interface. You can create a console application with a character-based interface. Finally, you can create a Web application that

resides on a Web server and uses Web pages for its interface.

You can create three types of programs that are not full-fledged but provide components that other programs can use. First, you can create a class library program so you can provide classes for other programs. Second, you can create a Windows control library for creating form controls such as buttons. Third, you can create a Web control library program that provides Web controls for your Web-based C# programs.

You can also create two different types of programs for specific needs: a Windows service that is a long-running application that runs in its own Windows session and a Web service for integrating your Web site with a C# program.

OPEN A NEW C# PROJECT

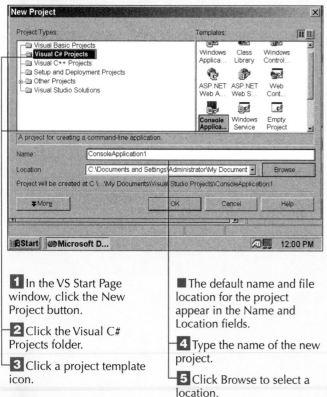

■1 In the VS Start Page window, click the New Project button.

■2 Click the Visual C# Projects folder.

■3 Click a project template icon.

■ The default name and file location for the project appear in the Name and Location fields.

■4 Type the name of the new project.

■5 Click Browse to select a location.

■ The Project Location window appears listing the project folders within your My Projects folder.

■6 Type the name of the folder in which you want to place the project.

■7 Click Open.

7

Extra

When the Open Project window appears, it shows all the projects in the default project folder, My Projects. By clicking one of the icons on the left side of the Project Location window, you can choose the folder from which a project is opened:

History	You can select from a folder that you used recently by clicking the History button.
Desktop	You can select from a folder on your desktop by clicking the Desktop button.
Favorites	You can select a folder within your Favorites folder by clicking the Favorites button.
My Network Places	Finally, you can search your network drives by clicking the My Network Places button.

In the Project Location window, you can also select any folder on your hard drive(s) by clicking the Down Arrow (▼) next to the Look in field and then selecting your drive. The folders on the selected drive appear in the window.

You can view all the templates in the Templates area by clicking the small button above and to the right of the Templates area.

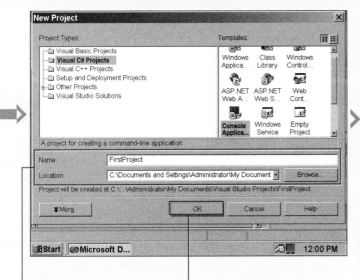

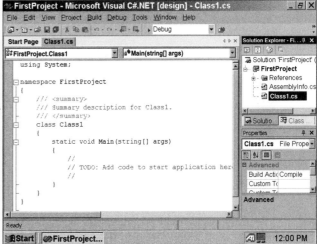

■ The New Project dialog box reappears with the name and location you selected in the Name and Location fields.

Note: If you know the name of the path location where you want to store the project, you can type it directly into the Location field.

8 Click OK.

■ The form or code that corresponds to the template you selected replaces the Start Page in the parent window.

VIEW .NET FRAMEWORK ONLINE RESOURCES

Visual Studio .NET contains minimal printed documentation. Most of the documentation for C# and Visual Studio .NET is contained within the MDE window itself. Having online documentation within the MDE window enables you to get the help you need quickly and conveniently.

The MDE window also contains links to help from both the Microsoft Web site and online newsgroups where you can leave and read messages from other C# programmers. You can also search the Microsoft Web site for help with specific topics.

Visual Studio .NET installs its self-contained help files when you install Visual Studio .NET. You can access self-contained help from the MDE menu bar, but you can only access

online help and resources from the Start menu. When you access help on the Web or newsgroups, the MDE parent window behaves as a window in your Internet browser would, so you can get your help directly from the MDE window without having to start an Internet browser.

If you have a continuous connection to the World Wide Web, such as a DSL or cable modem connection, then the Microsoft Web site help pages update automatically each time you access them. If you have a dial-up connection and you are not currently connected to the Web, then the MDE window will require you to connect before you can view the Microsoft Web site help pages.

VIEW .NET FRAMEWORK ONLINE RESOURCES

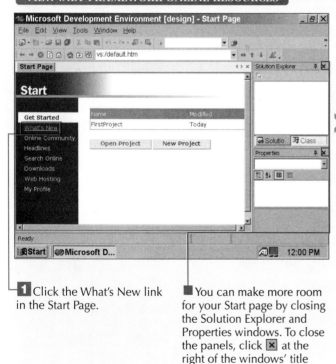

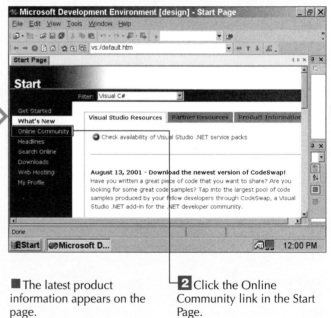

1 Click the What's New link in the Start Page.

■ You can make more room for your Start page by closing the Solution Explorer and Properties windows. To close the panels, click ✖ at the right of the windows' title bars.

■ The latest product information appears on the page.

2 Click the Online Community link in the Start Page.

Extra

If you want to see information just about C#, you can filter out information to see the information you want in the Filter drop-down list that appears at the top of the Start page.

The Filter drop-down list enables you to view Web information on the Microsoft Web site, view headlines, search for help, and view downloads that have information specific to the Visual Studio .NET language or topic that you want to view.

If you want to filter help results and information by topic, you have two options for doing so. You can limit your filter to topics that strictly mention C# or to C# topics and other topics that relate to C#.

If you access a newsgroup, your default newsgroup program, for example, the Microsoft Outlook Newsreader, loads automatically and displays new messages. If you do not have a newsreader, the MDE window reports that a newsreader cannot be started and that you cannot access the newsgroups.

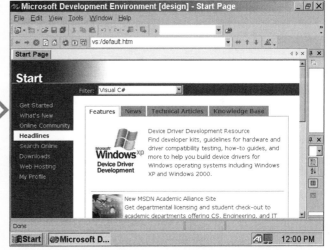

■ The Visual Studio .NET Web site and available newsgroups appear on the page.

3 Click the Headlines link.

■ A list of headlines with the latest information about Visual Studio .NET and its languages appear in the parent window.

OPEN A C# WEB PROJECT

C# contains several templates for creating Web-based projects so that you can integrate your C# programs with a Web site and share the projects with other members of a programming team. Sharing projects on a Web site or a corporate intranet speeds development of your C# program. Integrating a C# program with a Web site lets you accept input from users on a Web site and manipulate that data in the program.

A *graphical user interface*, GUI, is a window on the screen that lets users interact with the program. One key C# component for building a GUI program is the *Web form*. A Web form is a collection of tools that lets you create a

program GUI, and C# builds Web forms using Microsoft Active Server Pages (ASP) technology.

Active Server Pages are a Microsoft Web technology, and the latest ASP version, ASP .NET, integrates the Visual Studio .NET programming languages with Web browsers. C# lets you build two types of Web applications that use ASP.NET: *Applications* that use forms and *services* that use Web-based technologies such as XML.

You can also create two other types of Web-related projects: button controls and new Web projects. You can create button controls for use in Web forms, and start a new Web project from scratch.

OPEN A C# WEB PROJECT

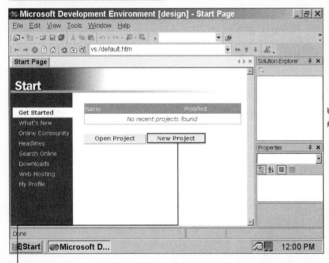

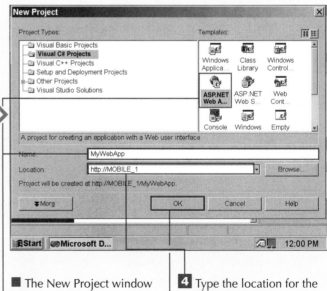

1 In the VS Start Page window, click the New Project button.

■ The New Project window appears.

2 Click the ASP.NET Web Application icon to create a Web application.

3 Type the name of the Web application to change it from the Visual Studio .NET default.

4 Type the location for the Web application.

■ If you do not have a Web site, Visual Studio .NET places the project in a Web folder on your computer called MOBILE_1.

5 Click OK.

Extra

When you create a new Web project and place it on a Web directory, you should ensure that the directory where you place your Web program is secure so that only people with certain access can view it. If the Web directory your program resides in is not secure, others can access, alter, and outright steal your code from both inside and outside of your network. Discuss these issues with your Webmaster before posting your code on the Web or an intranet.

When you create a Web project, you must install certain components onto your Web server. Without these components, you cannot develop your Web site. You can develop Web projects by installing the following components onto your Web server: Internet Information Server version 4.0 or later, FrontPage Server Extensions, the .NET Framework Common Language Runtime, and ASP.NET. Make sure that your Webmaster has installed these programs before you develop a C# Web application.

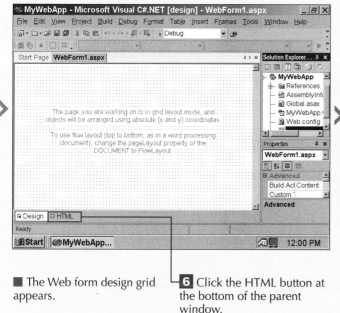

■ The Web form design grid appears.

6 Click the HTML button at the bottom of the parent window.

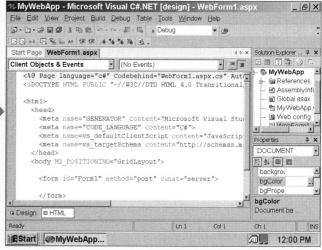

■ The Web code appears in the parent window.

SET JSCRIPT .NET AS THE DEFAULT SCRIPT LANGUAGE

Because Java is a progenitor of C# as well as a ubiquitous Web programming language, Microsoft provides Java support for Visual Studio .NET and C#. This support lets you integrate existing Java programs with your C# program so both programs appear to work seamlessly — that is, as one program.

Microsoft implements this support not through Java itself, but through a derivative scripting language called *JScript*. JScript is the Microsoft implementation of the JavaScript programming language, and it lets you link JavaScript in your Web page or XML document with your C# program and to other Java programs.

The only differences between JavaScript and JScript are minor, and there are no functionality differences with the JavaScript with which you may already be familiar. JScript .NET is not a full-fledged programming language. You can neither write standalone programs with it using ASP.NET nor view it with ASP-enabled Internet browsers.

Your C# program cannot automatically tell that your Web page has JScript or JavaScript code. Instead, you must create or edit a Web page from the MDE window and set the default client script for the HTML document. Then, you can enter JScript code into your HTML program and your C# program will be able to read the JScript-enabled HTML page.

SET JSCRIPT .NET AS THE DEFAULT SCRIPT LANGUAGE

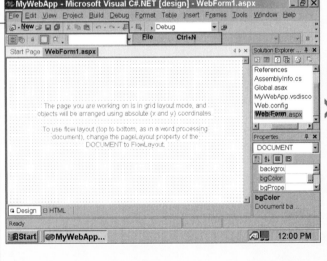

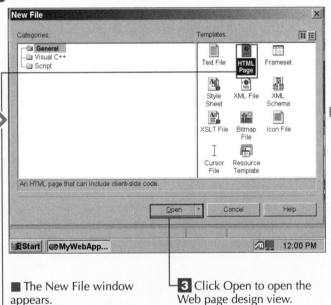

1 Click File ➪ New ➪ File on the Web forms code page.

■ The New File window appears.

2 Click the HTML Page icon.

3 Click Open to open the Web page design view.

Extra

You cannot take advantage of the MDE window's editing tools when you edit an HTML or XML page. If you want a full-fledged script debugger, Microsoft offers the Microsoft Script Debugger, which is a dedicated debugger for JScript and VBScript scripts.

The Microsoft Script Debugger and its companion Script Editor are separate programs that you can download from the Microsoft Developer Network Web site at http://msdn. microsoft.com/scripting.

If you are not certain about whether a program that you want to integrate into a C# program has JavaScript enabled, you can easily find out by opening your Web page in an HTML editor and checking for text that starts with `<SCRIPT LANGUAGE = "JavaScript"`. If you find this text, you have JavaScript in your Web page, and all you have to do is enable JScript .NET in that Web page within the MDE window.

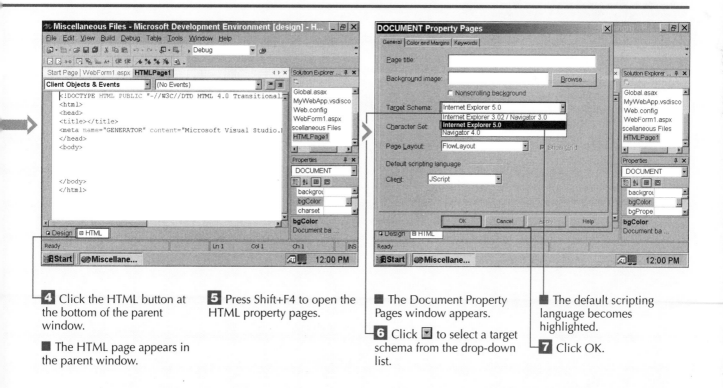

4 Click the HTML button at the bottom of the parent window.

■ The HTML page appears in the parent window.

5 Press Shift+F4 to open the HTML property pages.

■ The Document Property Pages window appears.

6 Click ▣ to select a target schema from the drop-down list.

■ The default scripting language becomes highlighted.

7 Click OK.

EXPLORE THE CLASS VIEW WINDOW

When you start a new C# project, C# creates default classes that define and categorize the elements in your new program. For example, if you start a new Windows application that has a form, C# creates default classes that define the form objects. The Class View window lets you view all your classes and their related components so you know exactly what is in your class code without having to search through the code.

The Class View window gives you a convenient way to see with which class an object in your program is associated without having to close or minimize your program code or form. The Class View window appears in the same space in the Microsoft Development Environment (MDE) window as the Solution Explorer window.

The class information appears in a tree format that you can expand to view all classes associated with a particular program component, such as a form. If you have more than one program in a project, the Class View window tree lets you access classes for all the programs in the project.

If you want to see classes that meet certain criteria, you can sort classes in the tree alphabetically, by type for viewing related classes in your program, or by access.

EXPLORE THE CLASS VIEW WINDOW

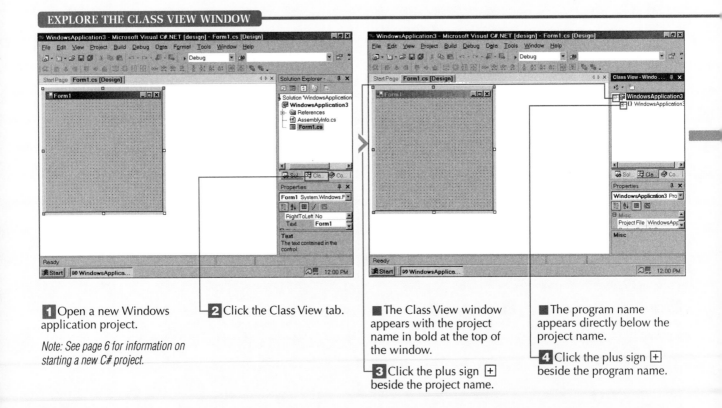

1 Open a new Windows application project.

Note: See page 6 for information on starting a new C# project.

2 Click the Class View tab.

■ The Class View window appears with the project name in bold at the top of the window.

3 Click the plus sign ⊞ beside the project name.

■ The program name appears directly below the project name.

4 Click the plus sign ⊞ beside the program name.

EXPLORING THE C# INTERFACE

Extra

If the Class View window is not available as a tab at the bottom of the Solution Explorer window, you can access the Class View window from the menu bar.

You can open the Class View window by clicking View and then Class View on the menu. You can also open the Class View window by pressing Ctrl+Shift+C. No matter if you access the Class View window using the menu or the keyboard, after you open the Class View window, it replaces the Solution Explorer in the upper-right corner of the parent window.

When you click a class, the properties for that class appear in the Properties window; the Properties window appears below the Class View window.

If you do not have the Properties window open, you can right-click the class and then click Properties from the pop-up menu. See page 26 to learn more about the Properties window.

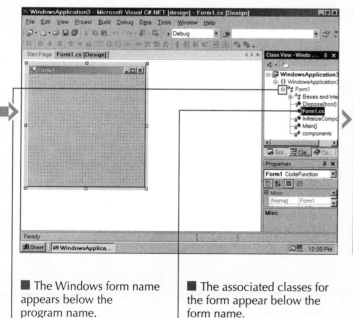

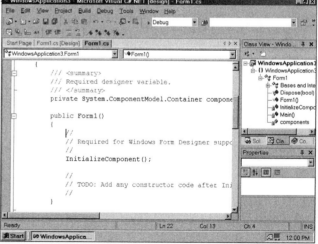

■ The Windows form name appears below the program name.

■ The associated classes for the form appear below the form name.

■ The class location appears in the code displayed in the parent window.

5 Click the plus sign ⊞ beside the form name.

6 Double-click a form class in the tree.

VIEW THE CONTENTS WINDOW

The Microsoft Development Environment (MDE) window provides several different types of online Visual .NET documentation, including the Contents window. When you access the Contents window, the window appears in the same space as the Solution Explorer window. If you have used Windows online help before, then the Contents window will be very familiar to you. The MDE organizes Visual Studio .NET information into different subjects that display in the Contents window in a tree format.

Microsoft has divided the Contents window into two main topic groups called *books:* Visual Studio .NET and MSDN Library. The online documentation displayed in each topic

contains subtopic groups. You can open each book in the tree that matches the subject you want more information about.

As you expand the tree, specific topics appear, enabling you to select your topic from this list. Many help pages also contain links to other help pages, in case you need related information.

The Filtered By drop-down list at the top of the Contents window lets you filter the type of information displayed in the tree. If you want to view only C# information, the Contents window tree will display those groups and topics that pertain only to C#.

VIEW THE CONTENTS WINDOW

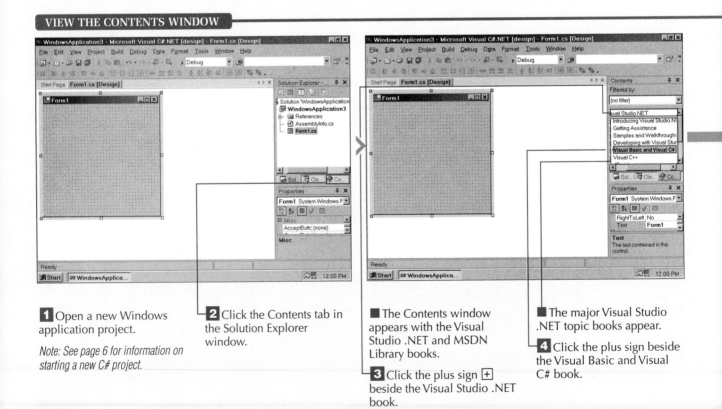

1 Open a new Windows application project.

Note: See page 6 for information on starting a new C# project.

2 Click the Contents tab in the Solution Explorer window.

■ The Contents window appears with the Visual Studio .NET and MSDN Library books.

3 Click the plus sign ⊞ beside the Visual Studio .NET book.

■ The major Visual Studio .NET topic books appear.

4 Click the plus sign beside the Visual Basic and Visual C# book.

Extra

With some topics, the Contents window may not be able to display the full names of the topics. The MDE window provides two ways to scroll through the entire topic name so you can determine if that is a topic you want more information about.

First, you can click the horizontal scrollbar at the bottom of the Contents window. This lets you view the entire window. Second, you can move the mouse pointer over the topic name and the full topic name will appear in a white box above the mouse pointer. The second option does not work if the name of the topic is too long.

In the Contents window tree structure, as with any tree structure in the MDE, you can close all the topics underneath a book in the tree by clicking the minus sign beside the topic. When you do, all the topics that appear under the book minimize.

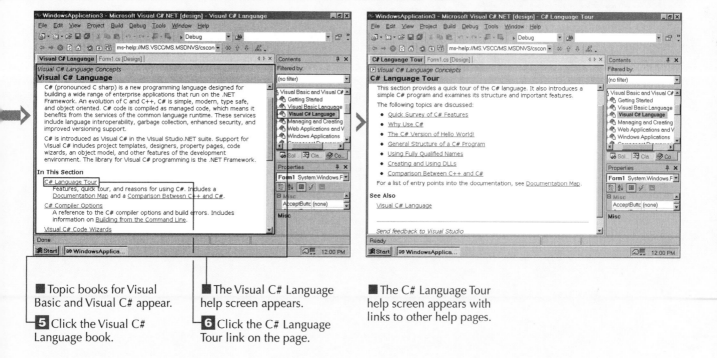

■ Topic books for Visual Basic and Visual C# appear.

5 Click the Visual C# Language book.

■ The Visual C# Language help screen appears.

6 Click the C# Language Tour link on the page.

■ The C# Language Tour help screen appears with links to other help pages.

GET HELP USING THE INDEX WINDOW

The Index window lets you search for specific topic information, instead of going through all the topics in the Contents window searching for what you need. The Index window lets you type in the topic that you are looking for and then finds the topic that best matches your description. Some topics contain subtopics that let you view different aspects of a topic. For example, if you want to learn more about properties, the Index window contains plenty of topics about how properties apply to different aspects of Visual Studio .NET, such as adding properties to forms.

As with the Contents window, you can filter the topics that appear in the Index window, according to different parts of Visual Studio .NET. If you want to view only C# information, you can set the filter so that the Index window presents only C# topics. You can also set the filter so the Index window presents topics about and related to C#.

You can view related information in any help topic page link and in the Index Results window directly below the help topic page. The filter that you set in the Index window does not affect these page and Index Results links.

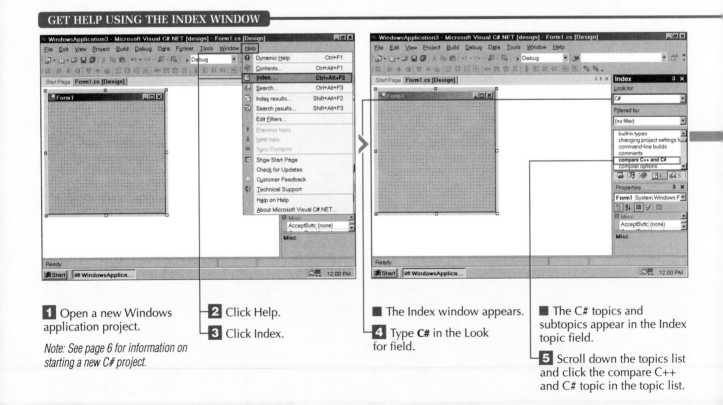

GET HELP USING THE INDEX WINDOW

1 Open a new Windows application project.

Note: See page 6 for information on starting a new C# project.

2 Click Help.

3 Click Index.

■ The Index window appears.

4 Type **C#** in the Look for field.

■ The C# topics and subtopics appear in the Index topic field.

5 Scroll down the topics list and click the compare C++ and C# topic in the topic list.

Extra

You can view the last five searches that you made in the Index window by clicking the down arrow to the right of the Look For: field. When you click the down arrow, the last five search topics will appear with the latest search topic at the top of the list.

Moving back and forth between help topics is an effective way to search for help that you have already viewed. You can view help topics that you viewed previously in one of two ways.

First, you can move back and forth between help topics that you have already viewed by pressing the Alt key and the left or right arrow key on your keyboard. The left arrow displays one previously viewed help topic, and the right arrow displays the next help topic you can view. Second, you can click either the left or right arrow in the upper-right corner of the help topic.

All the help topics you view disappear after you close the parent window, so when you start the parent window again you will have to begin a new search.

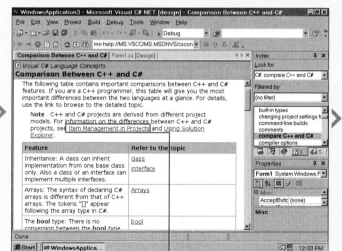

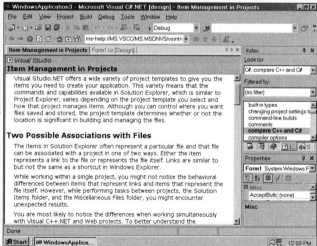

■ The Comparison Between C++ and C# help page appears with links to related topics in the page.

6 Click the Item Management in Projects link in the help page.

■ The Item Management in Projects help page appears.

Note: You can return to the Comparison Between C++ and C# help page by pressing Alt + the left arrow key.

SEARCH FOR HELP

The Search window lets you search by keyword in any help topic. If you need to find a particular word, such as *classes*, the Search window lets you narrow your search down to help pages that contain that word.

After you search for a word, the Search Results window displays the topics that contain that word. You can narrow the search down even further by using one of the Search window's nine filters and four search criteria check boxes.

The Search window has no preset filters when you search for a particular topic, which means that you automatically search through the entire Visual Studio .NET database. When you use filters, you search for words in help pages

that pertain to a specific topic. For example, you can look for the word *class* in all help pages that pertain to the C# topic.

You can limit the search even more by checking one of the four search criteria check boxes. These check boxes let you search words in specific locations, such as in a title, to speed your search.

Visual Studio .NET does not limit its search to its own database, but if you have an active Internet connection, Visual Studio .NET also accesses the Microsoft Developer Network (MSDN) Web site for information.

SEARCH FOR HELP

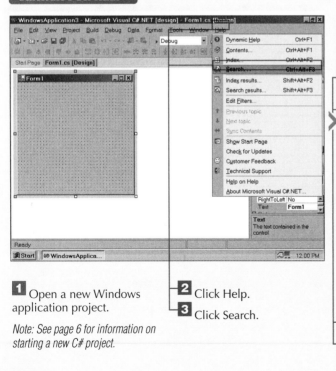

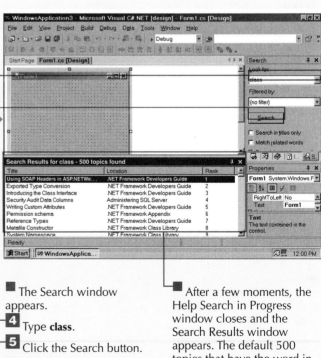

1 Open a new Windows application project.

Note: See page 6 for information on starting a new C# project.

2 Click Help.

3 Click Search.

■ The Search window appears.

4 Type **class**.

5 Click the Search button.

■ The Help Search in Progress dialog box appears in the center of your screen.

■ After a few moments, the Help Search in Progress window closes and the Search Results window appears. The default 500 topics that have the word in the topic appear.

Extra

The Search Results window automatically displays up to 500 topics that Visual Studio .NET thinks are the most relevant to your search. Going through 500 topics to find what you want is time consuming, so the Search window lets you limit your search even more (and save time) by checking one or more of its four search criteria check boxes.

When you click the Search in titles only check box, you can search for your keyword only in topic titles.

When you click the Match related words check box, you can display topic results with words and terms that are similar to the word that you are looking for. For example, if you search for topics with words related to C#, you will see topics that also relate to C++.

When you click the Search in previous results check box, you can search for the word in your previous search. For example, if you previously searched for the word *class*, and you want to search for the word *C#* in that previous search, you can do that.

When you click the Highlight search hits (in topics) check box, Visual Studio .NET will highlight all of the instances of the keyword you searched for in the help topic.

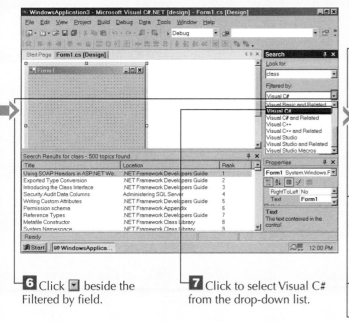

6 Click ▾ beside the Filtered by field.

7 Click to select Visual C# from the drop-down list.

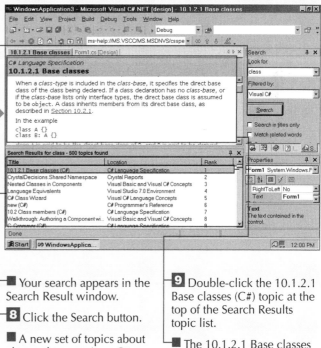

■ Your search appears in the Search Result window.

8 Click the Search button.

■ A new set of topics about classes that pertain to C# appear in the Search Results window.

9 Double-click the 10.1.2.1 Base classes (C#) topic at the top of the Search Results topic list.

■ The 10.1.2.1 Base classes help page appears.

ADD COMPONENTS FROM THE TOOLBOX

After you create a new Visual C# program in the MDE window, you can add functionality to the skeleton of your program in two ways: programmatically or by using the Toolbox. The Toolbox contains a variety of components so you can add them to your program and modify them.

Toolbox components can include design-time controls, HTML code fragments, text files, and .NET components. The Toolbox places these components into different groups. For example, Web form components appear in the Web Forms group.

The type of C# program you create determines the components the Toolbox displays. For example, if you create a Windows application that has a form, then the

Toolbox will display the Windows Forms component group that contains all the form components, such as a check box and a button.

The Toolbox always contains two groups: General and Clipboard Ring. The General group contains components that apply to any object. You can cut or copy components to the Clipboard Ring and then paste those components from the Clipboard Ring to another object such as a button from one form to another.

You can open a new group in the Toolbox and copy objects from a program into that group or from another group. You can also add components from Visual Studio .NET or another location on your computer or network.

ADD COMPONENTS FROM THE TOOLBOX

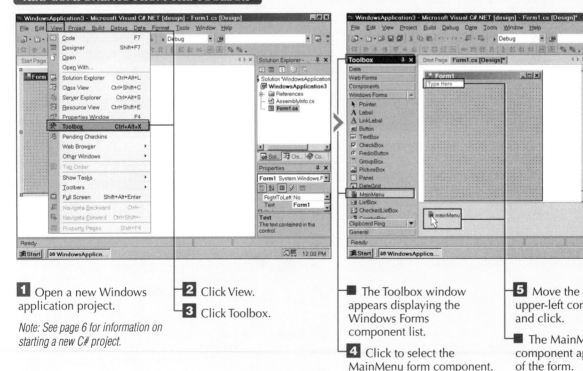

1 Open a new Windows application project.

Note: See page 6 for information on starting a new C# project.

2 Click View.

3 Click Toolbox.

■ The Toolbox window appears displaying the Windows Forms component list.

4 Click to select the MainMenu form component.

5 Move the cursor over the upper-left corner of the form and click.

■ The MainMenu component appears at the top of the form.

Extra

You can delete any component from the Toolbox by right-clicking the component and then clicking Delete in the pop-up menu that appears. The only component you cannot delete is the Pointer component in the General group.

You can quickly cut, copy, and paste Toolbox objects by pressing the following keyboard combinations: Ctrl+X to cut, Ctrl+C to copy, and Ctrl+V to paste. When you access the Clipboard Ring, you can press Ctrl+Shift+V to move to the next item in the clipboard until you arrive at the object you want to cut, copy, or paste.

You can display all group tabs in the Toolbox window by right-clicking anywhere in the Toolbox window and selecting Show All Tabs from the pop-up menu that appears.

If you want to view only the object icons and not their descriptions, right-click anywhere in the Toolbox window and then select List View in the pop-up menu. Return to the list view by right-clicking in the Toolbox window and then selecting the List View option in the pop-up menu.

You can also rearrange group tabs in the Toolbox window and objects within a group by clicking and dragging the group tab or object to a new location in the window.

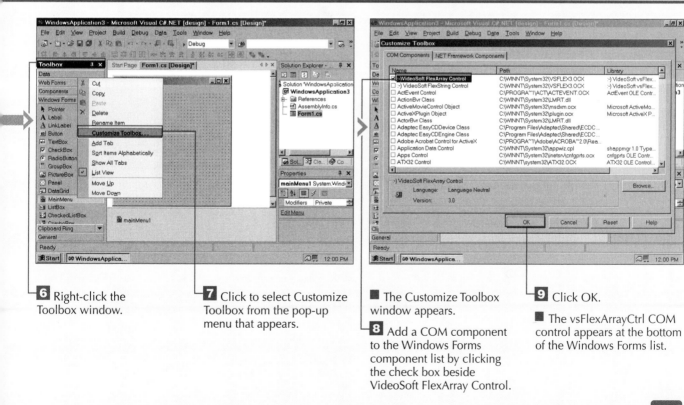

6 Right-click the Toolbox window.

7 Click to select Customize Toolbox from the pop-up menu that appears.

■ The Customize Toolbox window appears.

8 Add a COM component to the Windows Forms component list by clicking the check box beside VideoSoft FlexArray Control.

9 Click OK.

■ The vsFlexArrayCtrl COM control appears at the bottom of the Windows Forms list.

ADD A TASK TO THE TASK LIST

During program construction, you probably write down errors and tasks on a piece of paper or on sticky notes. The Task List in the MDE eliminates the need for paper notes by letting you enter tasks that you need to complete within the MDE for easy reference.

If Visual Studio .NET encounters an error in a program, it automatically adds the problem to the task list for your information. If you want to add any other tasks to your list, you can log the task by identifying the task to complete, what program the task applies to, and the line you must apply the task to, if any.

You can also identify which tasks have been completed or not, and what priority each task will take. The Task List window presents the tasks in table form for easy viewing. After you populate your task list, you can sort it by different criteria. For example, you can sort the list so the high-priority tasks appear at the top of the Task List window.

You can also view certain tasks that you may be concentrating on. For example, if you have finished your program and you need only to add comments, you can have the Task View window display only the comment tasks.

ADD A TASK TO THE TASK LIST

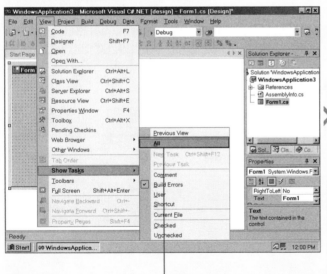

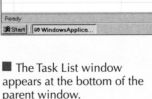

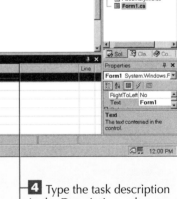

1 Open a new Windows application project.

Note: See page 6 for information on starting a new C# project.

2 Click View ➪ Show Tasks ➪ All.

■ The Task List window appears at the bottom of the parent window.

3 Click the first line in the task list table.

■ The first task highlights and the blinking cursor appears in the description field.

4 Type the task description in the Description column field and then press Enter.

5 Set the priority for the task by clicking the exclamation box beside the new task entry.

When you have a large number of tasks, the Task List window lets you show tasks of a certain type so you can see only the tasks you want. You can show tasks by right-clicking a task and then clicking Show Tasks from the pop-up menu that appears. The default selection is All (that shows all tasks), but you can also view comment tasks, tasks that report build errors, user-inspired tasks, shortcut tasks, tasks in the current file, checked tasks (that is, completed), and unchecked tasks.

If you have used any word-processing program recently, you know about the benefit of having red squiggly underlines that appear under misspelled words so you can correct the misspellings quickly. Visual Studio .NET uses the same approach for code errors so you can fix those errors quickly; Microsoft calls this feature IntelliSense.

If you make a coding mistake, such as adding a matching brace, then the MDE window automatically adds the error to the Task List with a red squiggly icon next to it that identifies that there is a coding problem to fix.

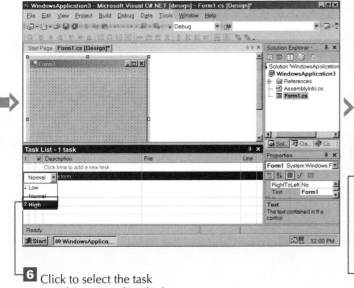

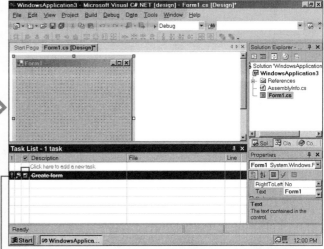

6 Click to select the task priority (low, normal, or high) from the drop-down menu.

7 To mark the task as completed, click the check box beside the task.

■ A strikethrough line appears through the task description that denotes that the task has been completed.

CHANGE FORM PROPERTIES IN THE PROPERTIES WINDOW

The Properties window appears in the lower-right corner of the parent window. The Properties window contains the information that pertains to a specific object. For example, if you create a Windows application, the form appears in the parent window; a form lets a user input information so your C# program can manipulate it. The form properties, including the form name, appear in the Properties window. When you change the form name, that name will appear on the form when you run your program.

The Properties window reflects information in the currently selected object. The Properties window contains a list of all objects in the program that you can alter in the properties window.

Many objects contain names or values that you can edit directly in the Properties window. Some object attributes have check boxes that you can click to enable or disable the object attribute. The Properties window also provides a description about a selected object attribute in case you are not familiar with what an attribute does.

Some object attributes in the Properties window contain more information than what the attribute value provides, such as font size, that you can edit in the Properties window. You can also sort the attributes in the Properties window if you want to see certain types of properties, such as events.

CHANGE FORM PROPERTIES IN THE PROPERTIES WINDOW

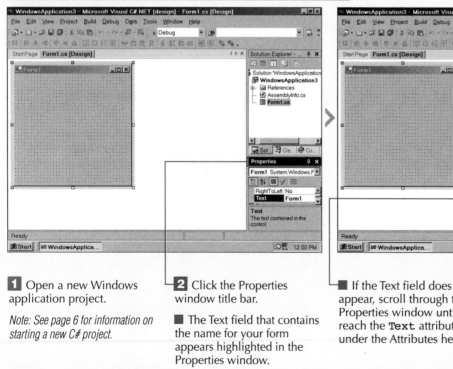

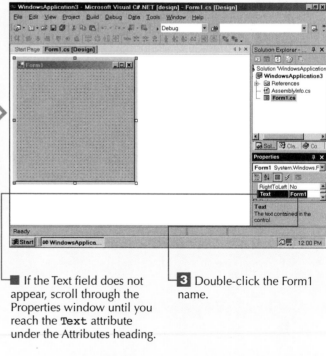

1 Open a new Windows application project.

Note: See page 6 for information on starting a new C# project.

2 Click the Properties window title bar.

■ The Text field that contains the name for your form appears highlighted in the Properties window.

■ If the Text field does not appear, scroll through the Properties window until you reach the **Text** attribute under the Attributes heading.

3 Double-click the Form1 name.

Extra

If you do not see the Properties window in the parent window, you can open it in one of three ways: you can click the folder in the Solution Explorer window, click View ⇨ Properties, or press the F4 key.

The buttons in between the object name field and the properties table let you sort and view different properties. The two sort buttons at the left of the window let you sort properties alphabetically and by category. The Properties window automatically categorizes certain object attributes into their own groups. For example, a form has a Design category that includes such attributes as the form grid size.

The two buttons directly to the right of the sort buttons let you view the properties and events that are related to the selected object.

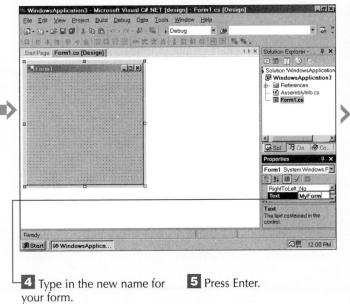

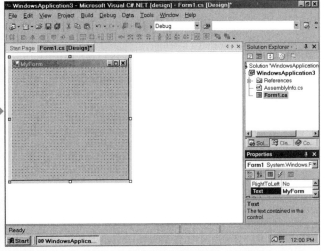

4 Type in the new name for your form.

5 Press Enter.

■ The name of the form changes in the Properties window and in the form title bar in the parent window.

ADD A CUSTOM TOOLBAR

Toolbars appear near the top of the MDE window, enabling you to access commands that you use most often without having to remember where a specific command is in a menu; instead, you can just click a button. The MDE window has 25 built-in toolbars; the Standard toolbar appears by default and others appear when you perform a particular function. For example, the Layout toolbar appears when you edit a form. You can also add your own custom toolbars to access the features you use.

Custom toolbars can reduce the number of active toolbars in the parent window. If you prefer accessing commands using the keyboard, Visual Studio .NET also lets you set keyboard combinations for different commands.

Visual Studio .NET also lets you determine how information on the toolbar appears on your screen. For example, you can determine if you want the toolbar icons to also contain their text descriptions. Doing so makes it much easier to determine what a command does, especially if you are not familiar with all of the toolbar buttons, but they do add additional space to your toolbar that will take away from other space in your window. An alternative method that saves space is to have ScreenTips on toolbars active so a button description appears when you move the mouse pointer over a toolbar button.

ADD A CUSTOM TOOLBAR

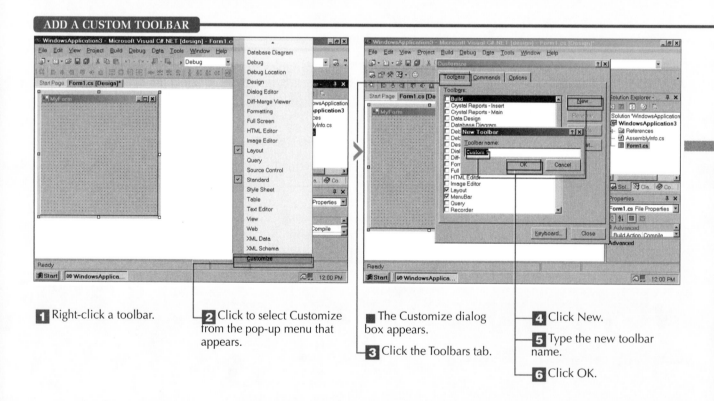

1 Right-click a toolbar.

2 Click to select Customize from the pop-up menu that appears.

■ The Customize dialog box appears.

3 Click the Toolbars tab.

4 Click New.

5 Type the new toolbar name.

6 Click OK.

28

Extra

You can reset the number of toolbars to the Visual Studio .NET default — the Standard and Web toolbars — by clicking the Reset button in the Customize window's Toolbars tab.

Visual Studio .NET has default settings for what drop-down menu options appear when you click an option on the menu. The most recent options that you used appear first, and then the rest of the options appear after the drop-down menu has been open for a short time. You can reset this information by clicking the Reset my usage data button in the Customize window's Options tab.

If you want to know what the keyboard shortcuts are for certain tabs without having to look them up in the Customize window, you can click the Show shortcut keys in ScreenTips check box in the Customize window's Options tab. After you check the check box, you can move the mouse pointer over a Toolbar button and the description and keyboard shortcut (if there is one) will appear in the ScreenTip next to the pointer.

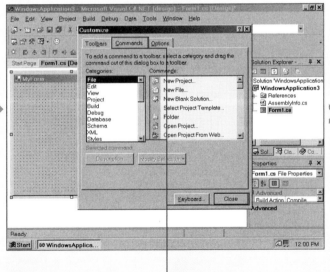

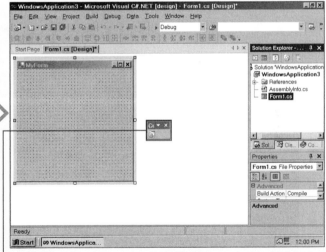

■ The custom toolbar appears in the middle of the parent window. You can click and drag to another area.

7 Right-click the custom toolbar.

8 Click to select Customize from the pop-up menu that appears.

9 Click the Commands tab in the Customize window.

10 Click to select a command category.

11 Drag the command you want to add to the custom toolbar.

12 Click the Close button in the Customize window.

■ The command appears in the custom toolbar.

■ You can access the command button in the custom toolbar by clicking.

DELETE A TOOLBAR

If you find that you no longer use a toolbar and you want to use the extra space for other features in the MDE window, like the parent window for editing code, the MDE window lets you delete a toolbar entirely from your system.

At the left of every toolbar is a series of dark gray lines or *hashmarks*. These lines indicate the start of the toolbar and where you can place the mouse pointer so you can move the toolbar around on the screen. You can determine whether the toolbar will remain at the top of the screen or float around the screen as its own window.

A down arrow appears at the far right of every active toolbar. This down arrow contains a menu that lets you conveniently add and remove buttons from the selected toolbar.

If you have more than one toolbar on the screen in the same toolbar row on the page, not all the buttons can fit on the toolbar row. If you want to have all the buttons visible in one toolbar row, move the toolbar to a new location or remove buttons from one or more toolbars so that all the toolbars fit, or increase your video resolution.

DELETE A TOOLBAR

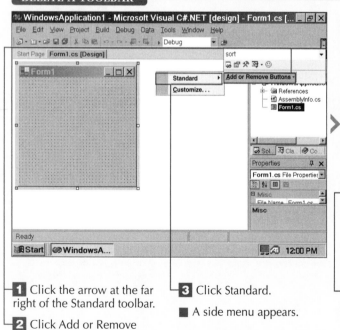

■ Click the arrow at the far right of the Standard toolbar.

■ Click Add or Remove Buttons.

■ Click Standard.

■ A side menu appears.

■ Remove the Solution Explorer command icon by clicking Solution Explorer to uncheck.

Note: All active toolbar buttons have check marks next to their names in the menu.

■ The Solution Explorer command icon disappears from the toolbar.

■ Close the menu by clicking a location outside of the menu.

Extra

You can also remove a toolbar by right-clicking the toolbar's hashmark and selecting the active toolbar from the pop-up menu that appears. You can tell which toolbars are active by looking for a check mark next to each toolbar.

If you have a truncated button bar, it displays two caret marks (>) above the down arrow. When you click either the caret marks or the down arrow, the functionality for both appears in the pop-up window. In this case, the Add and Remove Buttons option appears below the rest of the buttons in the button bar.

If you move a floating button bar around the perimeter of the screen, the button bar will immediately attach itself (or *dock*) to the perimeter in its own vertical or horizontal bar. This approach helps ensure that you get the maximum window space for all the other windows in the parent window.

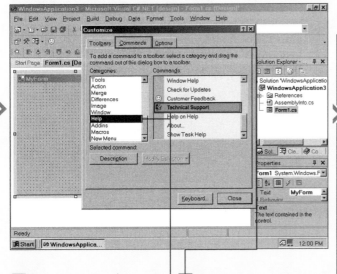

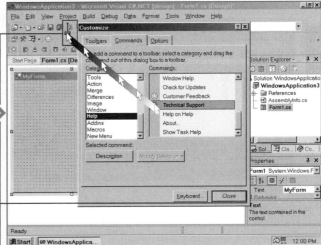

6 Repeat steps 1 and 2.

7 Click Customize.

■ The Customize window appears.

8 Click the Commands tab.

9 Click to select Help in the Categories list box.

10 Scroll down the Commands list box until you see Technical Support.

11 Click and drag the Technical Support entry to the Standard toolbar.

12 Click the Close button in the Customize window.

■ The Technical Support icon appears on the Standard toolbar.

■ You can now access the Technical Support command icon from the Standard toolbar.

CHANGE THE VISUAL STUDIO ENVIRONMENT

The MDE window gives you several methods for accessing commands including windows, toolbars, and shortcut keys. This modular approach to the user environment lets you add and remove windows, toolbars, and shortcut keys to the MDE window to create a working environment designed for you.

The MDE parent window provides a dozen environmental categories that you can alter. These categories contain different attributes that you can change. For example, if you want to change the keyboard shortcuts to mimic those in the previous version of Visual Studio (version 6), or shortcuts for a particular Visual Studio component (such as

Visual Basic), you can do this so you do not have to spend time learning new keyboard shortcuts (or adding them).

These environmental attributes also contain the active defaults denoted by information that appears in a text box or choices denoted by selected (or unselected) check boxes or radio buttons. The Options window presents the object categories and attributes so you can make changes and view settings quickly.

Some attributes and settings also contain descriptions so you can make more informed choices. Some attributes also let you set choices more precisely by offering buttons to more advanced settings.

CHANGE THE VISUAL STUDIO ENVIRONMENT

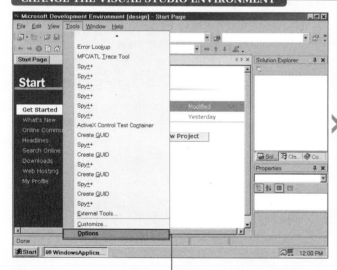

1 Start Microsoft Visual Studio .NET 7.0.

2 Click Tools ➪ Options.

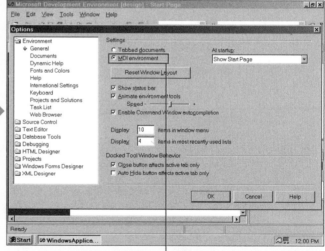

■ The Options window appears with the Environment folder open.

3 Click to select the MDI environment radio button to change the MDE window environment to MDI.

Extra

Two of the features that you will probably be interested in changing are the fonts and colors that appear in the parent window. Visual Studio .NET gives you a lot of control over how the visual elements on your screen appear in the parent window. When you access the Fonts and Colors option in the Options window, you can change the font and color scheme for more than 65 different elements that appear in a wizard. The sample area displays how the element font and type look before you apply them.

Changes that you make to the Options window do not take effect until you click the OK button. Unfortunately, if you make a change that you did not want to make and you cannot change it, you must click the Cancel button (and lose any other changes you made), open the Options window again, and make your changes.

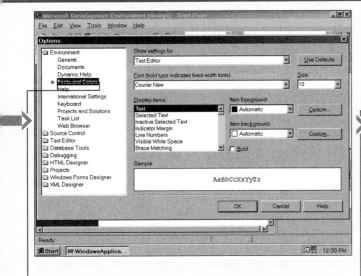

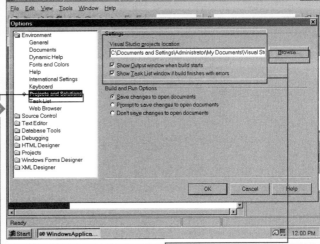

■4 Click to select the Fonts and Colors attribute to change the MDE window fonts and colors.

■ The Sample area shows how different elements will appear on screen.

■5 Click to select the Projects and Solutions attribute to change the file locations of projects and project build and run options.

■ You can change the default location on your disk for all projects in the Visual Studio projects location text box.

■6 Click OK after you finish viewing and making any changes.

MANAGE OPEN WINDOWS

The parent window is the area where you edit your program by either typing in code or editing forms. When you run your program, the changes you make in the parent window will appear.

The parent window is comprised of several windows that appear within it. The parent window displays documents in one of two interface modes: the Tabs on documents mode, which is the default interface mode, and the Multiple Document Interface mode.

The Tabs on Documents mode presents document windows in tabbed panes within the parent window. When you click a different tab at the top of the window, the information for that tab appears in the parent window.

The Multiple Document Interface mode presents document windows one at a time in the parent window. You can switch between document windows through the menu bar much as you would if you switched between open documents in a Windows word-processing program.

The windows that appear around the parent window provide information that you need to work, but you can also hide these windows automatically. The window titles will appear as tabs at the edge of your screen, and the window that corresponds to each tab does not open until you move the mouse pointer over the tab.

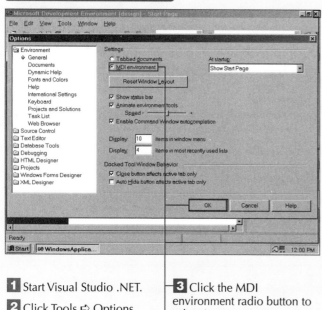

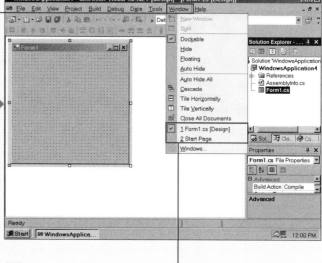

1 Start Visual Studio .NET.

2 Click Tools ➪ Options.

■ The Options window appears with the Environment folder open.

3 Click the MDI environment radio button to select it.

4 Click OK to close the Options dialog box.

5 Apply the MDI environment changes by closing Visual Studio .NET.

6 Restart Visual Studio .NET and open a new Windows application.

7 Click Window.

■ The Form and VS Start Page window entries appear at the bottom of the Window drop-down menu.

Extra

One common error when you change between the Tabs on Documents and Multiple Document Interface modes is not saving your work before you close Visual Studio .NET. The remedy is to select File ⇨ Save, if you have a project open, before you close Visual Studio .NET.

If you find it easier and faster to cycle through all the tabbed panes in the parent window using a keyboard rather than the mouse, all you need to do is hold down the Ctrl key and press the Tab key to move to the next tabbed pane. You can use this keyboard method in either the Tabs on Documents or Multiple Document Interface mode.

When you hide windows, the parent window resizes to the maximum space available. If you reopen a hidden window, the parent window does not resize. You can fix this by clicking the Auto Hide icon in the affected window again.

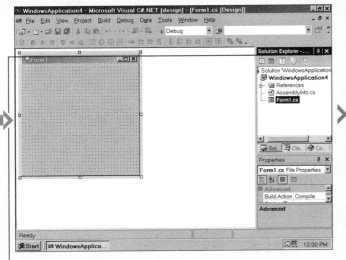

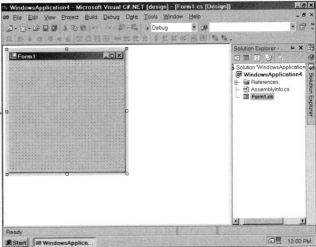

8 Click the Auto Hide icon in the Solution Explorer title bar to change the appearance of the Solution Explorer window.

■ Tabs appear to the right of the Solution Explorer window. Moving the mouse pointer over each tab opens the associated window in place of the Solution Explorer window.

OPEN A PROJECT

Visual Studio .NET places your C# program and related files, such as binary files, within a *project*. When you open a project, Visual Studio .NET opens all of the project components so you can edit and run your C# programs. When you start Visual Studio .NET you can open an existing project in one of two ways: from the Start page or from the File menu option.

You can open a project file from any directory on your computer or your network. As with other Windows software programs, such as Microsoft Office, you can open files within commonly-used folders including the default My Projects folder and your Favorites folder.

You can also change your default directory within the MDE window so you can save and access files from that directory. When you change your default directory before you create your first C# program, you will save the time it takes to move all your programs to that new default directory.

The Look in field contains a directory tree so you can navigate throughout your computer and/or network file and directory structure. After you select the directory in the Look in field, the Open Project window displays the directory files.

OPEN A PROJECT

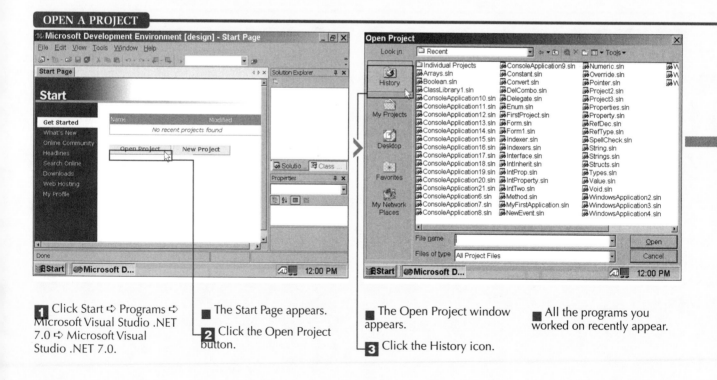

1 Click Start ➪ Programs ➪ Microsoft Visual Studio .NET 7.0 ➪ Microsoft Visual Studio .NET 7.0.

■ The Start Page appears.

2 Click the Open Project button.

■ The Open Project window appears.

3 Click the History icon.

■ All the programs you worked on recently appear.

Extra

If you install the Visual Studio .NET upgrade over an older version of Visual Studio with its directory structure, Visual Studio .NET will move your existing project files to the default Visual Studio Projects folder on your computer without affecting the files in any way. However, you should back up your files before you install Visual Studio .NET in case you run into any installation problems. Of course, you should also back up your project files to another media, such as a Zip drive or tape drive often in case of serious computer trouble.

When you open Visual Studio .NET, the VS Home Page displays a list of recently modified projects at the top of the page. The most recent project you worked on appears at the top of the list. You can open a project in the list by clicking the project title link in the list. If you are uncertain about when you last worked on a recent project, the list contains the date and time the project was saved.

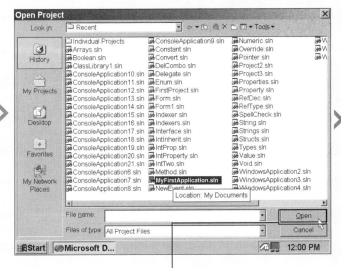

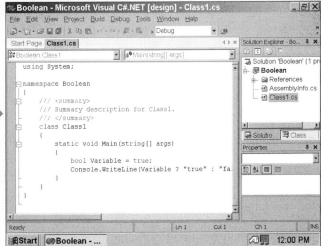

4 Click an application file in the list.

5 Click Open.

Note: If you leave your mouse pointer over the filename, the directory location of the file will appear in a pop-up box.

■ The program code appears in the parent window.

VIEW THE MAIN METHOD

The MDE window automates some code generation so you can better use your time writing the meat of your code.

After you create a new C# program, the MDE window creates the basic structure of your program based on the program you want to create. For example, if you create a console application, then the MDE window will create one class with a `Main method` included so you can perform functions such as specify variables, perform calculations, and output results on the screen.

The `Main` method is the block of code where you perform many of your functions. Without a `Main` method your C#

program cannot run, so no matter what type of C# project you want to create, the MDE window will always include a *skeleton* `Main` method — a `Main` method that does not have any functional code within it.

The default state for the `Main` method is void — the method returns no values of its own. Instead, the method processes the code within it. For example, you can add two numbers and output the result.

Depending on the type of project you create, the `Main` method contains comments that tell you to replace the comments with the functional code.

VIEW THE MAIN METHOD

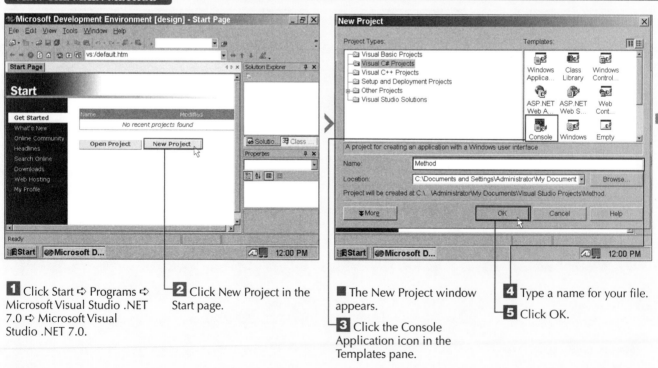

1 Click Start ➪ Programs ➪ Microsoft Visual Studio .NET 7.0 ➪ Microsoft Visual Studio .NET 7.0.

2 Click New Project in the Start page.

■ The New Project window appears.

3 Click the Console Application icon in the Templates pane.

4 Type a name for your file.

5 Click OK.

Apply It

The `Length` property lets you test the `Main` method that contains the string arguments to see if the method works as it should.

TYPE THIS:

```
using System;
class Class1;
{
    public static void Main(string[] args)
        if (args.Length == 0)
        {
        Console.Writeline("Please enter a numeric
argument: ");
        return 1;
        }
}
```

RESULT:

Please enter a
numeric argument: 1

The `return` statement is the last statement in the `Main` method and returns the number 1 as the output.

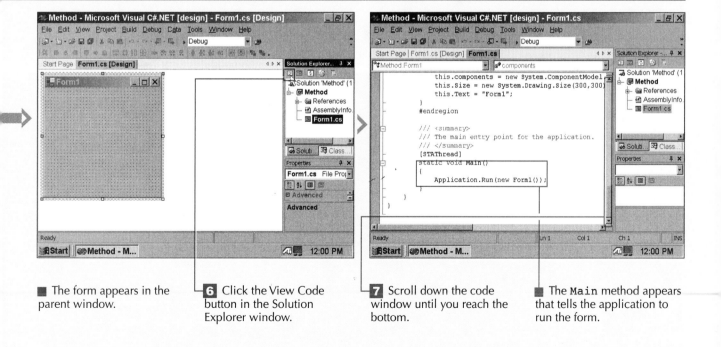

■ The form appears in the parent window.

6 Click the View Code button in the Solution Explorer window.

7 Scroll down the code window until you reach the bottom.

■ The `Main` method appears that tells the application to run the form.

COMBINE PROGRAM TYPES

C# categorizes the elements it uses, such as numbers and characters, into types. These types include predefined basic types, such as numeric and Boolean types, and user-defined types that include structs and enumerated types. Basic types include numbers and the type the number belongs to identifies the kind of number it is. For example, a number that is an integer can only be a whole number in a range from –2,147,643,848 to 2,147,483,647. Integers cannot have decimal places; numbers with decimal places belong in the decimal type. You declare these types when you equate a number with a variable, such as declaring that the number 5 is an integer.

As with other programming languages, C# requires that you declare the correct type for its associated number.

Numeric types belong to the struct category that is one of the two large C# type categories. The other is the enumeration type. The enumeration type lets you specify a list of constants and then assigns numbers to those constants so you can select one of the constants for use in your program. For example, you can specify months of the year in an enumeration and then output a month on the screen by calling the enumeration number associated with that month.

COMBINE PROGRAM TYPES

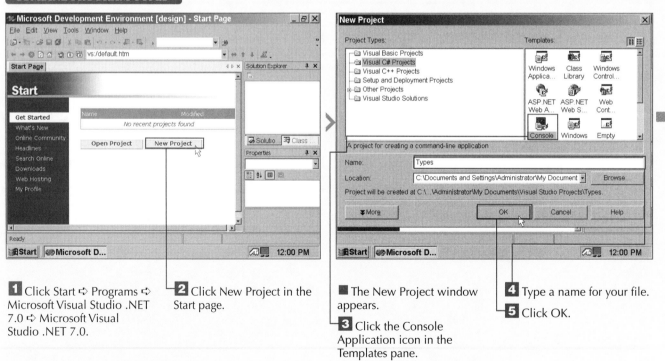

1 Click Start ➪ Programs ➪ Microsoft Visual Studio .NET 7.0 ➪ Microsoft Visual Studio .NET 7.0.

2 Click New Project in the Start page.

■ The New Project window appears.

3 Click the Console Application icon in the Templates pane.

4 Type a name for your file.

5 Click OK.

Apply It

You can determine the value of your constants by assigning constants to the first enumeration element.

TYPE THIS:

```
using System;
public EnumClass
{
    enum WeekDays {Mon=1, Tues, Wed, Thurs, Fri, Sat, Sun}
    public static void Main()
    {
        int x = (int) WeekDays.Wed;
        Console.WriteLine("The Wednesday enum value is {0}", x);
    }
}
```

RESULT:

The Wednesday enum value is 3.

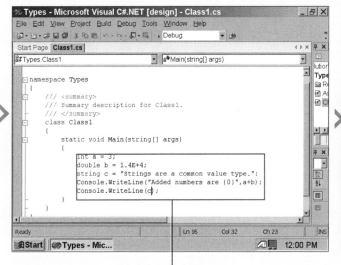

■ The Class1.cs code appears in the parent window.

Note: You can make more room for your Start page by clicking and dragging the right edge of the Start page until you reach the maximum size for the Start page.

6 Delete the comments within the Main method.

7 Type the code that defines some numeric and string types, adds the numeric types, and outputs the result.

8 Run the program by pressing the F5 key.

■ The combined numeric types and string types appear on the screen.

9 Save the program as the filename.

ADD REFERENCE TYPES

C# categorizes elements refer to data elsewhere in a program as `reference types`. Reference types let you access data that you need within different places in your program. For example, you may have several blocks of code that need to refer to the boiling temperature of water.

The reference type category contains several smaller categories including declarative and built-in types.

Declarative reference type elements include classes, interfaces, and delegates. These elements contain values and code that performs certain functions such as arithmetical operations.

Built-in reference types include objects and strings. An *object* is a collection of data and functionality. For example,

an object can be a variable with a value assigned to it, such as $x = 1$.

A string is a collection of characters for displaying output on screen. With string reference types, you can compare the values of the strings using the Visual C# equality operators — the == or =! operators — or other operators such as the additive operator, the plus sign, +. For example, you can define two strings and see if they are equal as shown below:

```
string a = "Tigger"
string b = "is a cat."
Console.WriteLine ( a + b );
```

The above code block would return with the output `Tigger is a cat.`

ADD REFERENCE TYPES

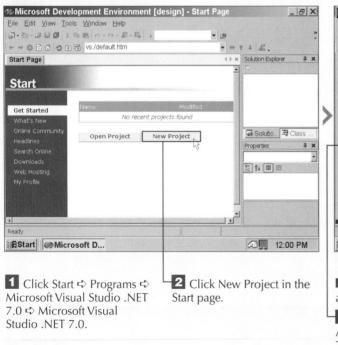

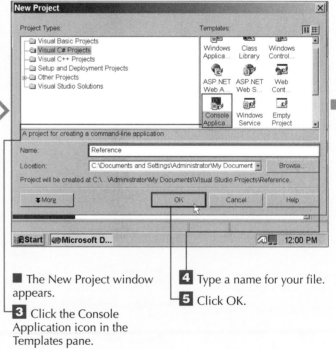

1 Click Start ➪ Programs ➪ Microsoft Visual Studio .NET 7.0 ➪ Microsoft Visual Studio .NET 7.0.

2 Click New Project in the Start page.

■ The New Project window appears.

3 Click the Console Application icon in the Templates pane.

4 Type a name for your file.

5 Click OK.

Apply It

You can reverse the boxing process by using a process called *unboxing.* Unboxing converts an object to a value type. When Visual C# unboxes an object, it checks the object instance to make sure that the instance is the boxed value of the given value type (such as an integer), and then Visual C# copies the value of the instance into the value type variable.

TYPE THIS:

```
using System;
public BoxClass
{
    public static void Main()
    {
        int TiggerAge = 11;
        object box = TiggerAge; // boxes the TiggerAge
value
        int UnBoxedAge = (int)box;  // Unboxes the
value
        Console.WriteLine("The unboxed value is {0}",
UnBoxedAge);
    }
}
```

RESULT:

The unboxed value is 11.

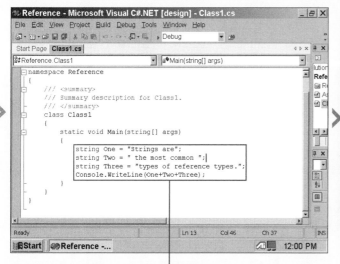

■ The `Class1.cs` code appears in the parent window.

6 Delete the comments within the `Main` method.

7 Type the code that specifies strings and concatenates them.

8 Run the program by pressing the F5 key.

■ The concatenated string appears on the screen.

9 Save the program as the filename.

ADD OPERATORS

Your program cannot operate without *operators,* which are mathematical symbols that perform a wide variety of functions. These operators compare, combine, and contrast values so your program can make choices. For example, your program can refuse to perform a particular action if a user-entered value such as a password is not the same as a stored password in a program.

C# places operators into sixteen different categories. Some operators calculate arithmetical algorithms such as number addition and subtraction. Some arithmetical operators let you control calculation overflow errors, such as divide by zero errors, that can cause a program crash.

Some operators are logical — they calculate whether a condition is true or not such as a user ID number matching the ID number on file within the program. Other operators are relational and determine whether a value is greater than, equal to, or less than another value.

Other operators assign values to variables by using the equals sign or a combination of the equals sign and another operator. For example, if you have the arguments $x = 1$ and $x + = 6$, then that is the equivalent of $x = 1 + 6$.

The most important operator of all is the new operator that lets you create new objects, such as classes and variables, in your program.

ADD OPERATORS

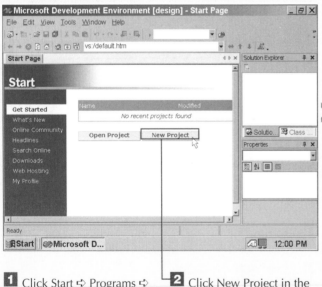

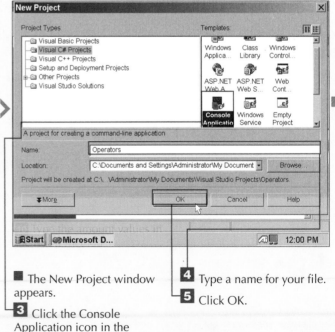

1 Click Start ➪ Programs ➪ Microsoft Visual Studio .NET 7.0 ➪ Microsoft Visual Studio .NET 7.0.

2 Click New Project in the Start page.

■ The New Project window appears.

3 Click the Console Application icon in the Templates pane.

4 Type a name for your file.

5 Click OK.

Apply It

Visual C# gives you the ability to overload operators. You can create your own operations when one or both of the operands are of a user-defined class or struct type.

TYPE THIS:

```
using System;
class Multiply {
    int number;
    public Integer(int number) {

        this.number = number; }

    public static Multiply operator *(Multiply x, Multiply y) {

        return new Multiply(x.number * y.number); }

class Output {

    public static void Main() {

    Multiply a = new Multiply(3,5);
    Multiply b = new Multiply(1,2);
    Console.WriteLine("Multiply Value: {0}", (a * b)); }

}
```

RESULT:

```
Multiply Value: 30
```

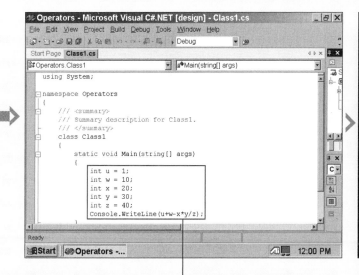

■ The Class1.cs code appears in the parent window.

6 Delete the comments within the Main method.

7 Type the code that specifies integer values and combines them using four arithmetic operators.

8 Run the program by pressing the F5 key.

■ The concatenated string appears on the screen.

9 Save the program as the filename.

INSERT ATTRIBUTES

C# provides attributes so you can specify additional information about the functionality of a string of code. For example, you can add an attribute to a string of code that points to another file for the program to open or to a type in another program.

Attributes retrieve information by using the reflection process. When your C# program runs, the attributes obtain information about program assemblies — the collection of types used in your program — and the types within those assemblies including classes, interfaces, and value types.

When your C# program encounters an attribute in a string of code, the program invokes the attribute. For example, if

your C# program encounters an attribute for accessing an external file, such as a text file, the file will open when you and your users access that string of code.

C# contains three reserved attributes: AttributeUsage, which decribes how a custom attribute class is used; Conditional, which marks a conditional method; and Obsolete, which marks a piece of unusable code. You can also create your own custom attributes by definining an attribute class. C# gives you the building blocks of attribute creation by deriving all custom attributes from the built-in System.Attribute class.

INSERT ATTRIBUTES

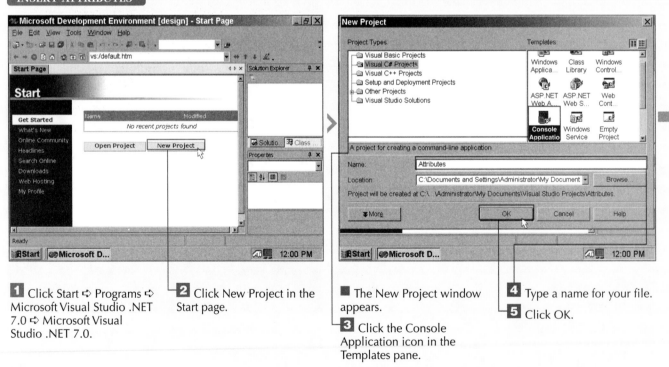

■1 Click Start ➪ Programs ➪ Microsoft Visual Studio .NET 7.0 ➪ Microsoft Visual Studio .NET 7.0.

■2 Click New Project in the Start page.

■ The New Project window appears.

■3 Click the Console Application icon in the Templates pane.

■4 Type a name for your file.

■5 Click OK.

The Visual C# reflection system comes in the form of a built-in method called GetCustomAttributes. The GetCustomAttributes class returns those custom attributes as an array of objects that you can view in your program output.

TYPE THIS:

```
using System;
[Obsolete]
class GetAttribute
{
    static void Main(string[] args)
    {
        Type x = typeof(GetAttribute);
        object[] xget = x.GetCustomAttributes();
        Console.WriteLine("The custom attribute is:");
        foreach (object y in xget)
        Console.WriteLine (y);
    }
}
```

RESULT:

The custom attribute is System.ObsoleteAtt ribute.

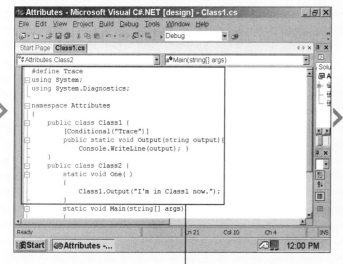

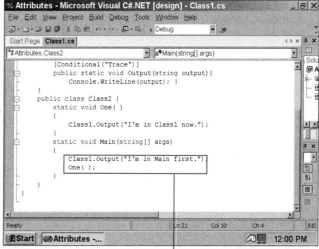

■ The Class1.cs code appears in the parent window.

6 Delete the summary description code for Class1.

7 Type the preprocessor and additional System namespace at top, the class to output data, and the output statement for the first method.

8 Remove the comments within the Main method.

9 Type code that outputs a string from the Main method and then gives permission to access the One method.

CONTINUED ▶

INSERT ATTRIBUTES

C# provides three built-in attributes. One provides the necessary building block for creating custom attributes. The other two attributes provide common attribute functions in C# programs: making a method conditional and marking a string of code that is obsolete. For example, you can set an attribute that will run a method only if the user-entered password matches the password in your program.

The AttributeUsage attribute lets you define where you can apply your attributes. Visual C# contains built-in attribute values called AttributeTargets that let you determine what elements should include the attribute, such as a class.

The Conditional attribute lets you determine whether a string in your program will let a method execute. The Conditional attribute looks for a preprocessing identifier, such as input from the user, that tells the program whether it should execute a particular method or skip the entire method.

The Obsolete attribute lets you mark a section of code as that not to be used. You can set the Obsolete attribute to display a message when you encounter the code in your program (which is the preferred method so you can inform users about other options), or as a Boolean false attribute that will generate a compiler warning when you access that part of the program.

INSERT ATTRIBUTES (CONTINUED)

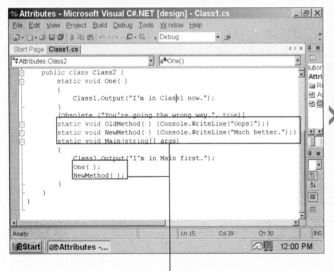

10 Add the Obsolete attribute code within Class2.

11 Add the Main method code that calls NewMethod.

12 Run the program by pressing the F5 key.

■ The Main method string appears first followed by the One method string and the NewMethod string.

The `AttributeTargets` class not only lets you specify the attribute target for an assembly or module but also for classes.

TYPE THIS:

```
using System;
[AttributeUsage(AttributeTargets.Class)]
class information Info : SystemAttribute
{
    public Info(string name);
}
```

The `AttributeTargets.Class` argument within the `AttributeUsage` attribute tells your program that the program attributes apply to a class and not to any other target.

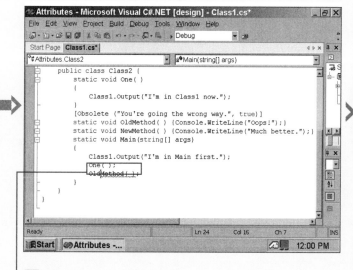

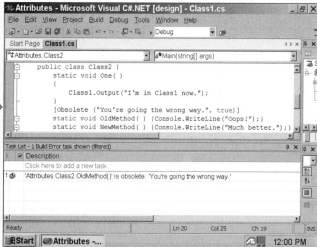

13 Change the `NewMethod` code in the Main method to `OldMethod`.

14 Run the program by pressing the F5 key.

■ The obsolete method prompts the Task List to report that you are going the wrong way.

15 Save the program as the filename.

ENTER CLASSES

Classes provide the functionality your C# program needs to perform its tasks. Three types of members comprise a class: data members, such as user-entered fields; function members that include methods, properties, and operators; and type members such as value types.

Visual C# lets you add classes using the Add Class Wizard. This three-page wizard asks you questions about the types of classes that you want to add, and after the wizard finishes, Visual C# enters the class types in your program automatically without making you put in the extra work of defining the classes in code.

Before you add the class in the Add Class Wizard, you have to tell Visual C# to add a class in the Class View window. When you add a class in the Class View window, the Add Class Wizard appears so you can enter the class information. After you enter the information, the class code appears in the parent window.

The Solution Explorer window in the MDE window provides the most direct way of adding a class to your project. When you add a class into the Solution Explorer tree, the class code appears in the parent window so you can edit it. The class does not, however, have as many elements defined as if you created a class using the Add Class Wizard.

ENTER CLASSES

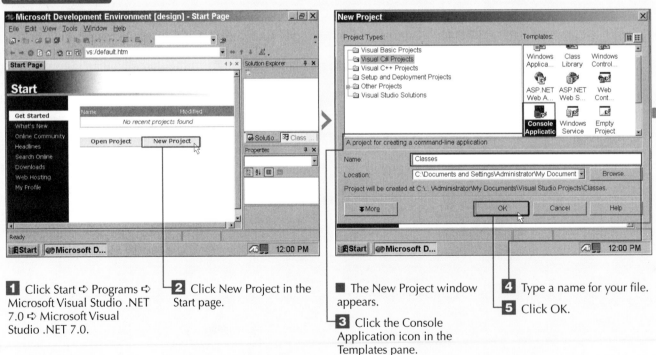

1 Click Start ➪ Programs ➪ Microsoft Visual Studio .NET 7.0 ➪ Microsoft Visual Studio .NET 7.0.

2 Click New Project in the Start page.

■ The New Project window appears.

3 Click the Console Application icon in the Templates pane.

4 Type a name for your file.

5 Click OK.

Extra

The Add Class Wizard converts your summary comments into XML documentation, but you can also add summary comments directly into your program code.

TYPE THIS:

```
using System;    /// <summary>
    /// The summary declaration for this class.
    /// </summary>

class Class1
```

RESULT:

The summary does not display on your screen, but when you or someone else displays the code for the program, the comments appear within the code.

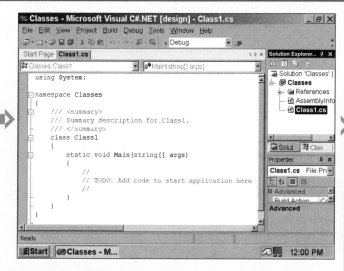

■ The default `Class1` appears in your code in the parent window and the Solution Explorer window also highlights `Class1` in the tree.

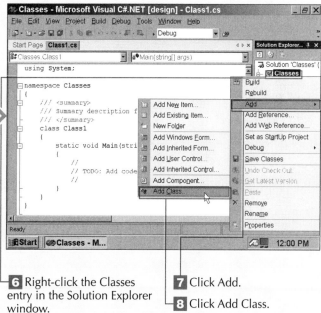

6 Right-click the Classes entry in the Solution Explorer window.

7 Click Add.

8 Click Add Class.

CONTINUED

ENTER CLASSES

fter you add your class name and its associated filename, you must create a namespace. A namespace organizes your Visual C# program so that it can present your program elements to external programs properly. A namespace is something like a box that you use to contain your entire program elements in.

When you create a Visual C# program that is something different than an empty project (such as a Windows application), Visual C# creates the namespace for you automatically and the namespace has the name of your program. The namespace is the first thing that appears in your program.

After you enter the namespace information, you can define both the accessibility level for the class and the class modifiers. The accessibility level lets you determine whether your class can be accessed by all elements in your program, and others, or accessed by certain components. The class modifiers let you determine whether your class will be a base class or a class that cannot be inherited by another class.

After you add any comments and finish with the wizard, the class code appears in the parent window already created so you can concentrate on writing the rest of your program.

ENTER CLASSES (CONTINUED)

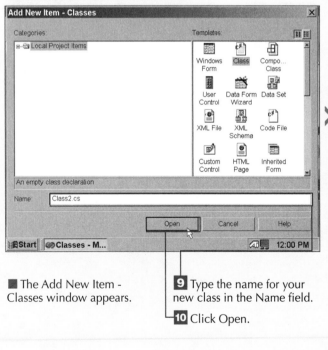

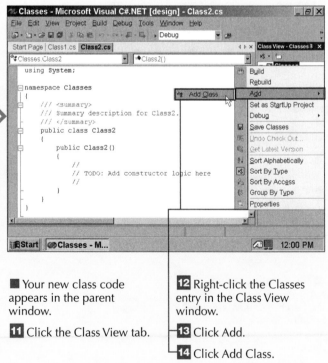

■ The Add New Item - Classes window appears.

9 Type the name for your new class in the Name field.

10 Click Open.

■ Your new class code appears in the parent window.

11 Click the Class View tab.

12 Right-click the Classes entry in the Class View window.

13 Click Add.

14 Click Add Class.

Apply It

When you determine the class accessibility level, you can determine whether the class will have elements that can only be accessed by files in the same *assembly*. An assembly is like a box that holds boxes containing your program components; these components come in the form of files, such as a class being stored in a `.cs` file. You restrict access to the same assembly by using the internal keyword.

TYPE THIS:

```
internal class IntClass
    {
    public int x = 5;
    }
```

RESULT:

When you tell your class that it has internal access, only the program components within the assembly box can access that class; components in other assemblies cannot.

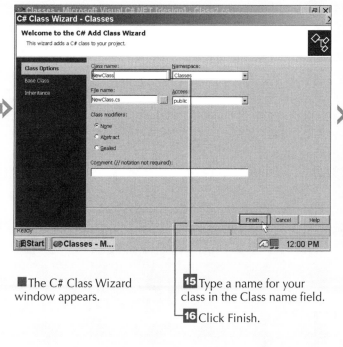

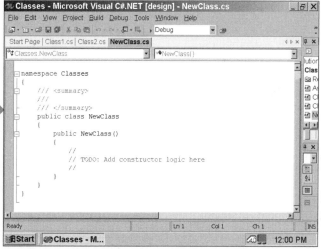

■ The C# Class Wizard window appears.

15 Type a name for your class in the Class name field.

16 Click Finish.

■ The C# Class Wizard window closes and your new class code appears in the parent window.

17 Save the program as the filename.

ADD COMMENTS TO CODE

C# lets you add comments to your code so you can remind yourself and tell others who view your code what you have done. If you update your code, comments can tell you what you did when you wrote that string of code. Comments also tell others what you did to the code in case someone else has to review or change your code. In sum, comments show that you are a polite programmer.

Like Java and C++, Visual C# indicates comments with two forward slash marks (//). Visual C# also marks comments in green and automatically adds comments to your code if you

create a new Visual C# project that is something other than an empty project (such as a form or console application). These comments provide information about what certain code does and also include "to do" information about what code you should add to the program skeleton.

If you have only a few words in your comments, you can add the comments to the right of the code line. If you want to say more, you can add multiple lines, although it is usually a good idea to break multi-line comments out onto their own lines so people can read your comments more easily.

ADD COMMENTS TO CODE

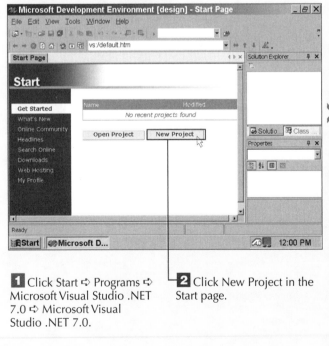

1 Click Start ➪ Programs ➪ Microsoft Visual Studio .NET 7.0 ➪ Microsoft Visual Studio .NET 7.0.

2 Click New Project in the Start page.

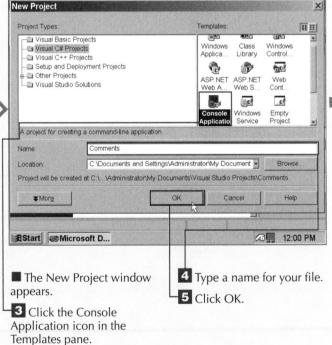

■ The New Project window appears.

3 Click the Console Application icon in the Templates pane.

4 Type a name for your file.

5 Click OK.

Extra

Like Java and C++, Visual C# begins its comments with the slash-and-asterisk combination (/*) and ends comments with the asterisk-and-slash combination (*/). However, there are some minor variations. Java and C# have the same comment structure, but C++ is slightly different. In case you want to copy comments from your Java and/or C++ program over to your Visual C# program. Here are examples of comments in Visual C#, Java, and C++.

VISUAL C#	JAVA	C++
//	//	//
/* comment */	/* comment */	/* comment */

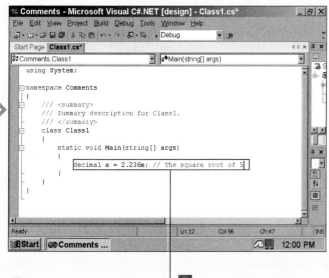

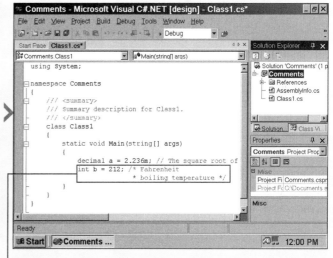

■ The `Class1.cs` code appears in the parent window.

6 Delete the comments within the `Main` method.

7 Type a decimal value with a two-slash comment immediately afterward.

■ The comment code color turns green to differentiate your comment from other code.

8 Type an integer value and a comment by placing /* at the beginning and an */ at the end of the comment.

■ The comment code turns green to differentiate your comment from other code.

Note: When you finish typing in an asterisk and slash, your comment appears in boldface; this signifies that you have a complete comment.

9 Save the program as the filename.

WRITE YOUR FIRST PROGRAM

Your first program lets you become acquainted with programming in the MDE window, gives you confidence in programming with C#, and provides the enjoyment of seeing your first program compile. The Hello, world! program is the ubiquitous first program that people write no matter what programming language you write the program in. Visual C# is brand new, so this task shows you how to write a Hello, world! program so you can announce your program, and Visual C#, to the rest of the world.

You can program your Hello, world! program in several different ways, though this task shows you only one of them. You can view all sample Hello, world! programs in the

Visual Studio .NET online help available in the MDE window. See page 18 for more information about using Visual Studio .NET online help.

You can also download the Hello, world! samples directly from the Hello World Tutorial page in Visual Studio .NET if you want to open and run them without having to type in all of the variants yourself. After you compile the program, the result appears in a `hello.exe` file that you can run from Visual C# or by opening the file in Windows and viewing the output in an MS-DOS, for Windows 9x and ME, or console, for Windows NT or 2000, window.

WRITE YOUR FIRST PROGRAM

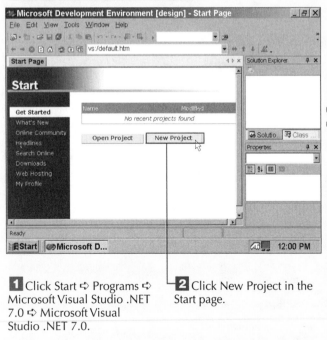

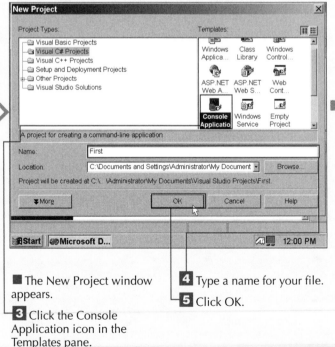

■1 Click Start ➪ Programs ➪ Microsoft Visual Studio .NET 7.0 ➪ Microsoft Visual Studio .NET 7.0.

■2 Click New Project in the Start page.

■ The New Project window appears.

■3 Click the Console Application icon in the Templates pane.

■4 Type a name for your file.

■5 Click OK.

Extra

If you are used to programming in C or C++, you will notice some changes in the Visual C# code, including the following:

- The program does not use a global `Main` method.

- The program does not support methods and variables at the global level, instead containing those elements within type declarations such as class and struct.

- The program does not use : : or -> operators. The former operator does not exist in Visual C# and the latter has limited use.

- The program uses a period (.) in compound names, the most common of which is Console.WriteLine.

- Because the declaration order is not significant in a Visual C# program, forward declarations do not exist.

- The program does not import text by using #include.

- Visual C# eliminates some inter-language barriers; for example, the `Console` class can be written in another language such as Visual Basic.

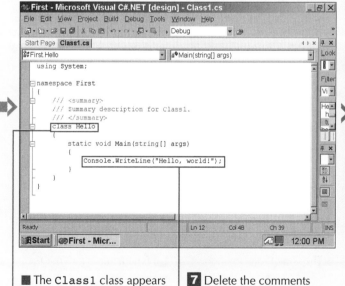

```csharp
using System;

namespace First
{
    /// <summary>
    /// Summary description for Class1.
    /// </summary>
    class Hello
    {
        static void Main(string[] args)
        {
            Console.WriteLine("Hello, world!");
        }
    }
}
```

Hello, world!

■ The **Class1** class appears in the parent window.

6 Rename **Class1** as **Hello**.

7 Delete the comments from the **Main** method.

8 Type the **Console.WriteLine** statement that announces your program to the world.

9 Run the program by pressing the F5 key.

■ The Hello, world! text appears.

10 Save the program as the filename.

ENTER XML DOCUMENTATION

A fter you document your code and compile it, C# automatically changes that code into Extensible Markup Language, XML, format. XML comments let you pass those comments easily if you want to share them with others, such as on a corporate Intranet, for feedback.

XML is a cross between HTML, Hypertext Markup Language, and the more powerful SGML, Standard Generalized Markup Language. XML contains greater flexibility than HTML but XML is not as hard to learn and use as SGML is.

XML is the default documentation language for Visual Studio .NET. You can compile the XML comments in your

program into an XML file that can then be shared on the Internet or on your company intranet using your Internet browser, provided that your browser is XML-capable. However, the job of processing the XML file so that it can create XML documentation is up to your site Webmaster.

XML documentation in your program starts with three slash marks, ///. Visual C# also includes 14 built-in XML tags for user documentation such as the <summary> tag. Visual C# processes the XML tags on types and type members such as classes, and that is why you will see some XML documentation when you view the code in a Visual C# project, other than an empty project, that is.

ENTER XML DOCUMENTATION

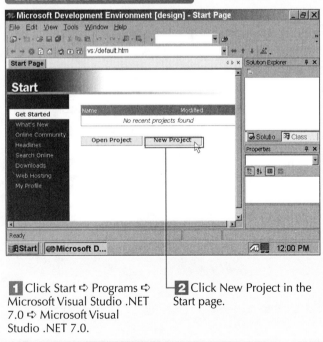

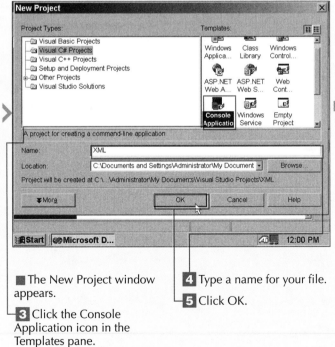

1 Click Start ➪ Programs ➪ Microsoft Visual Studio .NET 7.0 ➪ Microsoft Visual Studio .NET 7.0.

2 Click New Project in the Start page.

■ The New Project window appears.

3 Click the Console Application icon in the Templates pane.

4 Type a name for your file.

5 Click OK.

Apply It

You can also use the slash-and-asterisk combination — /* and */ — just as you do with Java and C++ if you prefer doing so.

TYPE THIS:

```
using System;

/* This is a comment about the following class. */

public class Class1;
```

As with Java and C++, remember that the asterisk always appears immediately before and after the comment text.

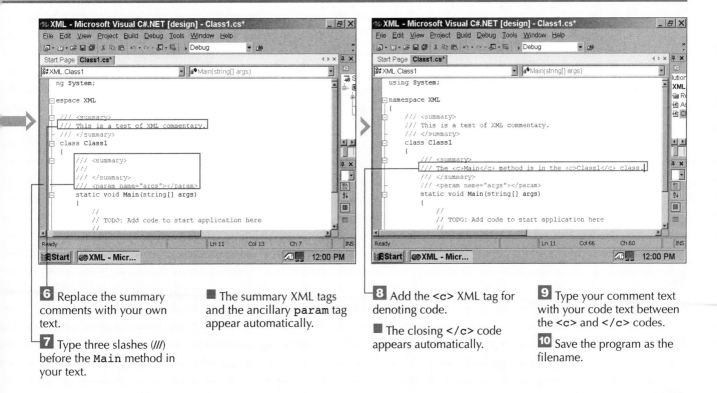

■ **6** Replace the summary comments with your own text.

■ **7** Type three slashes (///) before the **Main** method in your text.

■ The summary XML tags and the ancillary **param** tag appear automatically.

■ **8** Add the **<c>** XML tag for denoting code.

■ The closing **</c>** code appears automatically.

■ **9** Type your comment text with your code text between the **<c>** and **</c>** codes.

■ **10** Save the program as the filename.

ACCESS DOCUMENTATION

The MDE window gives you access to many different sources of help so you can get the answers you need quickly and get back to programming.

These sources include online text files that provide help and online resources from the Microsoft Web site. The online help files and Web pages appear directly within the MDE window so you do not have to close the MDE window and open a new one.

Visual Studio .NET installs online help as part of its installation process. You can access these files directly from the MDE window menu bar. Visual Studio .NET groups

these files by topic so you can find what you want easily. If you need more powerful search features, you can search by keywords and other criteria such as limiting results to Visual C# topics. When you view a help page, it appears in the parent window as another tab so you can switch between your help page and C# program.

When you view the online help features, those Web pages appear in the parent window as well. You can navigate these pages just as you would in a Web browser so you can find the information you want. The MDE window also includes a built-in online search feature so you can find what you need online more effectively.

ACCESS DOCUMENTATION

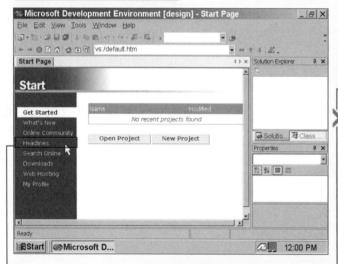

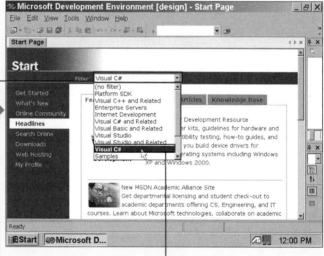

1 Click Start ➪ Programs ➪ Microsoft Visual Studio .NET 7.0 ➪ Microsoft Visual Studio .NET 7.0.

2 Click the Headlines link in the Start page.

Note: If you have a dial-up Internet connection, your dial-up connection window will appear so you can dial your Internet service provider. If you cannot connect to the Internet, the parent window displays an action cancelled message stating that Internet Explorer was unable to connect.

■ The Headlines screen appears in the Start menu with the Features tab selected.

3 Click ▼ to the right of the Filter field.

4 Filter the headline articles to show Visual C# articles only by clicking Visual C#.

Extra

If you decide to view a Webcast in MSDN Online that requires Windows Media Player and you do not have the Player, you can download the Player from the Webcast's opening HTML screen that contains an overview of the Webcast and links to download the Player.

You can send feedback directly from the MSDN Online site by clicking the Send Us Your Feedback link at the lower left-hand corner of the MSDN Online window. After you click the link, you can enter feedback on the MSDN articles or features or submit a bug report about the MSDN Web site, but not about Visual Studio .NET.

You can search for specific articles within MSDN Online by entering a search phrase in the Enter Search Phrase text box in the upper–left of the MSDN Online window and then click the Search button. The results will then appear in the MSDN Online window. If you need to conduct a more refined search, you can click the Advanced link below the Search button.

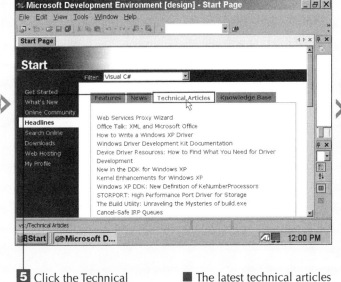

5 Click the Technical Articles tab.

■ The latest technical articles about C# appear.

6 Click the Knowledge Base tab.

■ Knowledge Base articles appear that contain the latest C# support issues.

LOG A BUG REPORT

It is inevitable that a product as sophisticated as Visual Studio .NET will have a few bugs in it. Microsoft wants your help in identifying bugs you have run into so the Visual Studio .NET team at Microsoft can fix your reported problem as quickly as possible. Microsoft makes it easy for you to send issues to Microsoft directly in the Microsoft Development Environment, MDE, window.

You log into the Visual Studio .NET Web site with your username and password. If you do not have a username or password, you can create one from the Web site. When you create a username and password, you will also have to enter your contact information that includes your name, mailing address, e-mail address, and telephone number.

After you log on successfully, you can read up on Visual Studio .NET news and information from the Visual Studio .NET site, and from here you can also log bug reports. After you enter a bug report, the Web site forwards the report to the appropriate personnel on the Visual Studio .NET team.

If the Visual Studio .NET team needs more information from you to replicate or fix the problem, they will contact you by e-mail using the contact information you entered when you created your username and password.

LOG A BUG REPORT

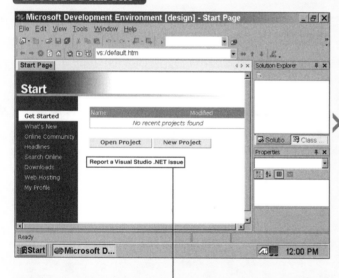

1 Click Start ➪ Programs ➪ Microsoft Visual Studio .NET 7.0 ➪ Microsoft Visual Studio .NET 7.0.

■ The Start page appears in the parent window.

2 Click the Report a Visual Studio .NET issue link.

■ The Login page appears in the parent window.

Note: If you have a dial-up Internet connection, your dial-up connection window will appear so you can dial your Internet service provider. If you cannot connect to the Internet, the parent window displays an action cancelled message stating that Internet Explorer was unable to connect.

3 Enter your login ID and password.

Note: If you do not have a login ID or password, sign up by clicking the Register Now link.

4 Click Submit.

Extra

It is easy to forget passwords, because you can have different passwords for each service, program, or operating system that requires a password. You should keep your passwords in a safe place, never on a network, so you can refer to them in case you forget them.

If you forget your password into the Visual Studio .NET site, you can click the I forgot my password link in the Login page. You will have to enter your user ID name and your e-mail address so Microsoft can e-mail you your password. If you forget your user ID name then you will have to open a new account with a different username so you can log on.

You can submit feedback directly to the Visual Studio .NET team at Microsoft without entering the Visual Studio .NET site. The Login page has a Feedback link at the upper right-hand corner of the site. When you click this link, a blank e-mail message to the Visual Studio .NET team e-mail address will appear so you can send the team an e-mail with your comments, suggestions, and/or problems.

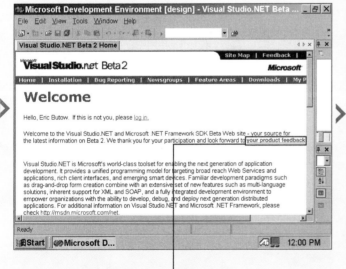

■ The Visual Studio .NET welcome page appears.

Note: Before you see the Welcome page, you may see a Security Alert dialog box informing you that you will be directed to a non-secure page. Click the Yes button in the box if it appears.

5 Enter a bug report by clicking the your product feedback link.

■ The bug report screen appears so you can give technical support detailed information about your problem.

VIEW INFORMATION ABOUT C# BUILDING BLOCKS

C# contains three different types of building blocks that define variables and functionality. You combine these building blocks — methods, classes, and structures — together to form a functioning program.

A *class* is the smallest building block, and it acts like a box for you to keep certain classes of elements such as the ages of your cats. You can also declare classes as base classes where a class can inherit characteristics from a base class. For example, you can have a base class of cats' names and have inheritor classes that contain more specific information such as fur color.

A structure is a value type. Unlike a class, which contains references to data in your program, a structure contains the data to which the classes refer. You can create structures using the struct keyword that you will learn about later in this chapter.

A module, the largest building block, is a portable executable file that can contain structures and classes. Modules have .exe (executable) or .dll (Dynamic Link Library) extensions; you can use modules to test various portions of your program before you integrate them and to integrate with other Windows programs that will reference the same DLL file.

VIEW INFORMATION ABOUT C# BUILDING BLOCKS

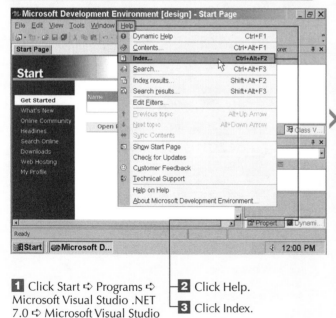

1 Click Start ⇨ Programs ⇨ Microsoft Visual Studio .NET 7.0 ⇨ Microsoft Visual Studio .NET 7.0.

■ The Start page appears.

2 Click Help.

3 Click Index.

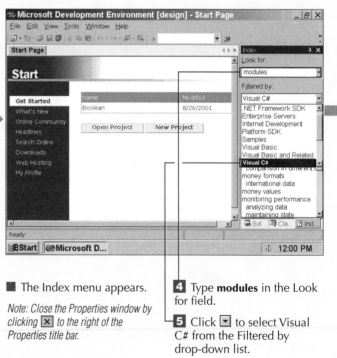

■ The Index menu appears.

Note: Close the Properties window by clicking ☒ to the right of the Properties title bar.

4 Type **modules** in the Look for field.

5 Click ▼ to select Visual C# from the Filtered by drop-down list.

Extra

You can create a module with the class name `Module` so your program knows the module will integrate with other parts of a program with a namespace such as a class. This ensures that your module and a class in your program work together.

If you want to create modules as separate programs, you can give each one a separate namespace name, or if you want to have the modules integrated, you can give several modules the same namespace name.

Classes help your program run more quickly. A class has the extra advantage of being a reference type — you can pass along a class that contains data instead of passing the data itself. Structs have the advantage of requiring less memory because moving a struct means that the program does not have to keep referencing data and using memory for that purpose.

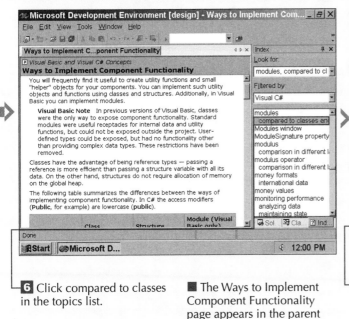

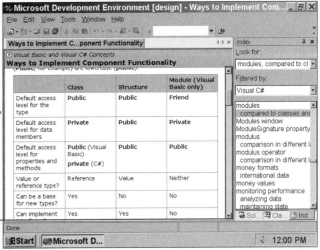

◢ **6** Click compared to classes in the topics list.

■ The Ways to Implement Component Functionality page appears in the parent window.

◢ **7** Scroll down the page until you reach the comparison table.

■ The comparison table compares the different components.

PROGRAM CLASSES

Object-oriented programming languages use classes that act as containers for data elements in your program. Classes let other elements in your program, such as methods, process that data and perform functions such as displaying a calculation result as output.

Object-oriented programming languages make use of classes, which are reference types that act as containers for data elements in your program. Classes include class member characteristics such as the method the member performs, the events the member performs, or the properties of the member.

A class usually includes definition of the object and the implementation of that object. However, a class can have no implementation information, and C# refers to the members of such a class as abstract members, and the class is called

an *abstract class*. You can use an abstract class when you want its instances to only have basic functionality that you can override or augment with information from other classes.

C# refers to the members of a class as an object. When your program invokes the object, the program refers to the class and receives the object properties as well as any implementation methods, such as whether the program uses the object as an event.

You can determine how your program accesses objects in your class. For example, one object within a class can only access another object within that class. However, any class can access objects in any other class.

PROGRAM CLASSES

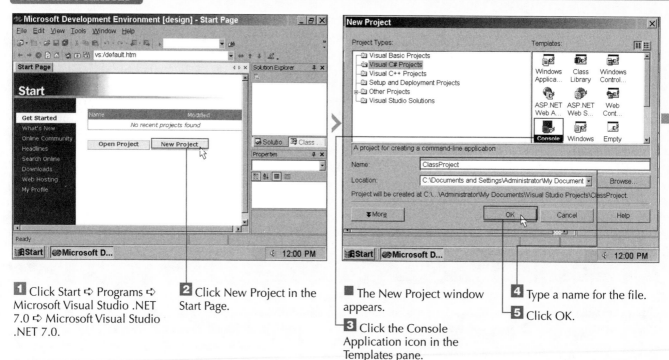

1 Click Start ➪ Programs ➪ Microsoft Visual Studio .NET 7.0 ➪ Microsoft Visual Studio .NET 7.0.

2 Click New Project in the Start Page.

■ The New Project window appears.

3 Click the Console Application icon in the Templates pane.

4 Type a name for the file.

5 Click OK.

When you add a class in the Add Class Wizard, one of the first things you must do is identify a namespace. C# automatically adds a new namespace when you create a new class, but if you add a class within a class, you can specify a new namespace.

TYPE THIS:

```
using System;
namespace NewSpace
{
class NewClass
{
public static void Main(string[] args)
{
    Console.WriteLine("This class has the namespace
NewSpace.");
}
}
```

RESULT:

This class has the namespace NewSpace.

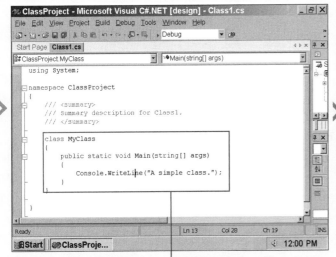

■ The Class1.cs code appears in the parent window.

Note: You can make more room for your Start page by clicking and dragging the right edge of the Start page until you reach the maximum size for the Start page.

6 Delete the Class1 code from the program.

7 Type the MyClass code.

8 Run the program by pressing the F5 key.

■ The output string appears on the screen.

9 Save the program as the filename.

ADD A CLASS

After you open a new C# project, the MDE window automatically creates a new class so you can save time and enter the class code immediately. If you need to add more classes you can do so in one of two ways: programming the class in code or accessing the Add Class Wizard from the Solution Explorer or Class View windows.

The Class View window lets you create a class using the Add Class Wizard. The Add Class Wizard also lets you determine if the class you are creating will inherit information from another class. If you want your class to inherit data from another, you must determine whether your class inherits from a base class or another class.

A *base class* is a single class from which all other classes will inherit. For example, if you set up class B to inherit from the base class A, you can set up class C to inherit from class B, and that way, class C will inherit all of the properties from class B as well as the base class A.

ADD A CLASS

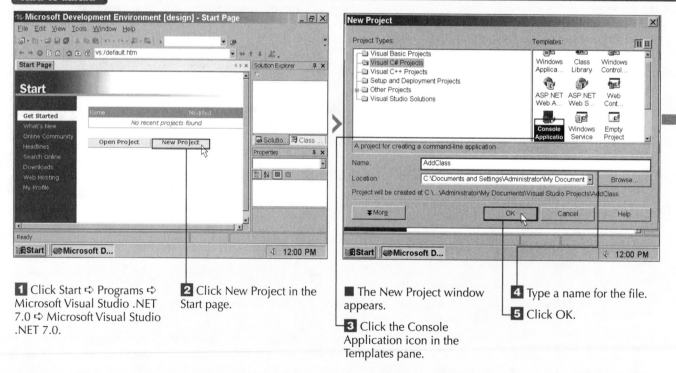

1 Click Start ➪ Programs ➪ Microsoft Visual Studio .NET 7.0 ➪ Microsoft Visual Studio .NET 7.0.

2 Click New Project in the Start page.

■ The New Project window appears.

3 Click the Console Application icon in the Templates pane.

4 Type a name for the file.

5 Click OK.

Extra

If you have programmed in C++ or Java before, you should be aware of changes in C# so you are not surprised. Because C# is closely related to C++ and Java, here are examples of the differences between several class-related keywords.

REFER TO A BASE CLASS	
Java	super
C++	__super
C#	base

SPECIFY THAT A CLASS CAN BE INHERITED	
Java	abstract
C++	abstract
C#	abstract

DERIVE A CLASS FROM A BASE CLASS	
Java	class A extends B
C++	class A public B
C#	class A B

SPECIFY THAT A CLASS CANNOT BE INHERITED	
Java	final
C#	sealed

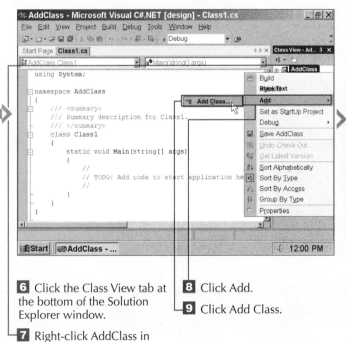

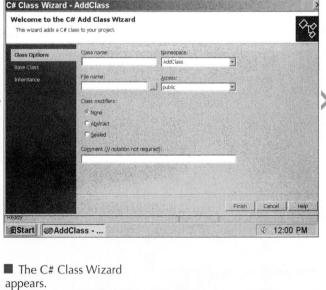

6 Click the Class View tab at the bottom of the Solution Explorer window.

7 Right-click AddClass in the Class View window.

8 Click Add.

9 Click Add Class.

■ The C# Class Wizard appears.

CONTINUED

ADD A CLASS

I f you decide to add a class using the Solution Explorer, the procedure is different than adding a class from the Class View window. The most obvious difference is that you do not use the Add Class Wizard. Instead, you tell C# that you want to create a new class object. After you create the class object, the class appears with the class skeleton already written for you so you can edit the class.

You can add as many classes to your program as you want. The class structure contains the namespace information, sample XML commentary, the class constructor, and comments telling you to add the constructor logic in place

of the comments. The class structure appears no matter what project you have created — even an empty Web project. You can edit the class to your content in the MDE parent window.

You can change the properties of the added class by using the Properties window below the Solution Explorer window. If you want to change the name of your class you can do that in the Solution Explorer as well. When you finish editing your class, it remains as part of your project unless you click the Exclude From Project option when you right-click the class name.

ADD A CLASS (CONTINUED)

-10 Type the name of the class in the Class name field.

■ The class name automatically appears in the File name field.

-11 Click ▾ to select the access level from the drop-down list.

-12 Click to select a class modifier in the Class modifiers area.

-13 Type a class comment in the Comment field.

-14 Click Finish.

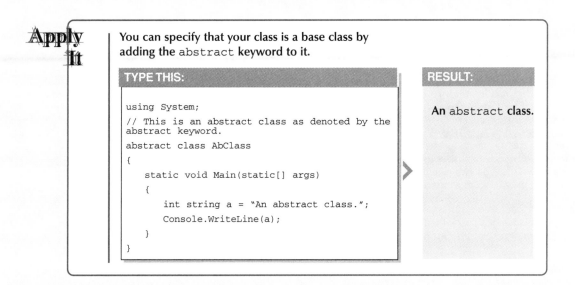

Apply It

You can specify that your class is a base class by adding the abstract keyword to it.

TYPE THIS:

```
using System;
// This is an abstract class as denoted by the
abstract keyword.
abstract class AbClass
{
    static void Main(static[] args)
    {
        int string a = "An abstract class.";
        Console.WriteLine(a);
    }
}
```

RESULT:

An abstract **class.**

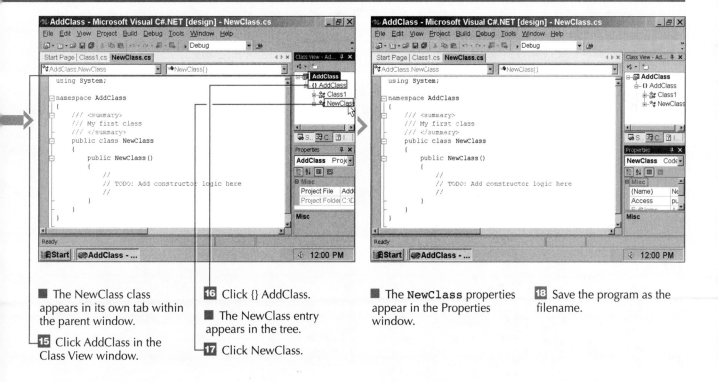

■ The NewClass class appears in its own tab within the parent window.

15 Click AddClass in the Class View window.

16 Click {} AddClass.

■ The NewClass entry appears in the tree.

17 Click NewClass.

■ The **NewClass** properties appear in the Properties window.

18 Save the program as the filename.

EMPLOY CLASS INHERITANCE

You can create classes with objects that more than one class can refer to. Class inheritance lets you define objects in a class once and then have other classes in your program refer to those objects.

Class inheritance speeds up the programming process by reusing code from a base class in other inheriting classes without adding extra code. You can also change objects in your base class that apply to all the inheriting classes.

Inheritance is not the best solution for all programming circumstances — interfaces can provide a better solution. See page 110 for more information on class inheritance and interfaces.

C# only gives you the ability to inherit classes from one base class. The base class is the very first class that all other classes inherit from. Like C++, you can have nested classes. Nested classes let you create classes within the class that you are programming in the MDE parent window. A nested class directly inherits from its parent class. Having nested classes makes it faster for you to create inheriting classes than if you created new classes one at a time.

You can override some base class information such as methods in your inheriting class, but for the most part inheriting classes observe the base class rules.

EMPLOY CLASS INHERITANCE

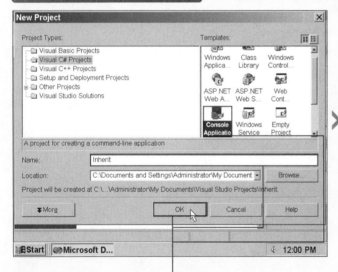

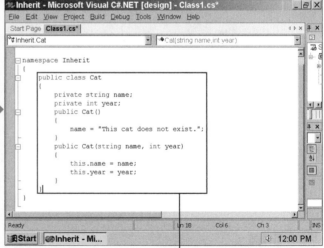

1 Click Start ➪ Programs ➪ Microsoft Visual Studio .NET 7.0 ➪ Microsoft Visual Studio .NET 7.0.

2 Click New Project in the Start page.

■ The New Project window appears.

3 Click the Console Application icon in the Templates pane.

4 Type a name for the file.

5 Click OK.

■ The Class1.cs code appears in the parent window.

6 Delete all code after the **namespace Inherit** code.

7 Type the code that establishes the variables and constructors.

Extra

The rule in C# is that there is only one base class. If you try to create classes with the same name that inherit from different base classes, C# will not let you do so.

Example:
```
abstract class A  // Base class A
{
}
class B : A  // Inherits from class A
{
}
class C: B // C inherits from B that inherits from A
{
}
abstract class D // new base class
{
}
class C: D // Error; you cannot inherit from two base classes at once
{
}
```

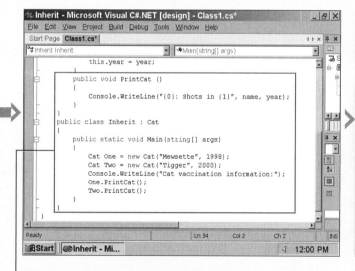

8 Type the code that outputs the information
and the inheriting class that processes the information for output.

9 Run the program by pressing the F5 key.

■ The output strings appear on the screen.

10 Save the program as the filename.

Note: You may want to change the summary comment in the class to note to others that NewClass inherits from Class1.

PROGRAM INSTANCE CONSTRUCTORS

A class has two key parts: constructors and destructors. A constructor is a declaration that tells the compiler what type of class you have created, the features of your class, and how you will treat every instance of your class.

An instance is a variable of an object in the class. For example, two separate instances in the Cat class can be Mewsette and Tigger. Every member that belongs to your class has a status associated with it: static or instance.

A *static* member of a class belongs to the class itself, not any specific instance, and maintains a current value. This is useful if you want to have a class of passwords with information that does not change. An *instance* lets you input different variables for your class. For example, if you have a Cat class, you can include various types of information such as name, weight, breed, and so on.

The instance constructor initializer is a piece of code that implements initialization of an instance of a class — in short, the piece of code that makes your class work. If you do not have a constructor in your class, C# adds one automatically — constructor initializers are that important. When you add a new class, C# adds the constructor initializer automatically.

PROGRAM INSTANCE CONSTRUCTORS

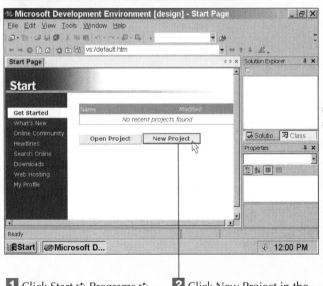

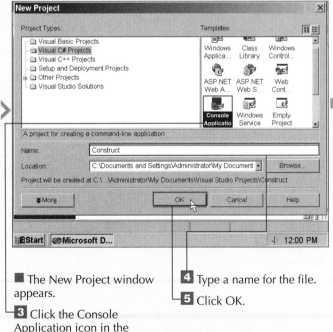

1 Click Start ➪ Programs ➪ Microsoft Visual Studio .NET 7.0 ➪ Microsoft Visual Studio .NET 7.0.

2 Click New Project in the Start page.

■ The New Project window appears.

3 Click the Console Application icon in the Templates pane.

4 Type a name for the file.

5 Click OK.

Apply It

You can add the `this` keyword so a class or struct can overload existing constructors and call one of its own constructors instead.

TYPE THIS:

```
using System;
class Class1 {
    public int a;
    public Class1() : this (2) //gives a the value of 2 { }

    public Class1(int b) {

        a = b //overloads the existing constructor }

        static void Main(string[] args) {

        Class1 x1 = new Class1();
        Class1 x2 = new Class1(4); // 4 is the new value per
the overloaded constructor
    Console.WriteLine(x1.a);
    Console.WriteLine(x2.a);
}
}
```

RESULT:

```
2
4
```

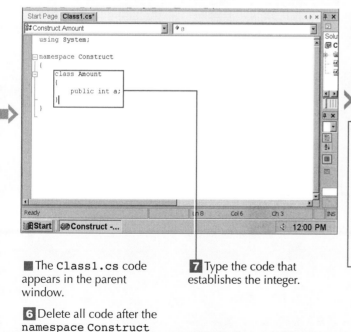

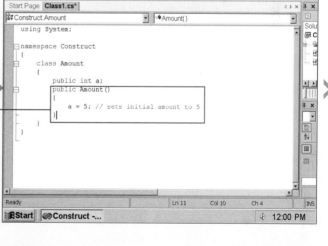

■ The `Class1.cs` code appears in the parent window.

6 Delete all code after the `namespace Construct` code.

7 Type the code that establishes the integer.

8 Type the `Amount` constructor that sets the initial value.

CONTINUED ▶

PROGRAM INSTANCE CONSTRUCTORS

The constructor declaration can include a set of attributes that help define what it is the class is doing. For example, if your class is creating a method, you can set attributes that determine how your class can be accessed. You can also add access modifiers to the class no matter what type of class you construct. These five access modifiers — public, protected internal, protected, internal, or private — determine your class accessibility.

The constructor initializer is only meant as the starting (and defining) point for the constructor itself. If you have a nested class, that nested class constructor initializer can access the parameters in the parent class constructor

initializer. For example, you can have a class with the constructor class One and the constructor of the second class can be class Two: One. The constructor initializer cannot, however, access any parameters in the constructor itself.

If you have an object in an inherited class, you can determine what class the object accesses — the base keyword tells the object to access class information from the base class, and the this keyword tells the object to access class information from the class in which it resides. If a constructor has no initializer, C# creates a base variable automatically.

PROGRAM INSTANCE CONSTRUCTORS

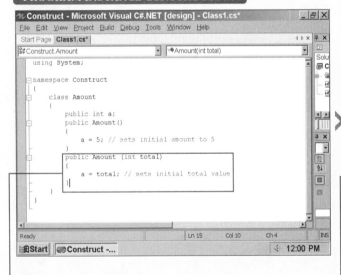

■9 Type the second Amount constructor that sets the initial total value.

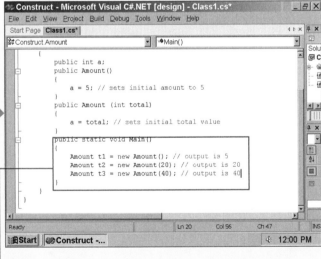

■10 Type the amount values in the Main method.

Apply It

You can create two separate classes in one by creating an internal class and then accessing the internal class from another class.

TYPE THIS IN CLASS1:

```
internal class Base {
    public static int x = 0;
}
```

TYPE THIS IN CLASS2:

```
class Test
{
    public static void Main()
    {
        Base thisBase = new Base();
    }
}
```

RESULT:

The MDE window reports an error because your class Test is trying to create a new instance from the abstract class Base.

```
Construct - Microsoft Visual C#.NET [design] - Class1.cs*
File  Edit  View  Project  Build  Debug  Tools  Window  Help
Start Page  Class1.cs*
Construct.Amount                            Main()
    {
        public int a;
        public Amount()
        {
            a = 5; // sets initial amount to 5
        }
        public Amount (int total)
        {
            a = total; // sets initial total value
        }
        public static void Main()
        {
            Amount t1 = new Amount(); // output is 5
            Amount t2 = new Amount(20); // output is 20
            Amount t3 = new Amount(40); // output is 40
            Console.WriteLine(t1.a);
            Console.WriteLine(t2.a);
            Console.WriteLine(t3.a);
        }
    }
Ready                    Ln 23    Col 37    Ch 28    INS
Start    Construct -...                        12:00 PM
```

```
5
```

11 Type the output code for all three values in the **Main** method.

12 Run the program by pressing the F5 key.

■ The value appears on the screen.

13 Save the program as the filename.

INSERT DESTRUCTORS

When you create constructors you are setting the stage to place your objects somewhere in memory. However, there may be times where you have to remove those objects from memory either to free up the space for other objects or because you want to clean out those objects that no longer apply to your program. C# gives you the ability to delete these objects by using destructors.

As the name suggests, a destructor destroys objects that you specify. The good news is that C# employs destructors automatically when it discovers that an object is no longer being used by the code.

Destructors are also helpful when you have objects that take up absolute addresses in your memory. The end result is that you have cleaner code that runs more efficiently and you do not have to go on a search and destroy mission. The lack of explicit destructors is a bit of bad news, but because C# takes care of it, you have one less thing to worry about.

When your program compiles, C# checks to see if any code in your program does not use a particular object any longer. If C# finds such an instance it adds the destructor code with the void return type automatically.

INSERT DESTRUCTORS

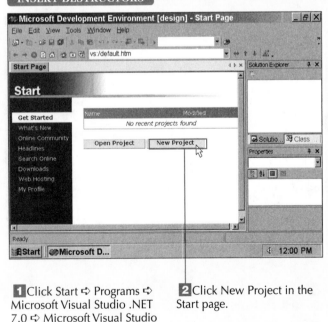

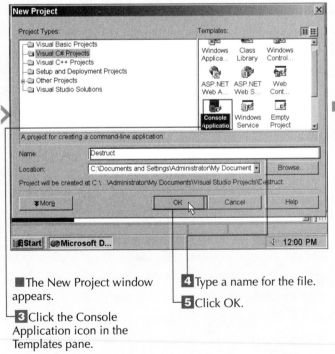

1 Click Start ➪ Programs ➪ Microsoft Visual Studio .NET 7.0 ➪ Microsoft Visual Studio .NET 7.0.

2 Click New Project in the Start page.

■ The New Project window appears.

3 Click the Console Application icon in the Templates pane.

4 Type a name for the file.

5 Click OK.

Extra

C# destroys objects completely and thoroughly. Destructors are not inherited — that is, when C# determines that your project is no longer using the object in a base class, it will not go to any other inherited classes to see if the objects exist in those inherited classes. Instead, C# goes through every class one by one. If C# finds an inherited class with the same object, then C# places that object higher on its list of objects to destroy.

After C# finishes its check of objects in all classes, it creates a list of objects to destroy with the objects in inherited classes first on its task list. Then C# goes through its list and destroys the orphan objects one by one. This all happens behind the scenes, but when you open your classes after your project compiles, you can see the destructor code.

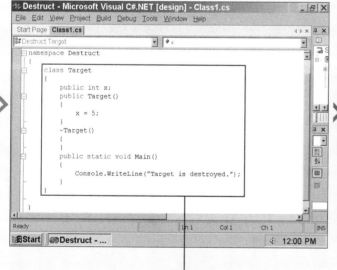

■ The `Class1.cs` code appears in the parent window.

6 Delete all code after the `namespace Destruct` code.

7 Type the code that establishes the constructor, then destroys the constructor with the destructor, and outputs a report.

8 Run the program by pressing the F5 key.

■ The string appears on the screen.

9 Save the program as the filename.

PROGRAM STRUCTS

A struct is a value type that is short for structure. As you may have guessed, a structure contains many different types of data including constants, constructors, fields, methods, and properties. A struct differs from a class in that a class is a reference type where an object created in your program refers to the class information to which the object belongs.

In contrast, a struct contains all of the information the object needs within itself. A struct is most useful if you have a limited range of values for a particular object such as the color of a cat's fur or the types of model trains you have

available. The Visual Studio .NET team at Microsoft recommends that if you have a class that is smaller than 16 bytes then your C# program is more likely to handle a struct more efficiently than a class.

The structure of your struct code block is very similar to that of a class code. For example, a struct uses the same accessibility modifiers that let you determine how your project and other programs access your struct code. However, you build your struct code within the main portion of your program and not as a separate class file.

PROGRAM STRUCTS

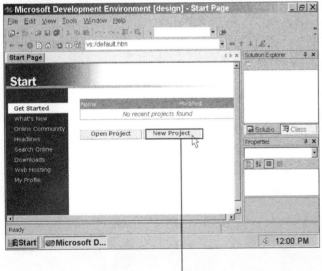

1 Click Start ➪ Programs ➪ Microsoft Visual Studio .NET 7.0 ➪ Microsoft Visual Studio .NET 7.0.

2 Click New Project in the Start page.

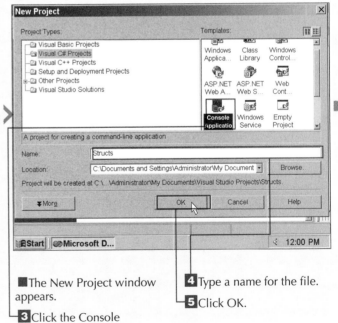

■ The New Project window appears.

3 Click the Console Application icon in the Templates pane.

4 Type a name for the file.

5 Click OK.

Apply It

Structs have one important limitation — they cannot inherit from another struct or class the way that a class does. You can implement an interface from a struct just as you do from a class.

TYPE THIS:

```
using System;
class BaseClass
{
    public static void Main()
    {
        Console.WriteLine("The base class.");
    }
}
struct Inherit : BaseClass
```

RESULT:

An error in the MDE window appears because you cannot have a struct inherit from a base class.

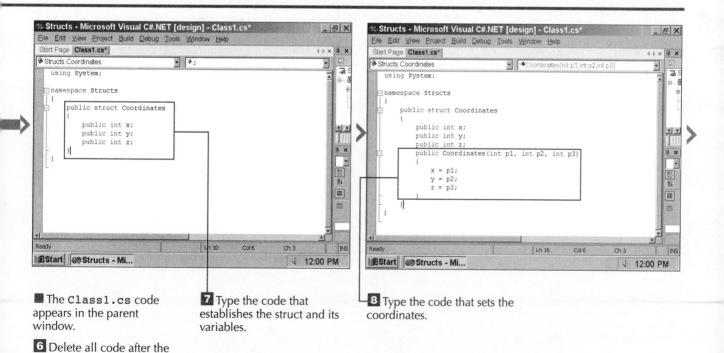

■ The Class1.cs code appears in the parent window.

6 Delete all code after the namespace Structs code.

7 Type the code that establishes the struct and its variables.

8 Type the code that sets the coordinates.

CONTINUED ▶

PROGRAM STRUCTS

Structs are more efficient when you have only a limited range of values that an object must refer to. This makes a struct a good choice when you define an array of values because a struct will process only the array, not each separate value in the array.

Unlike classes, C# does not include a Struct Wizard like the Add Class Wizard, which helps you create classes. What is more, when you create structs you do not do so in its own component as with classes. Instead, you create structs within the main body of your project programmatically.

Structs can include constructors like classes can, but these struct constructors must include parameters. These

parameters include the name of the struct and if the struct depends on or implements an interface. If you try to create a struct that has no parameters, C# will let you know that you are in error and your project will not compile.

There are some other differences between structs and classes. There is also no inheritance for structs as there is for classes because structs are self-contained. Structs cannot inherit information from most classes, and structs cannot function as a base class.

PROGRAM STRUCTS (CONTINUED)

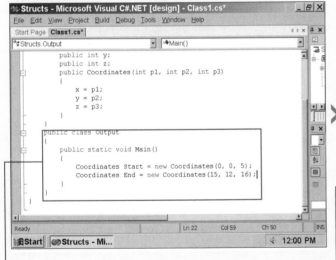

9 Type the class and the `Main` method for providing screen output and enter the coordinates at the start and the end.

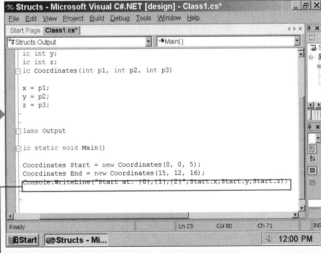

10 Type the output line for the `Start` coordinates.

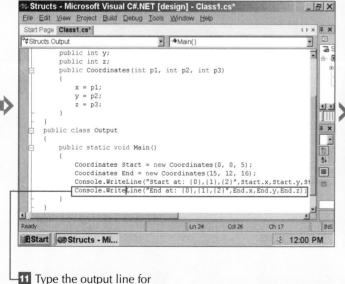

Apply It

You can create a built-in union attribute in C# so that all fields in your program start at the same point in memory.

TYPE THIS:

```
using System.Runtime.InteropServices;
[StructLayout(LayoutKind.Union] // Place the struct attribute before declaring the struct.
struct Union
```

RESULT:

Declaring your struct information and the `System.Runtime.InteropServices` namespace ensures that you can run your program. After you declare your struct you can enter the struct constructor.

Structs - Microsoft Visual C#.NET [design] - Class1.cs*

File Edit View Project Build Debug Tools Window Help

Start Page **Class1.cs***

Structs.Output   ▼   ◆Main()

```
        public int y;
        public int z;
        public Coordinates(int p1, int p2, int p3)
        {
            x = p1;
            y = p2;
            z = p3;
        }
    }
    public class Output
    {
        public static void Main()
        {
            Coordinates Start = new Coordinates(0, 0, 5);
            Coordinates End = new Coordinates(15, 12, 16);
            Console.WriteLine("Start at: {0},{1},{2}",Start.x,Start.y,St
            Console.WriteLine("End at: {0},{1},{2}",End.x,End.y,End.z);
        }
    }
```

Ready   Ln 24   Col 26   Ch 17   INS

Start   Structs - Mi...   12:00 PM

```
Start at: 0,0,5
End at: 15,12,16
```

11 Type the output line for the **End** coordinates.

12 Run the program by pressing the F5 key.

■ The string appears on the screen.

13 Save the program as the filename.

83

DISPLAY HEAP AND STACK INFORMATION

C# allocates memory in one of two ways: heap and stack. The heap method provides more flexibility so classes usually use the heap method. The stack approach sets aside memory for processing. Structs use stack memory allocation because they are self-contained and know exactly how much memory to allocate for their operation.

A heap memory method is a term that describes the dynamic allocation and freeing of objects as the program runs. The heap method is best when you do not know the amount of objects ahead of time and/or the number of objects cannot fit into a stack. Because classes produce a large number of objects that cannot be known ahead of time, the compiler allocates new classes and operators on the heap.

A stack is an area of memory that holds arguments and variables. When the compiler compiles your project it automatically sets aside the stack memory it will need so your program will run properly. Because structs are self-contained, the compiler knows how much memory to use and sets aside the stack.

The heap method gives you more flexibility, and it is best when you use classes. However, you should use structs whenever possible to ensure that the amount of memory your project takes up is as low as possible, which means your project is reaching peak performance.

DISPLAY HEAP AND STACK INFORMATION

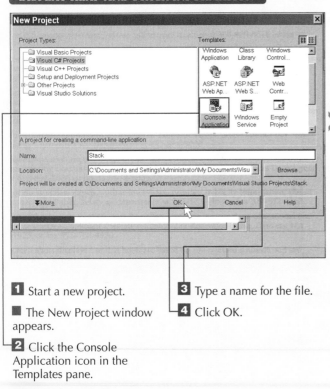

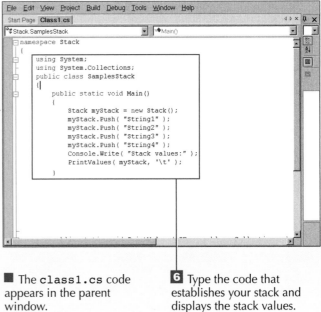

1 Start a new project.

■ The New Project window appears.

2 Click the Console Application icon in the Templates pane.

3 Type a name for the file.

4 Click OK.

■ The **class1.cs** code appears in the parent window.

5 Delete all code after the **namespace Stack** code.

6 Type the code that establishes your stack and displays the stack values.

Extra

Many performance factors depend on the platform that you run your program on. Most users run some flavor of Windows, and unfortunately Windows has yet to have perfect memory allocation. Depending on the version of Windows that you use, you may not get the performance that you expect or the same performance on every flavor of Windows.

The heap method of memory allocation can take time because the compiler is always opening, freeing up, and reorganizing memory blocks. Depending on how you construct your program, there may also be threads trying to access memory at the same time or other types of memory corruption that can cause your project (or even your computer) to crash.

There is no magic wand to fix heap memory problems, but Windows 2000, the most current version of Windows as of this writing, has the best memory allocation features. Windows XP promises to improve its memory allocation abilities. Program carefully so you do not have memory headaches no matter what Windows platform your project will run on.

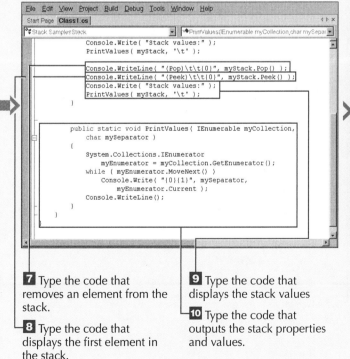

7 Type the code that removes an element from the stack.

8 Type the code that displays the first element in the stack.

9 Type the code that displays the stack values

10 Type the code that outputs the stack properties and values.

11 Run the program by pressing the F5 key.

■ The stack values appear at the top followed by the removed first string (**Pop**), the new first string in the stack (**Peek**) and the new stack values.

12 Save the program as the filename.

85

FIND TYPE INFORMATION

C# categorizes the elements that it uses to process information into types. *Types* indicate the elements within them and how they must be used. Because it can be hard to remember the elements associated with certain types, the MDE window contains type information for your reference.

Four type categories exist: `value`, `reference`, `pointer`, and `void`. Types in each category exist that perform a specific function.

`value` types store data within your C# program. Two categories of types comprise value types: `struct` and `enumeration`. `struct` types contain structs and built-in simple types, including `integral`, `floating-point`, `decimal`, and `Boolean` types. The `enumeration` type lets you declare a set of named constants.

`reference` types store references to data elsewhere in your C# program. `reference` type keywords include `class`, `interface`, `delegate`, `object`, and `string`.

`pointer` types let you point to a specific location in memory. You can only use `pointer` types in unsafe mode, where you specifically instruct the Visual Studio .NET compiler not to manage memory for a particular block of code, such as a class.

You use the `void` type in a method to specify that the method does not return a value. The MDE window online help contains complete information about types if you are uncertain about what type you must use in a specific situation.

FIND TYPE INFORMATION

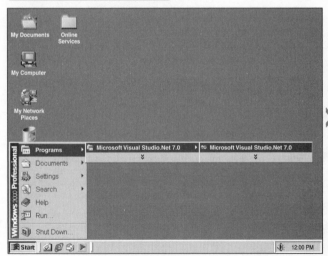

1 Click Start ➪ Programs ➪ Microsoft Visual Studio .NET 7.0 ➪ Microsoft Visual Studio .NET 7.0.

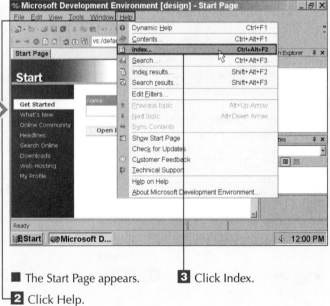

■ The Start Page appears.

2 Click Help.

3 Click Index.

Extra The MDE window online help contains more detailed reference information about types where you can learn about all the variables that are available for all the various types, particularly the value types. The reference information you can access includes the following help pages:

• The Default Values Table displays all of the available value types and their default values.

• The Built-In Types Table displays all of the built-in types and what their .NET counterpart keywords are. When the Visual Studio .NET compiler compiles your Visual C# project it converts the Visual C# types into the .NET keywords for final compilation.

• The Language Equivalent: Types page displays a table that has the storage size of each type and the equivalent type names for Visual Basic, Java, C++, Visual C#, Jscript, and Visual FoxPro.

• The Implicit Numeric Conversions Table and Explicit Numeric Conversions Table contained predefined implicit and explicit numeric conversion tables.

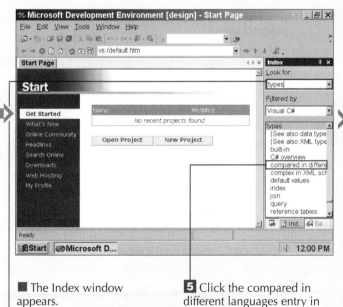

■ The Index window appears.

4 Type **types** in the Look for field.

Note: You can expand the Index window by closing the Properties window.

5 Click the compared in different languages entry in the Index list box.

■ The Look for field displays types, compared in different languages.

■ The Language Equivalents: Types help page appears displaying the type differences between Visual C# and other languages.

PROGRAM CONSTANT EXPRESSIONS

A *constant expression* describes a snippet of code that contains a constant value that the compiler evaluates when your project compiles. An example of a constant value is x = 5. A constant expression contains 1 of 16 types and 1 of 9 different constructs.

The type of a constant expression includes the following: sbyte, byte, short, ushort, int, uint, long, ulong, char, float, double, decimal, bool, string, any enumeration type, or null. Some of these types may be familiar to you, such as the int type declaring an integer. These types will be explored in more detail in this chapter, and you can also view all of the types and their associated value ranges in the MDE window online help.

The constructs you can use in a constant expression include literal keywords (null, true, and false), references to other constant expressions in classes and structs, references to members of enumeration types, nested constant expressions, cast expressions (the conversion of an expression into a type), predefined arithmetic operators (+, *, and /), and the ?: conditional operator that determines whether one or another value is true. You will not know the results from your constant expression until you compile and run your project.

PROGRAM CONSTANT EXPRESSIONS

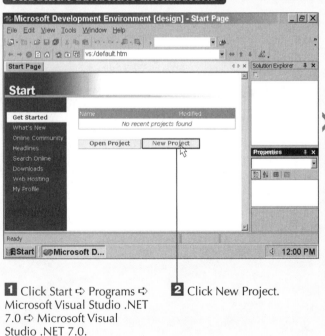

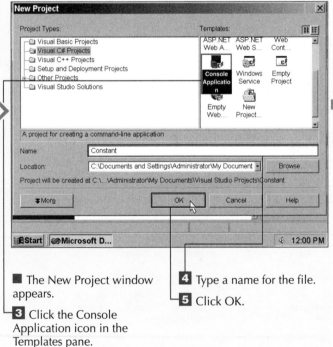

1 Click Start ➪ Programs ➪ Microsoft Visual Studio .NET 7.0 ➪ Microsoft Visual Studio .NET 7.0.

2 Click New Project.

■ The New Project window appears.

3 Click the Console Application icon in the Templates pane.

4 Type a name for the file.

5 Click OK.

Apply It

You can include a constant in another constant expression.

TYPE THIS:

```
using System;
class Zero
{
public const a = 5;
public const b = a + 10;
public static void Main()
{
Console.WriteLine(b
}
}
```

RESULT:

15

When the compiler checks for constant expressions, it will do so even if the constant expression is nested within a non-constant construct. If the constant returns an overflow, such as a divide by zero error, then the compiler will return a compile-time error for you to resolve.

The only constant expressions that can apply to reference types are `string` and `null` because reference types do not contain actual data — only references to that data.

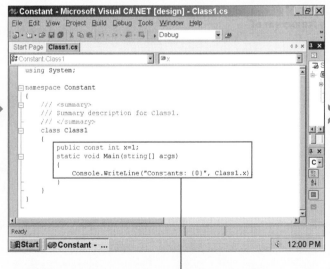

■ The `Class1.cs` code appears in the parent window.

6 Delete the comments within the `Main` method.

7 Type the code that specifies the constant expression and outputs the expression using the object name (`Class1`) and variable (`x`).

8 Run the program by pressing the F5 key.

■ The constant expressions appear onscreen.

9 Save the program as the filename.

SPECIFY VALUE TYPES

You cannot create a Visual C# project without value types. Value types come in two types: `struct` and `enumeration`.

Fourteen other value types exist besides the `struct` and `enum` types; Visual C# groups these types into *simple* types. Eleven of these twelve simple types are numeric, and the remaining simple value type, `bool`, is a Boolean value. These numeric types define the types of numbers that you have specified or you want the user to enter in a field.

Visual C# contains a built-in System namespace that contains all the reference information for predefined types.

The simple types act as aliases for these predefined types that the compiler uses when you compile your project. Visual C# also has two other predefined types, `object` and `string`, that are not simple types because they are used with reference types. Unlike reference types, value types cannot contain the `null` value.

Each value type contains an implicit constructor that tells the compiler to initialize the default value if you do not specify a value. The default values appear in the Default Values Table help page that you can access from online help in the MDE window.

SPECIFY VALUE TYPES

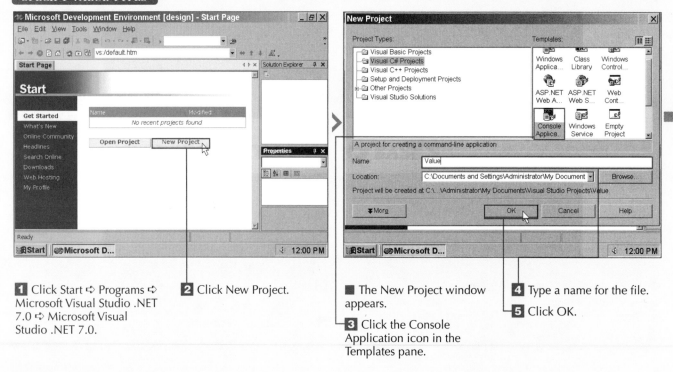

1 Click Start ➪ Programs ➪ Microsoft Visual Studio .NET 7.0 ➪ Microsoft Visual Studio .NET 7.0.

2 Click New Project.

■ The New Project window appears.

3 Click the Console Application icon in the Templates pane.

4 Type a name for the file.

5 Click OK.

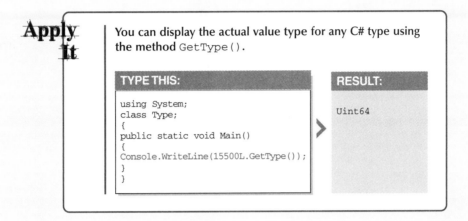

Apply It

You can display the actual value type for any C# type using the method GetType().

TYPE THIS:

```
using System;
class Type;
{
public static void Main()
{
Console.WriteLine(15500L.GetType());
}
}
```

RESULT:

```
Uint64
```

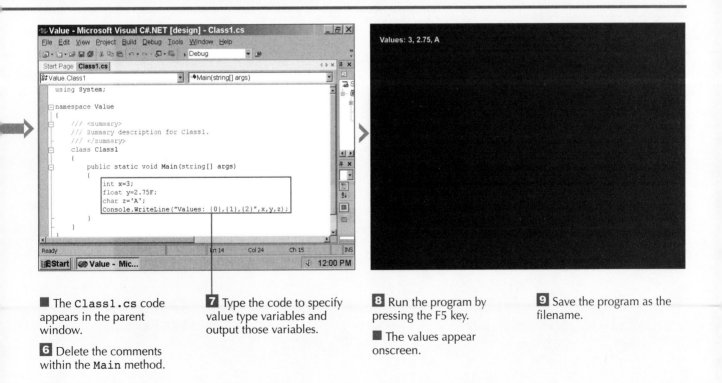

■ The Class1.cs code appears in the parent window.

6 Delete the comments within the Main method.

7 Type the code to specify value type variables and output those variables.

8 Run the program by pressing the F5 key.

■ The values appear onscreen.

9 Save the program as the filename.

PROGRAM NUMERIC TYPES

Numeric types let you specify the type of number you assign to a variable. By assigning numbers to variables, you can perform different calculations. Three different categories of types comprise the numeric types: integral, floating-point, and decimal.

The two most common numeric types are integral and decimal because we use those two number types most often. The integral type category has the most number of types because Visual C# categorizes integer types by the range of the integer. In one case, the char type, the integer is not a number at all.

Visual C# divides the integer ranges into four main groups: byte, short, int, and long. Of these four groups, you can specify whether the integer type is signed or unsigned. A *signed* integer type contains negative numbers in its

range and an *unsigned* integer contains a number range that starts with 0.

The number of digits in each integer group provides the most obvious information about the differences between the four groups. The byte group contains numbers up to three digits, the short type contains numbers up to five digits, the int type contains numbers up to ten digits, and the long type contains numbers up to 19 digits.

The char type is an integer that represents a Unicode character set value that ranges from 0 to 65535.

PROGRAM NUMERIC TYPES

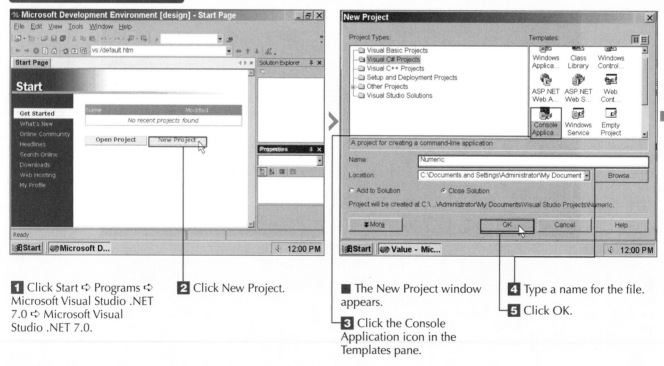

1 Click Start ➪ Programs ➪ Microsoft Visual Studio .NET 7.0 ➪ Microsoft Visual Studio .NET 7.0.

2 Click New Project.

■ The New Project window appears.

3 Click the Console Application icon in the Templates pane.

4 Type a name for the file.

5 Click OK.

Extra

You can determine whether an integer type is signed or unsigned by adding an s or a u before the type name. Only the `byte` type requires an s in front (thus `sbyte`) so you can signify the byte as signed. The other three types — `short`, `int`, and `long` — require you to precede those type names so you can signify those types as unsigned.

The Unicode character set is a worldwide standard set that applies numbers to different characters for most written languages throughout the world. When you declare a `char` variable, you can declare the variable as a letter or with the Unicode number that applies to that letter. For example, you can include a `char` line with `char Letter = 'X';`.

You can also provide the Unicode equivalent in place of X, as in `char Letter = '\u0058';`.

When you enter a Unicode character number you must include the Unicode number in single quotes, precede the number with a backslash and u, and also ensure that the Unicode number has four digits.

You can convert a `char` value to several other integer types including `ushort`, `int`, `uint`, `long`, and `ulong`. However, you cannot convert other integer types (or any other numeric type) to the `char` type.

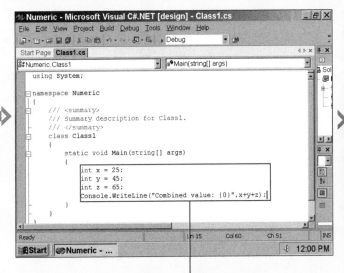

■ The `Class1.cs` code appears in the parent window.

6 Delete the comments within the `Main` method.

7 Type the code that adds two integral expressions and outputs the combined expression.

8 Run the program by pressing the F5 key.

■ The combined expression appears onscreen.

CONTINUED ▶

PROGRAM NUMERIC TYPES

Floating and decimal types make up the two other categories of numeric types that Visual C# supports. Visual C# offers two different floating point types: float and double. You can use the *float* type for very large numbers — the float range is from $\pm 1.5 \times 10^{-45}$ to $\pm 3.4 \times 10^{38}$, and the float type rounds off numbers to seven digits. You must denote a float type by using the suffix f after the floating point value.

If you need even larger numbers, the *double* type gives you a far greater range — $\pm 5.0 \times 10^{-324}$ to $\pm 1.7 \times 10^{308}$ — and it rounds off numbers to 15 or 16 digits depending on the number. Double numbers require no suffix after the value.

The *decimal* type does not give you the range of the floating point type — the decimal type ranges from 1.0×10^{-28} to 7.9×10^{28} — but it does give you greater precision by rounding off numbers to 28 or 29 digits depending on the number.

You must denote a decimal type by using the suffix m after the decimal value. If you do not use the f and m suffixes for floating-point and decimal values, the value will be treated as a double-value, and your project cannot compile.

PROGRAM NUMERIC TYPES (CONTINUED)

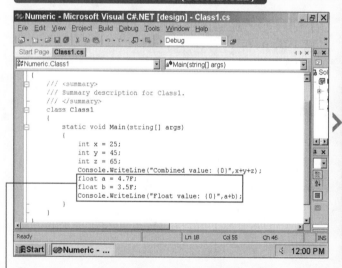

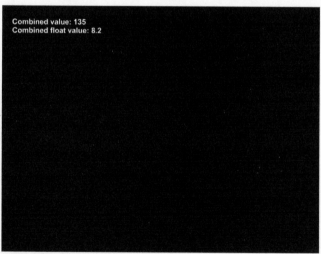

9 Add code to establish and output floating-point values.

10 Run the program by pressing the F5 key.

■ The integer and float values appear onscreen.

Apply It

If you want to enter a Unicode character, you can do so in C#. The Unicode character set is a worldwide standard set that applies numbers to different characters for most written languages throughout the world. When you declare a `char` variable, you can declare the variable as a letter or with the Unicode number that applies to that letter.

TYPE THIS:

```
using System;
class Character;
{
char Letter1 = 'X';
char Letter2 = '\u0058'
public static void Main()
{
Console.WriteLine(Letter1);
Console.WriteLine(Letter2);
}
}
```

RESULT:

```
X

X
```

You can mix integral and floating point types in one expression. When you mix types, the integral types will convert into floating point types. However, you cannot mix decimal types with integral or floating point types. Make sure to denote the decimal with the `m` suffix otherwise your project will not compile.

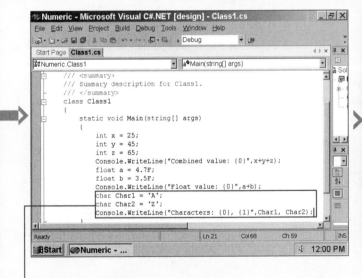

11 Add code to establish and output character values.

12 Run the program by pressing the F5 key.

■ The integer, float, and character values appear onscreen.

13 Save the program as the filename.

PROGRAM THE BOOLEAN TYPE

The Boolean type lets you determine if a variable or expression meets one of two criteria: True or False. Using the Boolean type is a good way to determine how your program functions depending on the values stored in one or more variables in your project.

The Boolean type uses the keyword bool, which is an alias of the System.Boolean type in Visual Studio .NET. You can use the System.Boolean type name as opposed to bool if you wish, but the functionality of the type name and the alias is exactly the same.

You can assign a Boolean value (that is, True or False) or a range of values to a bool keyword. For example, you can tell the bool keyword to check to see if the bool value is True where x > 5 and x < 10. If the value is between 6 and 9, the value will be true, and your project will determine what code block to execute next.

The default value of the Boolean type is False. Therefore, if you enter a bool statement and enter neither the True nor False variables in the statement, Visual C# automatically checks to see if the value in the bool statement is False.

PROGRAM THE BOOLEAN TYPE

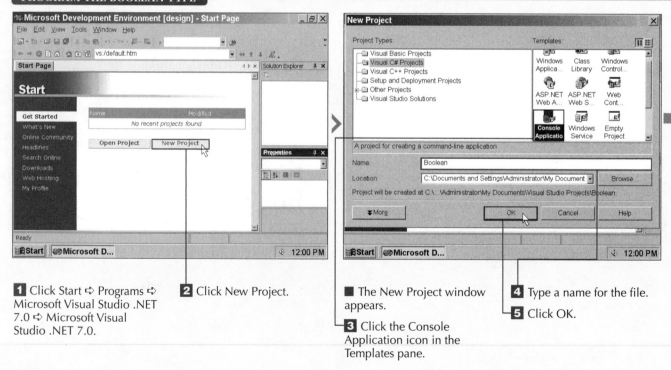

1 Click Start ➪ Programs ➪ Microsoft Visual Studio .NET 7.0 ➪ Microsoft Visual Studio .NET 7.0.

2 Click New Project.

■ The New Project window appears.

3 Click the Console Application icon in the Templates pane.

4 Type a name for the file.

5 Click OK.

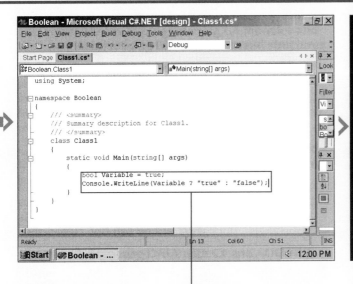

Apply It

You can determine whether a particular value meets a certain condition (for example, whether a value is greater than zero) by using Boolean types as the controlling expressions in `if` and `for` statements.

TYPE THIS:

```
using System;
class Boolean;
{
int x = 4;
public static void Main()
{
if (x!>= 0)
{
Console.WriteLine("The value of x is greater than zero.");
}
}
}
```

RESULT:

The value of `x` is greater than zero.

Unlike C++, which lets you convert a `Boolean` type to an `integer` type, Visual C# does not allow any `Boolean` type conversion. C++ lets you convert the false state to zero and the true state to a non-zero value. If you want to know if a variable is equal to zero or not, you have to create an `if` statement that checks if a variable is zero or not.

■ The `Class1.cs` code appears in the parent window.

6 Delete the comments within the `Main` method.

7 Type the code that specifies the Boolean value of `Variable` and outputs the state of the variable.

8 Run the program by pressing the F5 key.

■ The state of the `Boolean` variable appears onscreen.

9 Save the program as the filename.

DECLARE REFERENCE TYPES

Visual C# includes three reference type keywords: `class`, `interface`, and `delegate`. These keywords declare reference types, but they are not reference types in and of themselves. Visual C# includes two built-in reference types: `object` and `string`. These reference types act as keywords and also the declaration of a reference type in code.

You can assign values of any type to the variables that you include in the object statement. When you convert reference types to value types and vice versa, you do so by declaring those types within the object type before you convert.

The `string` type lets you define strings of Unicode characters that can include words, numbers, or any Unicode character. The string can be enclosed in two forms: quotation marks and quotation marks preceded by the @ symbol. The difference the @ symbol makes is that an escape sequence — the backward slash indicates a Unicode character number — is not processed. This makes it easier to enter a filename with all of its directory information that makes use of backward slashes.

The `string` type acts like a `value` type in that you can use equality operators for comparing strings and you can use other operators for combining and accessing string characters.

DECLARE REFERENCE TYPES

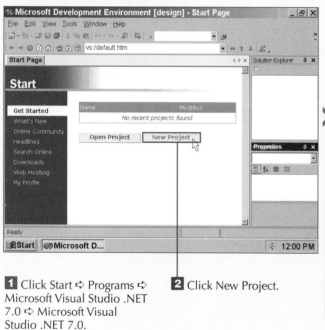

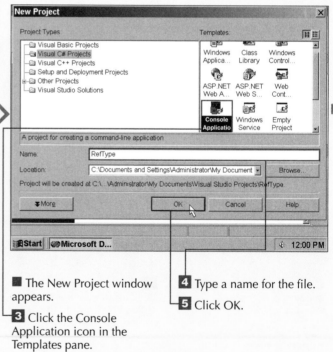

1 Click Start ➪ Programs ➪ Microsoft Visual Studio .NET 7.0 ➪ Microsoft Visual Studio .NET 7.0.

2 Click New Project.

■ The New Project window appears.

3 Click the Console Application icon in the Templates pane.

4 Type a name for the file.

5 Click OK.

Apply It

If you want to determine if two strings are the same, such as a user-entered password matching the stored password, you can use the equality (==) and inequality (!=) operators for testing whether two strings are the same as you would with two values in a value type declaration.

TYPE THIS:

```
using System;
class EqualityTest;
{
int x = 4;
int y = 5
public static void Main()
{
if (x != 0)
{
Console.WriteLine("The value of x is greater than zero.");
}
if (x == 0)
{
Console.WriteLine("The value of x is zero.");
}
}
}
```

RESULT:

The value of x is greater than zero.

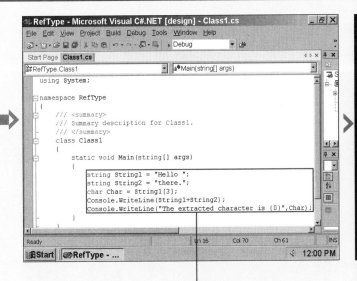

■ The `Class1.cs` code appears in the parent window.

6 Delete the comments within the `Main` method.

7 Type code that concatenates two strings and extracts a character from the first string.

8 Run the program by pressing the F5 key.

■ The string and extracted character appear onscreen.

9 Save the program as the filename.

ENTER REFERENCE TYPE DECLARATIONS

Visual C# offers three different keywords for declaring reference types: `class`, `interface`, and `delegate`. The `class`, `interface`, and `delegate` types have similar statement structures. They include optional class attributes and modifiers that further define your reference type and the identifier, which is the name of your reference type. After that the options change depending on the reference type you use. For example, with classes, you have the ability to specify a base class and any class member declarations. An interface and a class are also closely related in that they can rely on base versions of themselves that contain basic data but no members.

A class contains references about data. In contrast, an interface contains references about how that data should be used — that is, what methods, properties, events, and indexers should apply to that data. Interfaces contain only abstract members that have basic information about how data in a class or struct should behave.

Classes and structs can apply to more than one interface, and the class and/or struct must adhere to that interface much like you must adhere to a contract that you sign.

ENTER REFERENCE TYPE DECLARATIONS

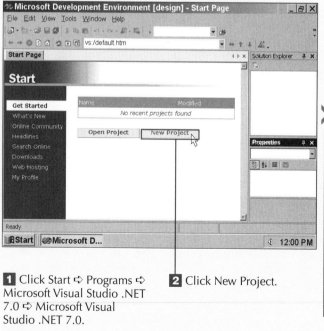

1 Click Start ➪ Programs ➪ Microsoft Visual Studio .NET 7.0 ➪ Microsoft Visual Studio .NET 7.0.

2 Click New Project.

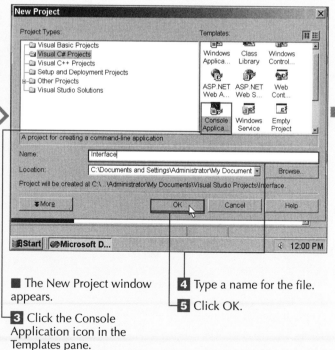

■ The New Project window appears.

3 Click the Console Application icon in the Templates pane.

4 Type a name for the file.

5 Click OK.

Apply It

To save keystrokes, you can implement an interface directly from a class.

TYPE THIS:

```
using System;
interface IntBase1
{
    void IBMethod1();
}
interface IntBase2
{
    void IBMethod2();
}
interface Int1: IntBase1, IntBase2
{
    void Method1();void Method2();
}

interface Int2: IntBase1, IntBase2
{
    void Method3(); void Method4(); void Method5();
}
class Class1: Int1, Int2
{
public static void Main()
{
Console.WriteLine("This class inherits from two interfaces that inherit
    from two base interfaces. No values are returned because all the
    interfaces do are return void methods.");
}
```

RESULT:

This class inherits from two interfaces that inherit from two base interfaces. No values are returned because all the interfaces return void methods.

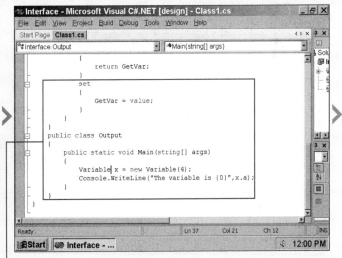

■ The `Class1.cs` code appears in the parent window.

6 Delete the comments within the `Main` method.

7 Type the code that establishes the interface, the fields, the constructor, and then implements the `get` method in the property implementation.

8 Type the code that implements the `set` method in the property implementation and the class that outputs the variable.

CONTINUED

101

ENTER REFERENCE TYPE DECLARATIONS

The delegate reference type serves two functions. First, a delegate object serves as the primary object in an event. An *event* tells your project about something that happens to an object in your program. Second, the delegate object contains method information that tells the affected object in the event what to do when the event occurs.

Delegates act like function pointers in other languages such as C++ and Pascal. Unlike other languages, Visual C# delegates are completely object-oriented so they are secure and type-safe. *Type-safe* code is code that accesses types in well-defined ways so as to prevent crashing programs that

can lead to other nasty things such as memory leaks and crashing operating systems.

When you create a delegate, you must enter two mandatory options. First, you must enter the result type that matches the return type of the method. Entering the result type lets you tie in the delegate with the method. Second, you must enter the delegate name. Without either of those options, the MDE window calls your attention to the error. You can add attributes and modifiers as you can with classes and interfaces.

ENTER REFERENCE TYPE DECLARATIONS (CONTINUED)

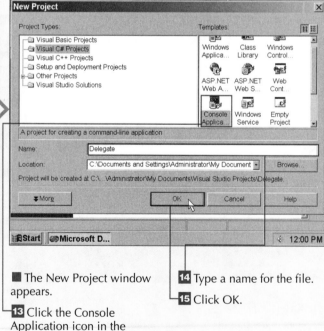

■9 Run the program by pressing the F5 key.

■ The constant expression appears onscreen.

■10 Save the program as the filename.

■11 Close the Interface project.

■12 Click the New Project button in the Start menu.

■ The New Project window appears.

■13 Click the Console Application icon in the Templates pane.

■14 Type a name for the file.

■15 Click OK.

Extra

No matter if you write your delegate before or after you write your method, avoid compilation errors by ensuring that the delegate result type and your method return type match before you compile your project.

The greatest similarity between delegates and interfaces is that they separate the specification of methods with the implementation of those methods. As with the class and struct, your decision about using a delegate or an interface depends on what you are trying to do.

If you need to call a single method or you want a class to refer to several methods, use the delegate. The delegate also has the added advantage of being easier to construct than the interface. However, the interface lets you specify the methods that an object in your project calls instead of general methods that a delegate includes. The interface is also a good choice if a class needs an inheriting interface as a jump point for accessing other interfaces or classes.

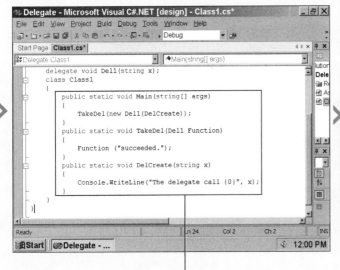

■ The `Class1.cs` code appears in the parent window.

16 Delete the comments within the `Main` method.

17 Type the code that establishes the delegate, calls the delegate, and outputs the result.

18 Run the program by pressing the F5 key.

■ The constant expression appears onscreen.

19 Save the program as the filename.

CONVERT VALUE TYPES TO REFERENCE TYPES

Visual C# enables you to convert value types to reference types and vice versa with a process called boxing. *Boxing* refers to the value type to reference type conversion process. *Unboxing* is the reverse procedure that converts reference types to value types.

Visual C# boxes value types, including struct and built-in value types, by copying the value from the value type into the object. After you box the value type, you can change the value of that value type. Boxing is useful when you need to copy a value from one value type to one or more value types. For example, you can copy an integer value to one or

more integers by having those other integers reference the object you created when you boxed the integer value.

Unboxing lets you convert an object into a value type or an interface type into a value type that implements that interface. When Visual C# unboxes the object, it checks the object to see if it is the same value type as the one you specify in the unboxing argument. If Visual C# sees that this is true, it unboxes the object value and places it into the value type.

CONVERT VALUE TYPES TO REFERENCE TYPES

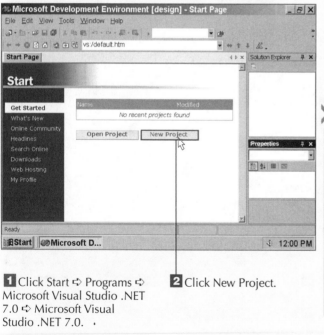

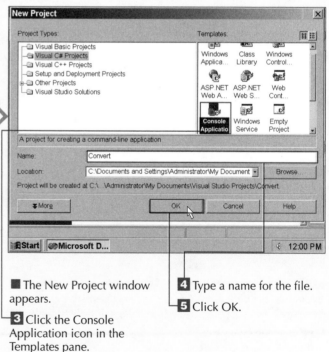

1 Click Start ➪ Programs ➪ Microsoft Visual Studio .NET 7.0 ➪ Microsoft Visual Studio .NET 7.0. ·

2 Click New Project.

■ The New Project window appears.

3 Click the Console Application icon in the Templates pane.

4 Type a name for the file.

5 Click OK.

You can unbox an object with a boxed object value. For example, if you see an object statement with $a = 5$, you want to move the number 5 from the object to an integer, or else the compiler will return an error. You can test whether an object value has been boxed correctly using the `try` and `catch` arguments.

TYPE THIS:

```
using System;
public class Unbox
{
int a = 5;
object x = a // boxes a into object x
try
{
int b = (int) x;
Console.WriteLine("The integer unboxed successfully.");
}
catch (InvalidCastException e) // If there is an error, the catch argument
catches it.
{
Console.WriteLine("{0} Unboxing error!",e);
}

}
```

RESULT:

The integer unboxed successfully.

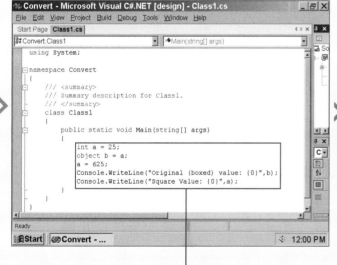

Original (boxed) value: 25
Square Value: 625

```
using System;

namespace Convert
{
    /// <summary>
    /// Summary description for Class1.
    /// </summary>
    class Class1
    {
        public static void Main(string[] args)
        {
            int a = 25;
            object b = a;
            a = 625;
            Console.WriteLine("Original (boxed) value: {0}",b);
            Console.WriteLine("Square Value: {0}",a);
        }
    }
}
```

■ The **Class1.cs** code appears in the parent window.

6 Delete the comments within the **Main** method.

7 Type the code that boxes the original value and outputs the boxed and changed values.

8 Run the program by pressing the F5 key.

■ The constant expression appears onscreen.

9 Save the program as the filename.

PROGRAM POINTER TYPES

When you compile a project, the Visual Studio .NET garbage collector manages all objects in your class and ensures that all objects handle memory correctly and have legitimate references. However, there may be times when you need to have an object access a particular memory address that you do not want the garbage collector to touch. Visual Studio .NET gives you this control with unsafe mode and pointers.

When you enter the `unsafe` keyword in code, you tell the compiler and the Visual Studio .NET runtime environment (the Common Language Runtime) that the garbage collector should not manage those memory blocks that have been allocated in the unsafe argument. You point to the memory blocks to reserve by using the pointer type.

The key portion of your unsafe code block is the fixed pointer type. The fixed pointer type pins down the memory you want to reference so the garbage collector will not allocate that memory block at random to other objects in your program.

Note that if you try to create pointer types and do not explicitly create the unsafe context in your code, the pointers will be considered invalid. In that case the MDE window will alert you to this error, and if you try to compile your project, the compiler will return an error.

PROGRAM POINTER TYPES

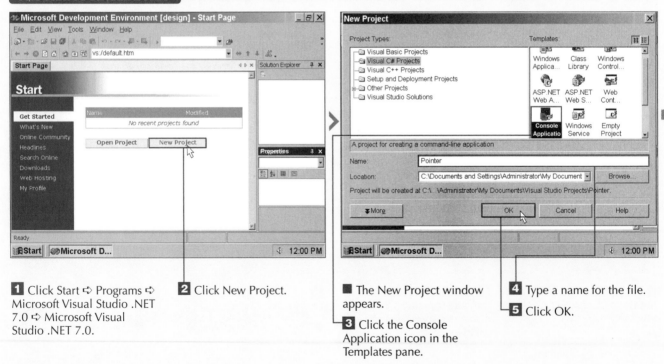

1 Click Start ➪ Programs ➪ Microsoft Visual Studio .NET 7.0 ➪ Microsoft Visual Studio .NET 7.0.

2 Click New Project.

■ The New Project window appears.

3 Click the Console Application icon in the Templates pane.

4 Type a name for the file.

5 Click OK.

Apply It

You can initialize pointers of different types by nesting fixed statements within each other. This approach saves time when you need to declare several different pointer types.

TYPE THIS:

```
using System;
class Pointer
{
int x, y;
unsafe static void Main()
{
Pointer test = new Pointer();
Fixed(int* p1 = &test.x)
Fixed (int* p2 = &test.y)
*p1 = 2;
*p2 = 4;
Console.WriteLine(test.x);
Console.WriteLine(test.y);
}

}
```

RESULT:

```
2
4
6
```

If you receive an error running unsafe code you have not told the compiler to compile unsafe code. You can do so by selecting the project name in the Solution Explorer window and pressing Shift+F4 on your keyboard. When the Property Pages window appears, you can click the Configuration Properties file folder in the left-pane and then change the Allow unsafe code blocks setting to True.

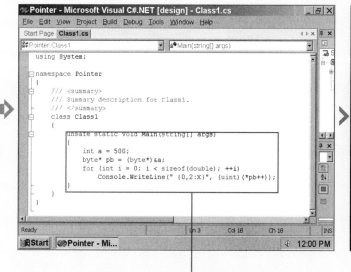

■ The `Class1.cs` code appears in the parent window.

6 Delete the comments within the `Main` method.

7 Type the code that changes the method into an unsafe one and displays the memory locations for values in a range.

8 Run the program by pressing the F5 key.

■ The memory blocks and the value types appear onscreen.

9 Save the program as the filename.

INSERT THE VOID TYPE

The void type is a new type introduced with Visual C# and the last of the four types available. Visual C# uses the void type with methods as well as functions that require methods including classes, events, delegates, and indexers.

The void type indicates that the method does not return a value and/or take any parameters. Many statements will use the void type that precedes the method so the program will understand that it will take the implementation information from your method and the method will not accept any parameters or return any value.

If you want a method to accept parameters from the code that accesses the method (such as a class) but not return any value, you can enter void as the return type. The void type cannot be used as a parameter in the method statement; void applies only to the method return type and as a precedent to the method statement.

The void type gets a lot of exposure because so many different components in Visual C# use methods. These can include indexers and events as well as other reference types including classes and delegates. See page 130 to learn more about using the void type with delegates.

INSERT THE VOID TYPE

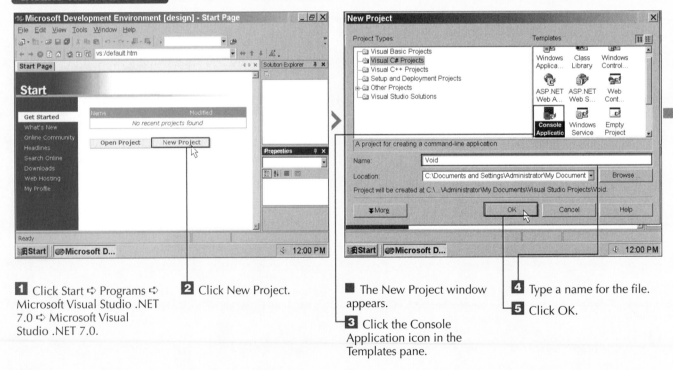

1 Click Start ➪ Programs ➪ Microsoft Visual Studio .NET 7.0 ➪ Microsoft Visual Studio .NET 7.0.

2 Click New Project.

■ The New Project window appears.

3 Click the Console Application icon in the Templates pane.

4 Type a name for the file.

5 Click OK.

Apply It

When you create a new class, you can use the new modifier for hiding an inherited member in the base class. You can do this by entering the name of the method preceded by the void type.

TYPE THIS:

```
using System;
public class Inherited : Base
{
new public void Main ();
}
```

RESULT:

This code hides the Main method in the base class so only the objects in the inherited class will receive the implementation instructions from the Main method. Because the void type precedes the Main method in the code, the method will not return any values or accept any variables.

You use the void type when the method has no return statement, but if you do not include a void type or a return statement within your method, the Visual Studio.NET compiler will return an error. The MDE window alerts you if a void type or return statement does not exist, so that you can fix the problem before you compile your program.

When you create a new class, you can use the new modifier for hiding an inherited member in the

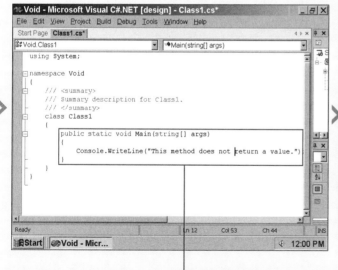

■ The Class1.cs code appears in the parent window.

6 Delete the comments within the Main method.

7 Type the code that specifies the constant expression and outputs the expression.

8 Run the program by pressing the F5 key.

■ The constant expression appears onscreen.

9 Save the program as the filename.

ADD INTERFACE PROPERTIES

The Visual C# Add Properties Wizard lets you enter properties information from the Class View window without entering any code. After you finish with the wizard, the properties information appears in your code in the proper location.

Properties provide basic information about how to read, write, and compute values of fields. Interface properties use the get and set accessors, statements that access information, for reading and writing information from a field, respectively.

When a user enters information into a text field in your program, you can use the get accessor to add that

information into your program and you can use the set accessor for assigning that user input to a value. The get accessor is similar to a method in that it must return a value of the property type. For example, if the property for the get accessor is character based, the value must be a string.

The set accessor is similar to a method that returns the void type. The set accessor is not designed to write information for output but to provide information acquired through the get accessor for use in the rest of the program. For example, a name acquired through the get accessor can be assigned to a value by using the set accessor.

ADD INTERFACE PROPERTIES

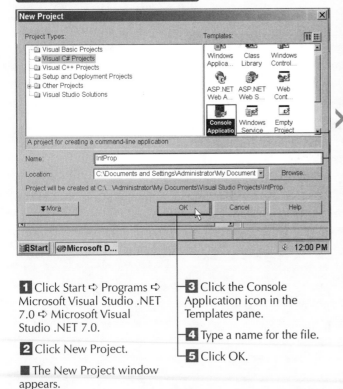

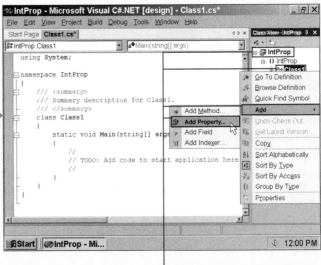

1 Click Start ➪ Programs ➪ Microsoft Visual Studio .NET 7.0 ➪ Microsoft Visual Studio .NET 7.0.

2 Click New Project.

■ The New Project window appears.

3 Click the Console Application icon in the Templates pane.

4 Type a name for the file.

5 Click OK.

6 Click the Class View tab in the Solution Explorer window.

■ The Class View window appears.

Note: You can also view the Class View window by pressing Ctrl+Shift+C on your keyboard.

7 Click the plus sign (+) to expand the tree until you reach the Class1 entry.

8 Right-click Class1.

9 Click Add.

10 Click Add Property.

Apply It

You can change the state of your object as the program runs within the get accessor, such as adding two plus (+) operators to an integer variable to change the variable value.

TYPE THIS:

```
using System;
class ChangeState
{
public int Number
get
{
return Number++;
}
}
```

RESULT:

The state of the object changes every time your project accesses the Number field.

Visual C# classifies the get and set accessors as read-only and write-only properties, respectively. *Read-only* properties cannot have any values written to them. *Write-only* properties have restricted reference access — only properties that can use the write-only property to perform a task can reference that write-only property.

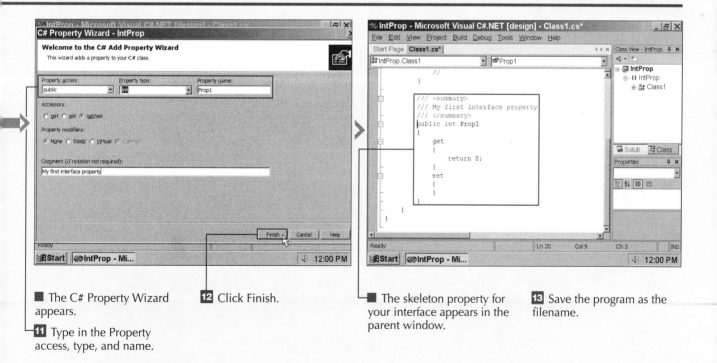

■ The C# Property Wizard appears.

11 Type in the Property access, type, and name.

12 Click Finish.

■ The skeleton property for your interface appears in the parent window.

13 Save the program as the filename.

ADD AN INTERFACE INDEX

Like interfaces, you can add an interface index in a class. The MDE window lets you create an interface index in your class. After you finish with the wizard, the index code will appear in the MDE window so you can edit it to your satisfaction.

An indexer works very much like an array, but the difference is that an array stores values and an indexer stores implementation information contained in one or more interfaces in your class. The interface index helps your program categorize and obtain interface information more quickly. This means that indexers are your friends because they increase the performance of your program.

The C# Indexer Wizard is a window containing several fields in which you can enter interface indexer information. This includes drop-down lists of default information that you can choose from and adding index parameters (such as the index name) to your index.

Visual C# bases the interface indexer type on the value or reference type that appears in your class. This lets you tie into the type of value that you want the index to affect. For example, if you have a variable with a `byte` value that you want the interface index to add its information to, be sure the indexer type is `byte`.

ADD AN INTERFACE INDEX

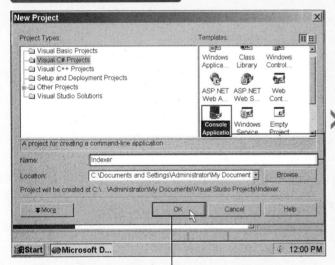

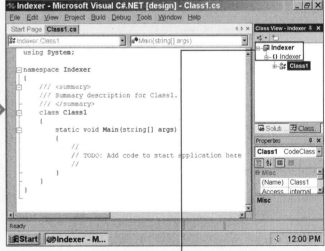

1 Click Start ➡ Programs ➡ Microsoft Visual Studio .NET 7.0 ➡ Microsoft Visual Studio .NET 7.0.

2 Click New Project.

■ The New Project window appears.

3 Click the Console Application icon in the Templates pane.

4 Type a name for the file.

5 Click OK.

6 Click the Class View tab in the Solution Explorer window.

■ The Class View window appears.

Note: You can also view the Class View window by pressing Ctrl+Shift+C on your keyboard.

7 Click the plus sign (+) to expand the tree until you reach the Class1 entry.

Extra

The public indexer access option in the C# Indexer Wizard lets you select the access modifier as you do when you create an instance constructor. You have your choice from one of five access modifiers.

• The public modifier is the default setting; this ensures that your entire project, as well as any other program that accesses your project, can access your class.

• The protected modifier limits access to the members of the base class and any inheriting classes.

• The internal modifier limits access to any element in your project.

• The protected internal modifier limits access to elements in your project or to the members of the base class and any inheriting classes.

• The private modifier limits access to members only within the class.

The default accessibility option is public and that is the choice you see when you create a new interface index in the wizard.

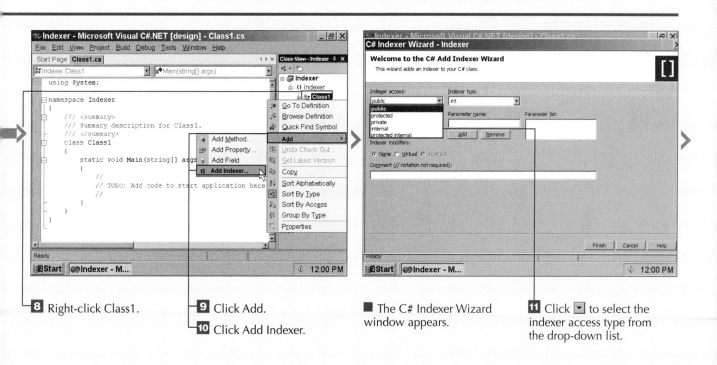

-8- Right-click Class1.

-9- Click Add.

-10- Click Add Indexer.

■ The C# Indexer Wizard window appears.

-11- Click ▾ to select the indexer access type from the drop-down list.

CONTINUED ▶

ADD AN INTERFACE INDEX

A fter you enter the indexer access level and type information, you can enter parameters that determine what type and name the indexer will have. The type of indexer must be the same as the value or reference type that the interface index accesses. For example, if the reference type in the class is an object, you should give the interface index the object parameter type.

From there you can enter the parameter name from a list of parameters that meet the object type requirements. For example, if your interface index is an object, the list of available parameter names will be those in the class that associate with the object type. You can add and remove as many parameters from the indexer list as you want.

The indexer modifiers let you determine if the indexer will be a regular indexer or will have special instructions. For example, the virtual indexer will check to see if there is an inheriting class that has its own index that will override the index you are currently adding. If the inheriting class has an index with an override modifier, your class will use the override index instead.

You can also add comments to your index if you want information about your index present in your code.

ADD AN INTERFACE INDEX (CONTINUED)

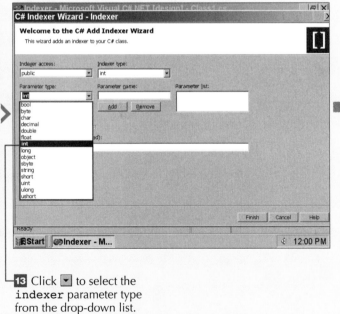

12 Click ▼ to select one of the 15 indexer types from the drop-down list.

13 Click ▼ to select the indexer parameter type from the drop-down list.

Extra

Properties and indexers have some similarities — the most obvious is that all of the rules defined for the properties `get` and `set` accessors also apply to the indexer `get` and `set` accessors.

Although properties and indexers are related, you should be aware of some significant differences:

- Visual C# identifies a property by its name and an indexer by its signature.

- You can access a property with a simple name. You must access an indexer through an element.

- A property can have a static object that does not change. An indexer must contain instance information generated by the class.

- The `get` accessor of a property has no additional parameters. The `get` accessor of an indexer has the same parameters as the indexer.

- The `set` accessor of a property contains the implicit value parameter. The `set` accessor of an indexer has the value parameter and the additional indexer parameters.

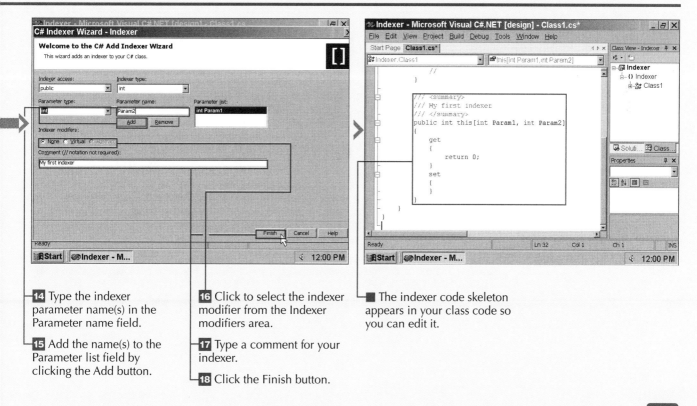

■14 Type the indexer parameter name(s) in the Parameter name field.

■15 Add the name(s) to the Parameter list field by clicking the Add button.

■16 Click to select the indexer modifier from the Indexer modifiers area.

■17 Type a comment for your indexer.

■18 Click the Finish button.

■ The indexer code skeleton appears in your class code so you can edit it.

VIEW INFORMATION ABOUT METHODS

A method is a piece of code that implements an action that a class or object can perform. Methods appear within a class and provide additional information that classes cannot handle.

C# supports two types of methods: static and non-static. All objects in a class can access the static methods in that class without creating any instance of that class. Instances of a class can only access non-static methods. For more information on adding static and non-static methods, see pages 6 to 13.

You can overload methods, which means that different methods can have the same name as long as each separate

method has a unique signature. C# identifies a signature by looking for specific method features including the method name and the method parameters.

You can only add a method when you are editing a class. When you program a method you can do so in one of two ways: in code or by using the C# Method Wizard. The C# Method Wizard contains fields with basic method information that you can enter and choose from. Once you finish entering information into the wizard, the basic method code information appears in your code so you can edit it.

VIEW INFORMATION ABOUT METHODS

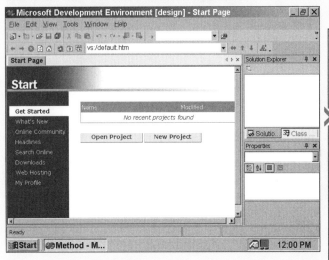

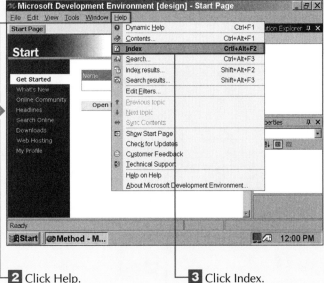

1 Click Start ⇨ Programs ⇨ Microsoft Visual Studio .NET 7.0 ⇨ Microsoft Visual Studio .NET 7.0.

■ The Start page appears.

2 Click Help.

3 Click Index.

Extra

When you add a new method, you can have several methods with the same name with different signatures in the same class. However, if you try to add a method and another class type such as an interface with the same name, the MDE window would register an error and the compiler would not be able to run the program. If you have the same name for the method and interface but the method and interface were in separate classes, then C# would have no problem.

Though C# looks for the module name and the formal parameter list when determining a module signature, it does not look for the return type or the names of the parameters. So if you receive an error from the MDE window about signatures, check to see that your module names and lists are different for each module.

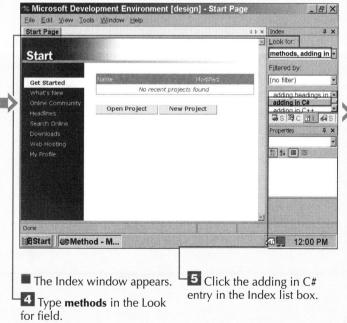

■ The Index window appears.

4 Type **methods** in the Look for field.

5 Click the adding in C# entry in the Index list box.

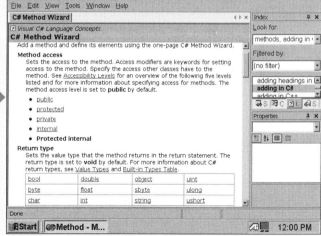

■ The C# Add Method Wizard appears so you can learn about adding methods.

ADD A METHOD

As with a property and an indexer, C# gives you two ways to add a method. If you like the step-by-step functionality provided by a wizard, the C# Add Method Wizard lets you add a method automatically. You can also add a method in code.

When you add a method in code you start with the method keyword. You can add information that precedes the keyword: whether the method is static or non-static (the default is non-static) and whether the method contains a void type. The void type renders the method invisible where it takes on no parameters and returns no values.

After you enter the method keyword, you can enter the optional method declarations. These declarations include various attributes, method modifiers, the return type, and then the name of the method itself. Then you begin to add the information within your method.

Attributes include names that you can enter in your class and refer to in your method. An attribute is a good way to identify information that you want to include in your class such as your company Web site. The method modifiers help determine the access to your method from your class and other code in your project.

ADD A METHOD

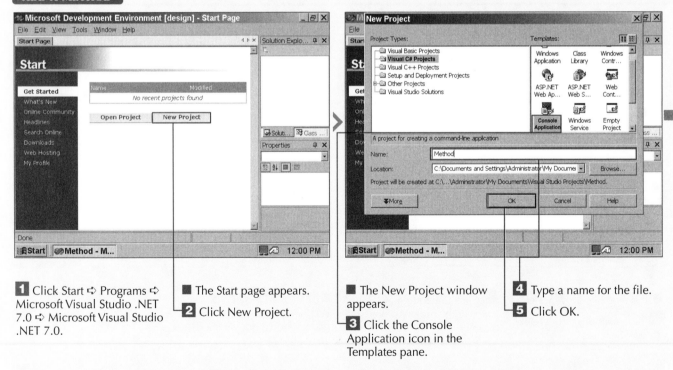

1 Click Start ⇨ Programs ⇨ Microsoft Visual Studio .NET 7.0 ⇨ Microsoft Visual Studio .NET 7.0.

■ The Start page appears.

2 Click New Project.

■ The New Project window appears.

3 Click the Console Application icon in the Templates pane.

4 Type a name for the file.

5 Click OK.

Apply It

You use the return keyword in all methods except one: the void type. When you specify the void method type, you do not need to include the return keyword because the return type is automatically void.

TYPE THIS:

```
using System;
class VoidTest
{
public static void Main()
{
int diameter = 25;
Console.WriteLine("The diameter is {0}", diameter);
}
}
```

RESULT:

```
The diameter is 25
```

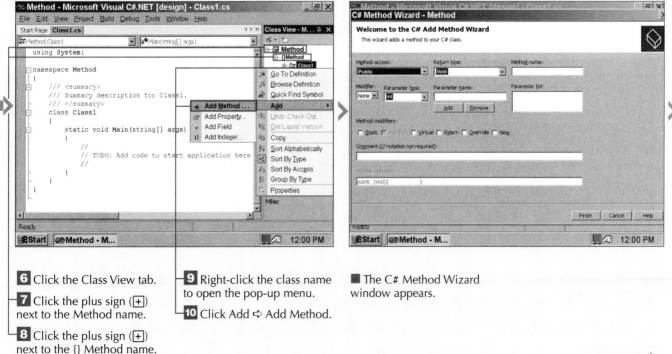

6 Click the Class View tab.

7 Click the plus sign (⊞) next to the Method name.

8 Click the plus sign (⊞) next to the {} Method name.

9 Right-click the class name to open the pop-up menu.

10 Click Add ➪ Add Method.

■ The C# Method Wizard window appears.

CONTINUED ▶

ADD A METHOD

After you include the attributes and method access modifiers, you can further define your method using several different modifiers.

If your method resides in an inheriting class and you also have a modifier in your base class, you can disregard the method in the base class by adding the new keyword. Using the new keyword in your method effectively hides the base class method so your class only pays attention to the method in its class.

You can determine if the method will have the static, virtual, override, abstract, or extern status. A static method lets all objects in its class access it. You can use a virtual

method in an inheriting class; a virtual method checks to see if any methods in any related class must override that method. An override method tells that method to override any methods in any related classes. The abstract method introduces a new virtual method but acts as a placeholder for a different method in a related class that will override the abstract method. The extern modifier lets you create an external method.

Once you add the modifier you can determine the return type and then enter the name of the method. After you add the method name you can begin work on the body of your method.

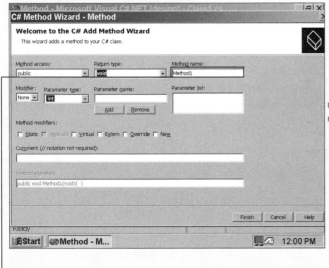

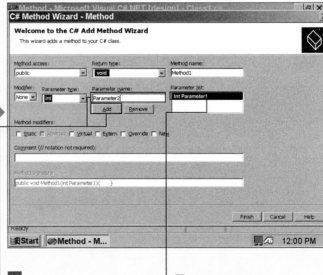

11 Type the method name in the Method name field.

Note: The Method signature field at the bottom reflects the changes to the method code as you type information into the wizard fields.

12 Type the parameter name in the Parameter name field.

13 Click Add.

■ The added parameter name appears in the Parameter list field.

Apply It

C# lets you return multiple values from one method by using the out parameter.

TYPE THIS:

```
using System;
public class OutTest
{
    public static int Output(out int a)
{
        a = 25;
        return 0;
    }
public static void Main()
{
        int a;
        Console.WriteLine(Output(out a));
        Console.WriteLine(a);
    }
}
```

RESULT:

```
0
25
```

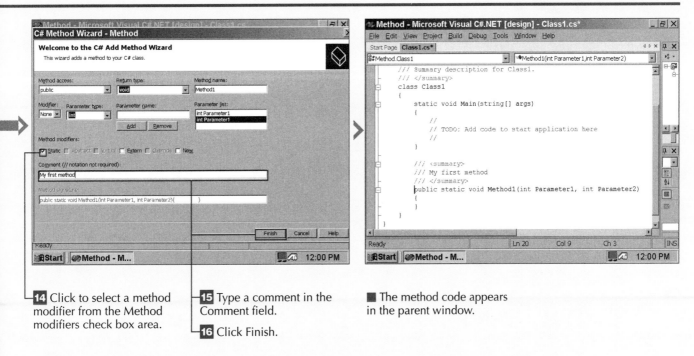

14 Click to select a method modifier from the Method modifiers check box area.

15 Type a comment in the Comment field.

16 Click Finish.

■ The method code appears in the parent window.

ADD STATIC METHODS

A static method maintains its information regardless of how many class instances are created; you can use static methods for maintaining a value such as the boiling temperature of water. Like classes, methods are either static or instance members of the class. A static method contains information that will remain constant so the class can use it repeatedly. This is useful when you want to make calculations in your class with a value that is always constant.

You must explicitly include the static option before typing in the method keyword in your code. If you do not, then C# will automatically consider the method to be non-static. This chapter discusses non-static methods in greater detail later on.

If you declare a static modifier with your method, then you cannot also include a virtual, abstract, or override modifier. If you try to, the MDE window will point out the error and your project will not compile. The static modifier remains with that class and only with that class — it does not rely on any methods in any other inheriting or base class. Because virtual, abstract, and override modifiers deal with inheriting classes, they do not apply to static modifiers.

You cannot access static members through object instances that occur when you run your project. That is what non-static methods are for. You can access static methods through both value and reference types.

ADD STATIC METHODS

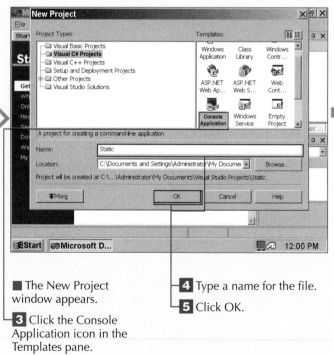

1 Click Start ➪ Programs ➪ Microsoft Visual Studio .NET 7.0 ➪ Microsoft Visual Studio .NET 7.0.

■ The Start page appears.

2 Click New Project.

■ The New Project window appears.

3 Click the Console Application icon in the Templates pane.

4 Type a name for the file.

5 Click OK.

Apply It

If you need to return more than one variable from your static method, you can do so using the `params` keyword.

TYPE THIS:

```
using System;
public class Params
{
    public static void Parameter(params int[] list)
{
            for ( int x = 0 ; x < list.Length ; x++
)
                Console.WriteLine(list[x]);
        Console.WriteLine();
            }
    public static void Main()
    {
        Parameter(10, 15, 20);
    }
}
```

RESULT:

```
10
15
20
```

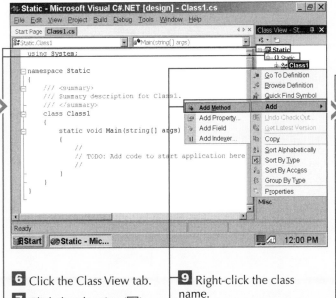

6 Click the Class View tab.

7 Click the plus sign (⊞) next to the Method name.

8 Click the plus sign (⊞) next to the {} Method name.

9 Right-click the class name.

10 Click Add ⇨ Add Method.

■ The C# Method Wizard appears.

11 Type the method name in the Method name field.

Note: The Method signature field at the bottom reflects the changes to the method code as you type information into the wizard fields.

CONTINUED ▶

123

ADD STATIC METHODS

C# uses simple names for accessing many different elements in a C# project, and methods are no different. However, if you have a static method then how you program static methods and other static information in your method determines if you can use simple names or not.

Simple names for a variable can be just one letter, such as x. When you declare variables and associate them with value types, the methods you include those declarations in determine whether your program can process those variables. For example, you can declare two variables of integers with the simple names a and b, with a declared as a non-static member and b declared as a static member.

If you place the two variables in a non-static method and evaluate them later in your class, you will have no trouble with your evaluation. However, if you put those two variables in a static method you will only be able to evaluate the static variable b because a static method cannot access a non-static variable.

If you decide to plunge ahead anyway and try to evaluate a non-static variable in a static method, you will find that the MDE window will protest that action and your program will not compile until you fix the problem.

ADD STATIC METHODS (CONTINUED)

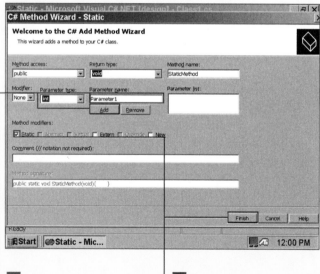

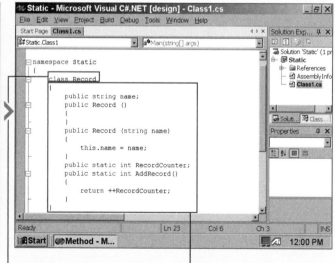

12 Type the parameter name in the Parameter name field.

13 Click Add.

■ The added parameter name appears in the Parameter list field.

14 Click to select a method modifier from the Method modifiers check box area.

15 Click Finish.

■ The **static** method code appears in the parent window.

16 Move the **static** method code above the **Main** method code.

17 Type the **Record** class code that establishes variables and static methods for adding to the number of records.

Extra

You can reference a static method in what Visual Studio .NET refers to as a *member-access* format. The member-access format contains the full version of the type and its associated identifier. The member-access format comes in the form of the type, a period, and then the identifier. For example, you can have the member access type int.number.

C# and the Visual Studio .NET suite do not force you to use the member-access format because many of the access types have aliases that C# refers to. If you reference your static method (or any other static member) in member-access form you must do so in the form E.M. The E must stand for the type that your method uses, not the object. The M stands for the type identifier. For example, if your method is of the type integer with the name `NumberOne`, then the member access form is `int.NumberOne`.

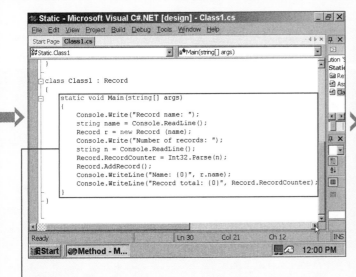

18 Type the `Main` method that lets the user input values and outputs the results.

19 Press the F5 key.

■ Type information at the prompts and the output appears.

20 Save the program as the filename.

INCLUDE NON-STATIC METHODS

The non-static status is the default for all methods. Non-static methods, also called instance methods, rely on an instance of the class — that is, the non-static method relies on the information it receives from an object generated by the class. Once the non-static method receives that object it provides the object with its implementation instructions and sends the object back out into the class for further processing.

The non-static method is best if you know that the class will generate an object for the method. If you create a method in an inherited class, then the non-static method is the only choice. A static method belongs to its class, but a non-static method can take objects from inheriting classes. You can also set non-static methods to override or be overridden by other non-static methods in other inherited classes in your class family or from the base class.

Your non-static method does not accept objects automatically. You must tell the method that you want to accept the value by using the this keyword. When you use the keyword this in your method, the referenced object receives a type that matches the object type and a value that acts as a reference to the object.

INCLUDE NON-STATIC METHODS

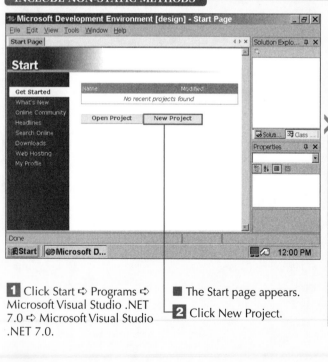

1 Click Start ➪ Programs ➪ Microsoft Visual Studio .NET 7.0 ➪ Microsoft Visual Studio .NET 7.0.

■ The Start page appears.

2 Click New Project.

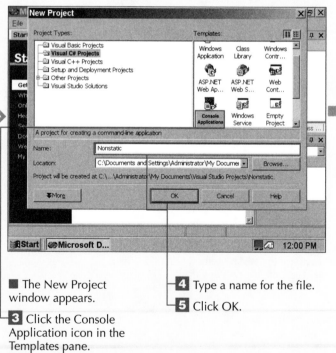

■ The New Project window appears.

3 Click the Console Application icon in the Templates pane.

4 Type a name for the file.

5 Click OK.

Apply It

You can reference a non-static method with the member-access format so you can point directly to the member you want the method to call.

TYPE THIS:

```
using System;
public class Name {
public string first;
public string last;public Person () { }
public Person (string first, string last) {
    this.first = first;
    this.last = last;
    }
class Main: Person {
public static void Main() {
    Console.Write("First name? ");
    String first = Console.ReadLine(); //accepts input
    Person a = new Person (name, id);
    Console.WriteLine("First name: {0}", a.first);
    }
}
```

RESULT:

```
First name? John
First name: John
```

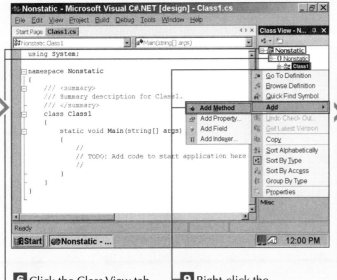

6 Click the Class View tab.

7 Click the plus sign (⊞) next to the Method name.

8 Click the plus sign (⊞) next to the {} Method name.

9 Right-click the class name.

10 Click Add ➪ Add Method.

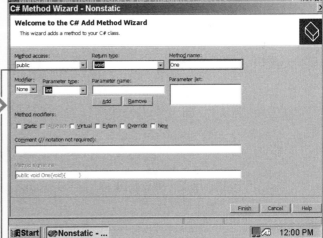

■ The C# Method Wizard appears.

11 Type the method name in the Method name field.

Note: The Method signature field at the bottom reflects the changes to the method code as you type information into the wizard fields.

CONTINUED ▶

INCLUDE NON-STATIC METHODS

When the non-static method processes the instance of a class, C# creates a copy of all instance (that is, object) fields for the method to process. This ensures that a copy of the instance remains in the class while your class is being instructed by the non-static method. Once the object leaves the non-static method, the method-trained copy replaces the original that was in the class.

The earlier discussion in this chapter about static methods included information about simple names and how the declaration of those names can affect processing in a static method. With non-static methods the same rules apply.

If you try to evaluate a static variable in a non-static method, you will receive an error and the MDE window will prohibit you from compiling your program.

If you have a non-static method that another method in another inheriting class can override, be sure that your overriding non-static method can process the variables in your class correctly. If you do not, you may encounter processing errors because the new, overriding method may not be able to process all the variables in your class. The same holds true if you override a non-static method in another inheriting class.

INCLUDE NON-STATIC METHODS (CONTINUED)

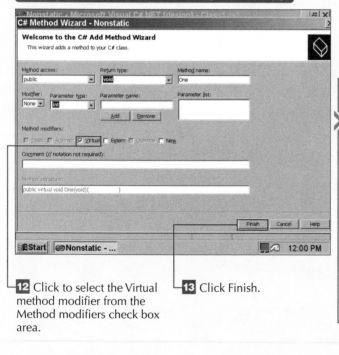

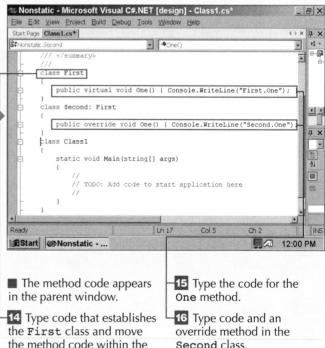

12 Click to select the Virtual method modifier from the Method modifiers check box area.

13 Click Finish.

■ The method code appears in the parent window.

14 Type code that establishes the `First` class and move the method code within the `First` class.

15 Type the code for the `One` method.

16 Type code and an override method in the `Second` class.

Extra

You can represent a class object in the member-access format as well for precise representation of your object. Though the member-access E.M format is the same as with static methods, the E cannot represent a type. Instead, the E must represent the class instance. Usually the member-access format does not include the identifier signified by M because the instance expression signified by E is all the information needed.

Another reason for using the member-access format is that you can perform a member lookup. A member lookup evaluates simple-name or member-access forms in an expression or statement.

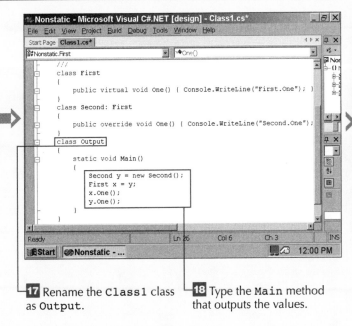

17 Rename the **Class1** class as **Output**.

18 Type the **Main** method that outputs the values.

19 Press the F5 key.

■ The **Second** class overrides the **First** class and produces two output lines of **Second.One.**

20 Save the program as the filename.

ENTER DELEGATES

Delegates act like pointers that you find in other languages such as C++, but delegates go several steps further in C#. Delegates provide object-oriented pointers to methods from other points in your project. This approach makes it easy for methods throughout your program to retrieve information from one source without having to enter that information repeatedly.

Delegates provide two key benefits. Delegates act as a central point where all pieces of your code that need objects refer to a specific method. It is quite inconvenient to have to write static methods for many different classes.

It is also inconvenient to refer to the same class for the same method, and that approach can also slow your project down when it runs. It is much more efficient to have one or a few delegates that can handle method operations for your entire project.

The second benefit of delegates is anonymity. The delegate does not care about what the method includes — whether it be static or non-static, what accessibility the method has, or any other information. The only thing the delegate cares about is if the method that it is looking for has the same signature as the delegate.

ENTER DELEGATES

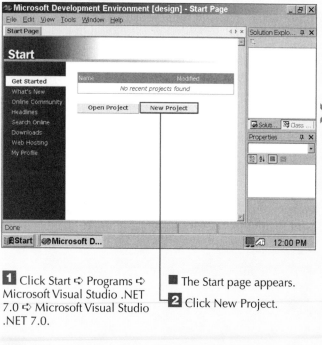

1 Click Start ➪ Programs ➪ Microsoft Visual Studio .NET 7.0 ➪ Microsoft Visual Studio .NET 7.0.

■ The Start page appears.

2 Click New Project.

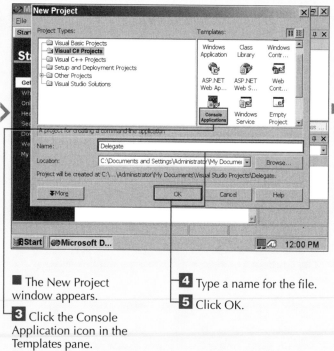

■ The New Project window appears.

3 Click the Console Application icon in the Templates pane.

4 Type a name for the file.

5 Click OK.

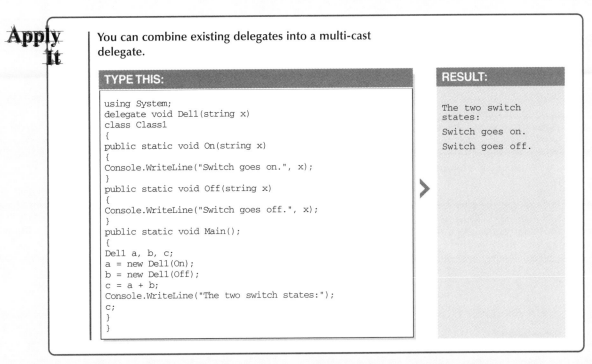

Apply
It

You can combine existing delegates into a multi-cast delegate.

TYPE THIS:

```
using System;
delegate void Del1(string x)
class Class1
{
public static void On(string x)
{
Console.WriteLine("Switch goes on.", x);
}
public static void Off(string x)
{
Console.WriteLine("Switch goes off.", x);
}
public static void Main();
{
Del1 a, b, c;
a = new Del1(On);
b = new Del1(Off);
c = a + b;
Console.WriteLine("The two switch states:");
c;
}
}
```

RESULT:

```
The two switch
states:
Switch goes on.
Switch goes off.
```

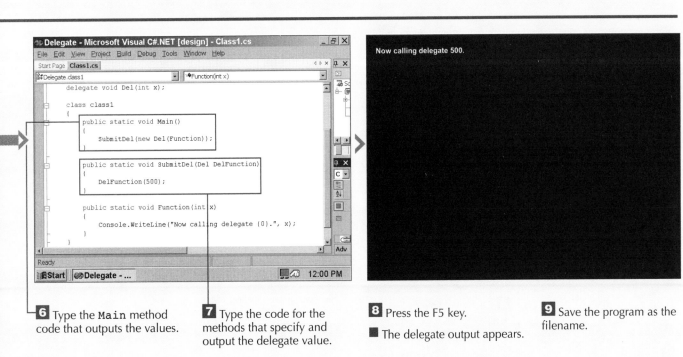

6 Type the **Main** method code that outputs the values.

7 Type the code for the methods that specify and output the delegate value.

8 Press the F5 key.

■ The delegate output appears.

9 Save the program as the filename.

PROGRAM EVENTS

I n object-oriented programming, an event lets clients of that class — clients can include delegates, other classes, methods, and indexers — know about something that happens to an object in a class. That something that happens is of great interest to the clients in the class and so the event lets those clients know about it and act accordingly.

By acting accordingly, the clients give the class delegates so the delegates can retrain those objects using the modules called by those delegates. Once the appropriate module retrains the changed object to behave properly, the object goes back to the class for further processing.

When you declare an event inside of a class you must declare the delegate inside the event. The class that the event resides in is the only class that calls the event. When the class calls the event, the class checks to see if a client has hooked up a delegate to the event, and if that is true then the class processes the event.

The previous task mentioned that C# declares events using delegates. If you have come to this task wanting to learn about events but you have not learned about delegates yet, skip back four pages and read about delegates before you continue on.

PROGRAM EVENTS

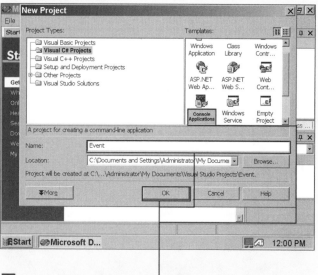

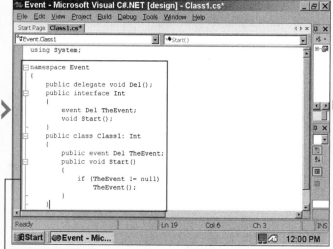

1 Click Start ➪ Programs ➪ Microsoft Visual Studio .NET 7.0 ➪ Microsoft Visual Studio .NET 7.0.

■ The Start page appears.

2 Click New Project.

■ The New Project window appears.

3 Click the Console Application icon in the Templates pane.

4 Type a name for the file.

5 Click OK.

6 Type the code that establishes your event delegate, interface, and class.

Extra

The facts that events can only be called from the classes they reside in and that classes can be inherited poses an interesting problem. C# does not let you invoke events in a base class from an inheriting class. This seems to defeat the purpose of having a class inherit all information from your base class. However, C# does offer a workaround to this problem.

C# can have an inheriting class call a base class event by creating a protected invoking method within the event. This method invokes the base class event and the project passes along the information from that base class event to the rest of the event. If you would rather not have the base class send its events, you can have this protected invoking method as a virtual method. An overriding method in an inheriting class can then take over from the virtual method and shut down the base class events.

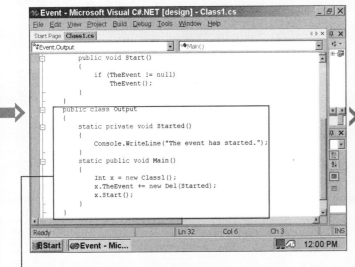

7 Type the code for the Output class that outputs the string when the event fires.

8 Press the F5 key.

■ The string appears on the screen when the event fires.

9 Save the program as the filename.

ADD AN EVENT-HANDLING METHOD

C# lets you bind an event and a method in the form of an event handler. When your program invokes an event, then the event handler calls the method associated with that event.

Event handlers are used with Windows forms in C# because they are well-suited for the events, such as a button click and the methods that follow, such as a window opening.

The event handler code contains two parameters for handling the event. The sender parameter references the argument that sent the event. The event object parameter sends an object specific to the handled event.

When you create an event handler, the calling event will produce a different object parameter type. There are some object parameter types with some built-in events in Visual Studio .NET such as mouse events.

These parameters help determine other information that is pertinent to a Windows form or any other graphical user interface that you want to program. For example, you may need information about where the mouse pointer is, where windows are on the screen, or where data is when you drag-and-drop.

ADD AN EVENT HANDLING METHOD

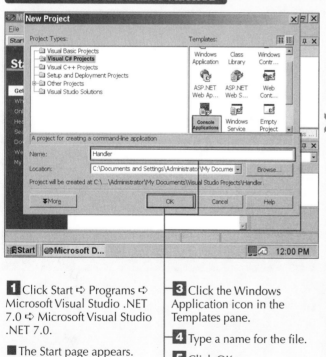

1 Click Start ⇨ Programs ⇨ Microsoft Visual Studio .NET 7.0 ⇨ Microsoft Visual Studio .NET 7.0.

■ The Start page appears.

2 Click New Project.

■ The New Project window appears.

3 Click the Windows Application icon in the Templates pane.

4 Type a name for the file.

5 Click OK.

■ A blank form appears in the parent window.

6 Access the Toolbox by pressing Ctrl+Alt+X.

■ The toolbox window appears with the Windows Forms tools open.

7 Click the Button entry.

8 Click and drag the outline of the button in the form.

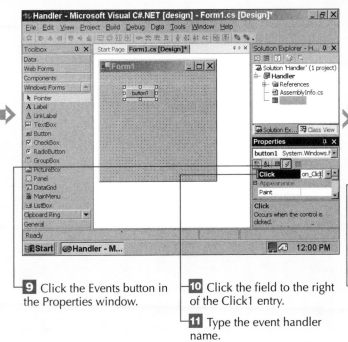

Apply It

You can create an event-handling method within code. Event-handling methods are always private and no matter what event-handling method you want to add, such as a mouse button click, the method arguments remain the same.

TYPE THIS:

```
private void Event1(object sender, System.EventArgs e)
{
button1.Click += new EventHandler(button1_Click);
}
```

RESULT:

When you run your program and the form appears, the form will click when you press down with the left mouse button.

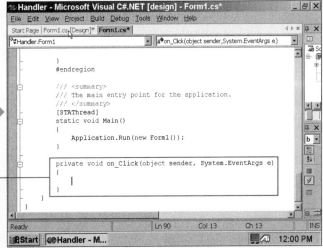

9 Click the Events button in the Properties window.

10 Click the field to the right of the Click1 entry.

11 Type the event handler name.

■ The event handler skeleton code appears so you can type in the event handler.

12 Save the program as the filename.

VIEW INFORMATION ABOUT ARRAYS

An array is a programming staple used in many different languages; arrays act as containers for elements in the same data type. For example, an array can contain a group of integers. C# treats arrays as objects that the program accesses through a reference variable.

You enter arrays using two square brackets ([]) after the array type and then enter the array identifier. C# indexes arrays starting with zero. For example, if you create an array that has ten elements in it, the array identifies the elements in the array from 0 through 9.

C# supports three different types of arrays: single-dimensional arrays, multidimensional (or rectangular) arrays, and array-of-arrays (jagged arrays).

A single-dimensional array is the simplest type. You can use single-dimensional arrays for storing simple lists like your friends' names or a set of numbers.

A multidimensional or rectangular array lets you store data information by x and y types much as you do when you store data in a spreadsheet column and row.

An array-of-arrays or jagged array lets you nest an array within one or more arrays so an element in one array can access elements in its partner arrays.

This chapter takes you through the different arrays and how to use each array type properly.

VIEW INFORMATION ABOUT ARRAYS

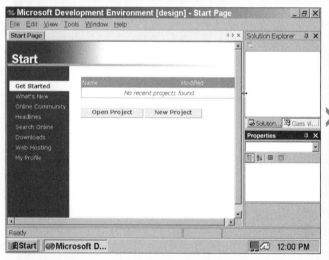

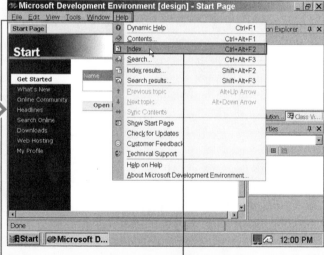

1 Click Start ➪ Programs ➪ Microsoft Visual Studio .NET 7.0 ➪ Microsoft Visual Studio .NET 7.0.

■ The Start page appears.

2 Click Help.

3 Click Index.

Extra

Several array declaration differences exist between C#, C/C++, and Java. The differences are more pronounced between C# and C/C++. The differences (and similarities) include:

- Declaring an array is the same in Java as it is in C#; you activate an array by including the new operator.

- You cannot place the bracket after the identifier as you can in C or C++. If you are an experienced C or C++ programmer, take care to ensure that your brackets appear after the type.

- The array is not part of its type as it is in C and C++. This feature lets you assign as many objects of a type, such as byte to an array no matter how long the array is.

- When you initialize an array, you include the array elements without entering the new int [] argument as you do in Java.

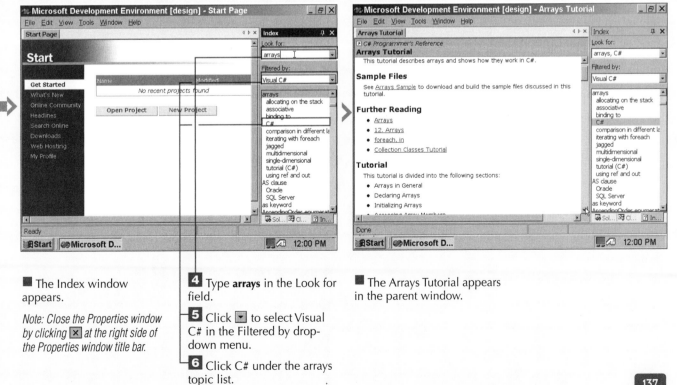

■ The Index window appears.

Note: Close the Properties window by clicking ☒ at the right side of the Properties window title bar.

4 Type **arrays** in the Look for field.

5 Click ▾ to select Visual C# in the Filtered by drop-down menu.

6 Click C# under the arrays topic list.

■ The Arrays Tutorial appears in the parent window.

ENTER SINGLE-DIMENSIONAL ARRAYS

Single-dimensional arrays let you define a set of variables and store them in one block of memory for easy retrieval. C# single-dimensional arrays can include defined sets of data. For example, you can enter a set of numbers or a set of string values such as the number of months in a year. You can use any value type as part of your array including integral, floating point, decimal, Boolean, struct, and enumeration.

After you declare your array, you must initialize it by using the new operator. When you initialize the array, you can give the array specific values such as numbers or specify the maximum number of elements in the array.

You give the array specific values as you do in C, C++, and Java — placing the values in curly braces at the end of the array argument. If you specify the maximum number of elements in an array instead, C# automatically assigns the first element in your array the number zero. For example, an array with six elements will be numbered 0 through 5.

Accessing an array in C# is very similar to what you find in C and C++. For example, you can create an integer array, then assign an integer to a particular location in that array.

ENTER SINGLE-DIMENSIONAL ARRAYS

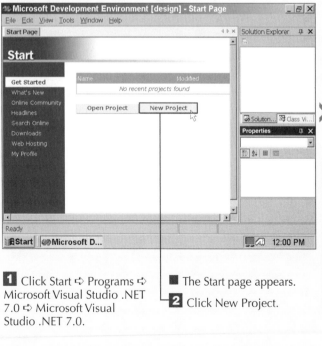

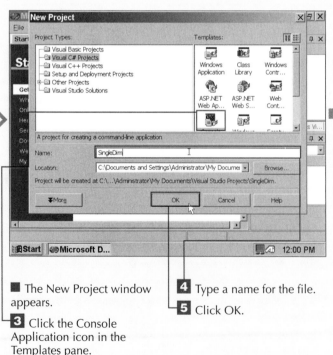

1 Click Start ➪ Programs ➪ Microsoft Visual Studio .NET 7.0 ➪ Microsoft Visual Studio .NET 7.0.

■ The Start page appears.

2 Click New Project.

■ The New Project window appears.

3 Click the Console Application icon in the Templates pane.

4 Type a name for the file.

5 Click OK.

Extra

You can omit optional parts of the single-dimensional array argument. One way is to omit the size of the array.

```
int[] values = new int[] {1, 2, 3, 5, 7, 11};
string[] letters = new string[] {"A", "B", "C"};
```

Another way is to omit the new statement altogether.

```
int[] values = {1, 2, 3, 5, 7, 11};
string[] letters = {"A", "B", "C"};
```

6 Type the code that outputs the opening string and establishes the array in the Main method.

7 Type the code that outputs the array by iterating through each element using the foreach statement.

8 Run the program by pressing the F5 key.

■ The prime number array appears on the screen.

9 Save the program as the filename.

ADD MULTIDIMENSIONAL ARRAYS

C# lets you declare multidimensional arrays for processing a large number of values in one argument. A multidimensional array arranges its data similar to the way a spreadsheet does.

C# multidimensional arrays let you specify two or three elements in the array for two-dimensional and three-dimensional arrays, respectively. You can use two-dimensional arrays for specifying coordinates such as with the row and column in a spreadsheet, on a map, or on a game board such as those for checkers and chess. Programmers use two-dimensional arrays for such tasks as image processing.

A three-dimensional array lets you specify three elements. For example, you can store a name in three dimensions — first name, middle name, and last name.

Just as with single-dimensional arrays, you can specify the number of elements in each dimension in the rectangular brackets after you declare the array type. If you think of the array as the table, C# lists the number of rows first and the number of columns second. If you have a three-dimensional array, then the third dimension appears last in the bracket.

You can also specify initial values for the array in the same order as you have them in the rectangular brackets. Like single-dimensional arrays, values appear in curly braces after you initialize the array with the new operator.

ADD MULTIDIMENSIONAL ARRAYS

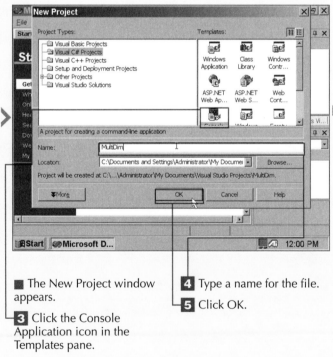

1 Click Start ➪ Programs ➪ Microsoft Visual Studio .NET 7.0 ➪ Microsoft Visual Studio .NET 7.0.

■ The Start page appears.

2 Click New Project.

■ The New Project window appears.

3 Click the Console Application icon in the Templates pane.

4 Type a name for the file.

5 Click OK.

Extra

C# contains rules about array structure that you must adhere to so your array can function properly. The rules include:

- Specify the size of your dimensions when you create a multidimensional array. If you have a particular array with the value x, you can specify the size of x-1 dimensions, but it is usually safer, not to mention less confusing, if you specify the information up front.

- When you create the array, it is a good idea to keep the same dimensions for every other array in your program. This approach can reduce confusion for users of your program.

- Microsoft recommends that you use the first dimension as the row and the second as the column, but you can define your dimension order however you like. Your dimension order must be consistent throughout your program.

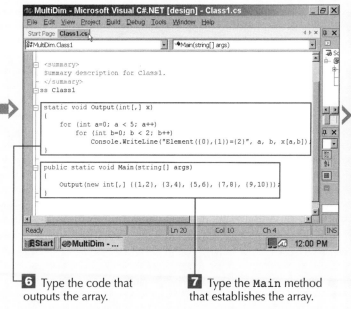

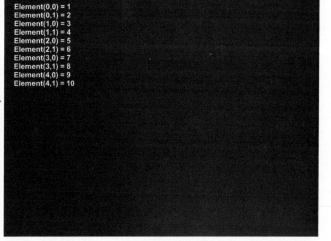

6 Type the code that outputs the array.

7 Type the **Main** method that establishes the array.

8 Run the program by pressing the F5 key.

■ Type information at the prompts and the output appears.

9 Save the program as the filename.

PROGRAM ARRAY-OF-ARRAYS

The most flexible type of array is the array-of-arrays, commonly called the jagged array. The jagged array lets you define an array with several different dimensions and sizes.

Multidimensional arrays have two or three dimensions that you can enter within the same rectangular braces that appear after the array value type. Array-of-arrays, however, let you nest single-dimensional arrays within one another. This approach lets you access a large number of arrays without the three-dimensional limit that multidimensional arrays provide.

When you initialize your array-of-arrays with the new operator, you must ensure that the number of brackets after

the new operator matches the number of brackets that appears after the array value type. If you do not, the MDE window will report the error.

Each single dimensional array must appear in its own rectangular braces that appear one after the other. You can also specify the initial element values in curly braces just as you do with single and multidimensional arrays. When you specify array values, you must ensure that the number of element values is the same as the number of arrays you specify after the array value type. For example, if you have four arrays, then you must specify four initial element values.

PROGRAM ARRAY-OF-ARRAYS

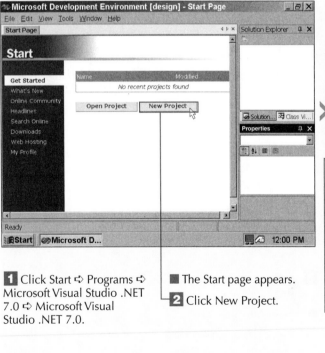

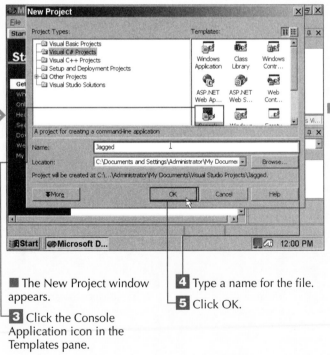

1 Click Start ➪ Programs ➪ Microsoft Visual Studio .NET 7.0 ➪ Microsoft Visual Studio .NET 7.0.

■ The Start page appears.

2 Click New Project.

■ The New Project window appears.

3 Click the Console Application icon in the Templates pane.

4 Type a name for the file.

5 Click OK.

Extra

Multidimensional arrays also go by the name of rectangular arrays, and if you have programmed in other languages, you may have seen these arrays referred to as ragged arrays. Microsoft has discarded the ragged moniker and has instead moved it over to the array-of-arrays corner. What is more, Microsoft changed ragged to jagged, though the change in name is only a means to set Microsoft and C# apart from other languages, because there is no change in definition from ragged to jagged.

C# refers to array-of-arrays as jagged because if you visualize the array as with in a multidimensional array, a jagged array is a series of rows for each single-dimensional array that looks like a bar chart. The height of each array bar depends on the number of elements in that array. All the bars in your array "chart" would not be of uniform height — in other words, jagged.

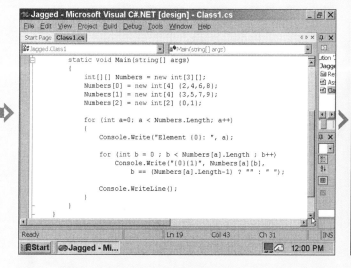

6 Type the code that establishes the array.

7 Type the code that iterates through the array and outputs the array elements that correspond with the array number.

8 Run the program by pressing the F5 key.

■ The jagged array elements appear as members of their associated array number.

9 Save the program as the filename.

ITERATE THROUGH ARRAY ELEMENTS

After you program an array, you may need to iterate through array elements in case you need to list all of them for another part of your program or in your output. C# lets you iterate through array elements by using the `foreach` statement.

The `foreach` statement is an easy way for you to display all of the elements contained in the class. The `foreach` statement acts as a loop that retrieves each array element. The loop follows the order that the elements appear in the array, and after the loop runs out of elements, the program moves on to the next statement.

The `foreach` statement appears immediately after the array statement. For example, you can view all of the elements in an array by assigning a `Console.WriteLine` statement after the `foreach` statement so you can see all of the array elements when your program runs. Another example is passing along integers from your array to a mathematical formula for further processing.

An array is a collections class that uses the System.Array base class. You can use the `foreach` statement for both arrays and collections. See page 150 for more information on implementing a collections class.

ITERATE THROUGH ARRAY ELEMENTS

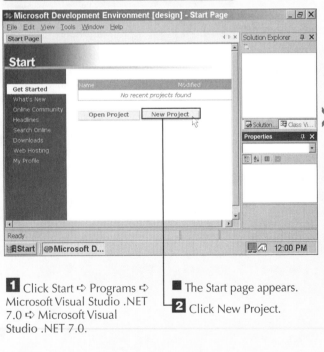

1 Click Start ➪ Programs ➪ Microsoft Visual Studio .NET 7.0 ➪ Microsoft Visual Studio .NET 7.0.

■ The Start page appears.

2 Click New Project.

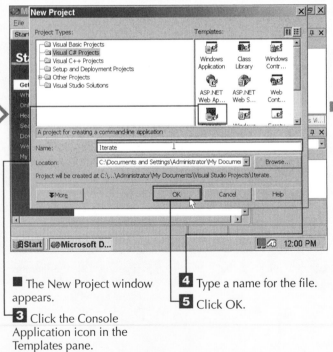

■ The New Project window appears.

3 Click the Console Application icon in the Templates pane.

4 Type a name for the file.

5 Click OK.

You can also iterate through an array using the `for` statement if you want. The `for` statement requires you to match the array with the indexing operation whereas the `foreach` statement does not.

TYPE THIS:

```
using System;
class Class1;
{
public static void Main()
{
int odd = 0, even = 0;
int[] arr = {1, 2, 3, 5, 7, 11};
for (int Index = 0; Index < arr.Count; Index++)
{
if (i%2 == 0)
even++;
else
odd++;
}
Class1 number = (Class1) arr[Index];
Console.WriteLine("There are {0} odd numbers and {1} even numbers.", odd, even);
}
}
```

RESULT:

There are 5 odd numbers and 1 even number.

```
namespace Iterate
{
    /// <summary>
    /// Summary description for Class1.
    /// </summary>
    class Class1
    {
        static void Main(string[] args)
        {
            int[] primes = new int[] {1,2,3,5};
            foreach (int x in primes)
            {
                int s = (x*x);
                Console.WriteLine("The square of {0} is {1}.",x,s);
            }
        }
    }
}
```

```
The square of 1 is 1.
The square of 2 is 4.
The square of 3 is 9.
The square of 5 is 25.
```

6 Type the code that establishes the array.

7 Type the **foreach** argument that squares each of the elements in the array and outputs that information to the screen.

8 Run the program by pressing the F5 key.

■ The element square information appears on the screen.

9 Save the program as the filename.

SORT ARRAYS

The Array.Sort method lets you sort elements in a single-dimensional array. You can use the Array.Sort method not only with single-dimensional arrays but also with jagged arrays because jagged arrays contain more than one single-dimensional array.

C# sorts arrays by using the IComparable or IComparer interface that each element in the array implements. The IComparable and IComparer interfaces are defaults that C# automatically invokes with the Array.Sort method, so you do not have to worry about programming the interface as well.

When you sort an array, C# orders the elements in that array in alphabetical order for strings and in numerical order for numerical types. You can then tie in the sort to a Console.WriteLine statement as shown in the task example so you can see how C# will sort the arrays.

For example, if you have a set of strings as your elements, and you want to write your sorted elements to the screen, the output will show the string with the first letter closest to the letter a and continue on in the list. If you have a numeric list, then the first number in the output will be the one that has the lowest amount, even if that amount is a negative number.

SORT ARRAYS

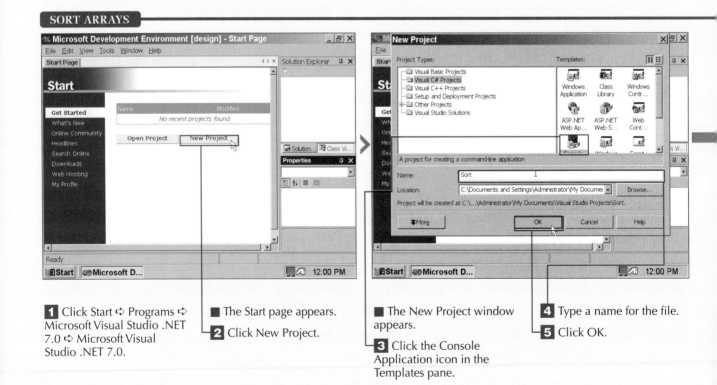

1 Click Start ➪ Programs ➪ Microsoft Visual Studio .NET 7.0 ➪ Microsoft Visual Studio .NET 7.0.

■ The Start page appears.

2 Click New Project.

■ The New Project window appears.

3 Click the Console Application icon in the Templates pane.

4 Type a name for the file.

5 Click OK.

Apply It

When you sort arrays that have strings that contain capital letters, C# considers those strings to be lower on the alphabetization list than strings with lowercase letters.

TYPE THIS:

```
using System;
class SortArray;
{
public static void Main()
{
string[] names = {"too", "two", "To", "Too"};
Array.Sort(names);
foreach (string value in names)
{
Console.WriteLine("The word is {0}", value);
}
}
}
```

RESULT:

```
The word is too
The word is two
The word is To
The word is Too
```

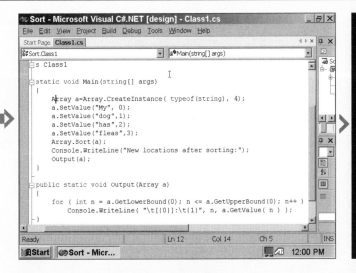

6 Type the code that creates an instance of your array, the elements in your array, the **sort** method, and outputs the results.

7 Type the **Output** method that outputs the information to the screen.

8 Run the program by pressing the F5 key.

■ The sorted array elements with their associated array locations appear on the screen.

9 Save the program as the filename.

SEARCH ARRAYS

C# lets you search for the first instance of an element in an array in case you need to pass a particular element in your array to another part of your program or if you need to get some specific information such as finding the number of times an element appears in an array.

You can search within an array using the `Array.IndexOf` method. This built-in method returns the index number of the first array element that you want to search for. For example, if you search for the third element in an array, then the `Array.IndexOf` method returns the index

number 2 because the default first index number in an array is 0. If you set the first index number yourself, then the index number returned for your found element will vary.

The `Array.IndexOf` method also lets you search for an array element within certain index positions. For example, you can search for an array element that is the string `and` that appears between index number 2 and 10. You can also search for an array element from an index position through the last element in the array.

The drawback to using the `Array.IndexOf` method is that you can only search within a single-dimensional array.

SEARCH ARRAYS

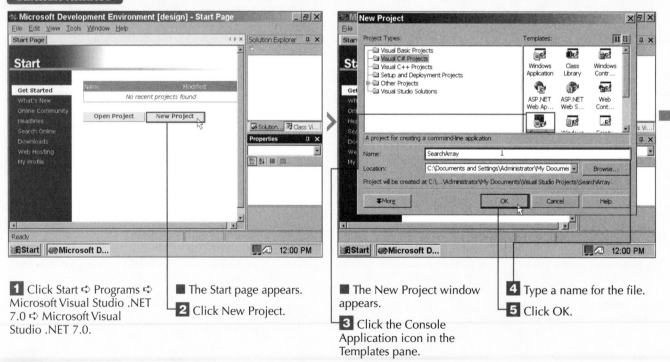

1 Click Start ➪ Programs ➪ Microsoft Visual Studio .NET 7.0 ➪ Microsoft Visual Studio .NET 7.0.

■ The Start page appears.

2 Click New Project.

■ The New Project window appears.

3 Click the Console Application icon in the Templates pane.

4 Type a name for the file.

5 Click OK.

You can use the `Array.LastIndexOf` method
to find the last occurrence in an array.

TYPE THIS:

```
using System;
public class Sample
{
public static void Main()
{
array Sample=Array.CreateInstance( typeof (String), 3);
Sample.SetValue( "Five", 0 );
Sample.SetValue( "by", 1 );
Sample.SetValue( "Five", 2 );
string String1 = "Five";
int Index1 = Array.LastIndexOf( Index1, String1 );
Console.WriteLine("The last occurrence of \"{0}\" is at index {1}.", String1, Index1);
}
}
```

RESULT:

```
The last occurrence of "Five" is at index 2.
```

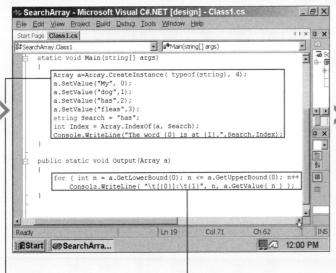

6 Type the code that creates
an instance of your array, the
elements in your array, the
`Array.IndexOf` search
method, and outputs the
results.

7 Type the `Output` method
that outputs the information
to the screen.

8 Run the program by
pressing the F5 key.

■ The element and its
associated number appear
on the screen.

9 Save the program as the
filename.

IMPLEMENT A COLLECTIONS CLASS

A collections class collects a number of elements that have a specific type, such as a set of numbers that represent the months of the year. C# provides two methods for declaring collections classes: programming arrays and programming the built-in IEnumerator and IEnumerable interfaces.

An array is built from the `System.Array` base class that is built into C#. C# identifies this base class as a collections class. You can also define a class as a collections class provided that you declare the `System.Collections` namespace in your program and include the IEnumerator and IEnumerable interfaces within the class.

The IEnumerator and IEnumerable interfaces let you enumerate elements in your collections class. Enumerations are discussed on page 156, but as a sneak preview, enumerations assign numbers to elements in your collections class so you and your program can keep track of your elements more easily.

Like an array, you can retrieve information from a collections class using the `foreach` statement. The `foreach` statement works on a collections class the same way it works in an array — the `foreach` statement iterates through each element in the collections class and can return that information to another statement or method in your program such as the `Console.WriteLine` statement for output.

IMPLEMENT A COLLECTIONS CLASS

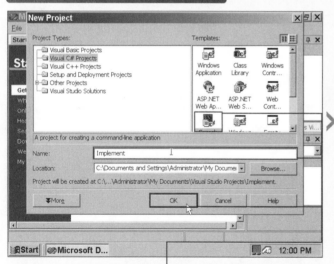

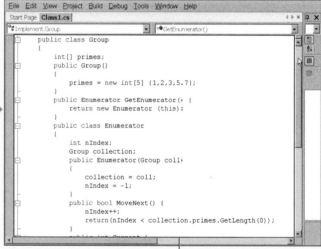

1 Click Start ➪ Programs ➪ Microsoft Visual Studio .NET 7.0 ➪ Microsoft Visual Studio .NET 7.0.

■ The Start page appears.

2 Click New Project.

■ The New Project window appears.

3 Click the Console Application icon in the Templates pane.

4 Type a name for the file.

5 Click OK.

6 Delete all code after the left brace directly below the `namespace Implement` code.

7 Type the code that establishes the array, establishes the `GetEnumerator` definition, and defines part of the `Enumerator` class.

Apply It

Like an array, you can use the `foreach` statement for iterating through a collections class. The following example acquires a collection in a *hashtable*, a predefined collection class.

TYPE THIS:

```
using System;
using System.Collections;
public class Class1
{
public static void Main(string[] args)
{
Hashtable areacode = new Hashtable();
areacode.Add("209", "Stockton");
areacode Add("559", "Fresno");
areacode Add("916", "Sacramento");
foreach (string code in areacode.Keys)
{
Console.WriteLine(code + "   " + areacode[code]);
}
}
}
```

RESULT:

```
209   Stockton
559   Fresno
916   Sacramento
```

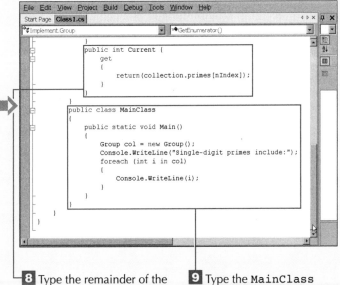

8 Type the remainder of the **Enumerator** class code.

9 Type the **MainClass** code that iterates through the collections class and outputs its elements.

10 Run the program by pressing the F5 key.

■ The collections class elements appear on the screen.

11 Save the program as the filename.

PROGRAM STRUCTS

The struct is a close relative of the class. A struct can have the same members of a class and can also implement interfaces. However, a struct is a value type so it will simply process information, such as integers passed through an array, as any other value type instead of instantiating objects for each element in the array as a class would. Using structs can save memory and help your program run faster.

You create an object in the struct by using the new operator. After you create the object, C# will create the object and call the value for the object. For example, you

can create an integer object that gets its value from a method contained in a class.

Because a struct is a value type, you cannot inherit from other structs and you cannot use a struct as a base class. A struct can inherit from an object in a base class but not from any inheriting classes.

When you create and run a program with a struct, C# creates the struct on the memory stack instead of the heap. Structs use attributes for specifying the memory areas the struct accesses. C# contains several different built-in struct attributes that you can use for certain tasks.

PROGRAM STRUCTS

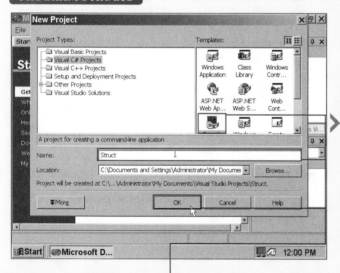

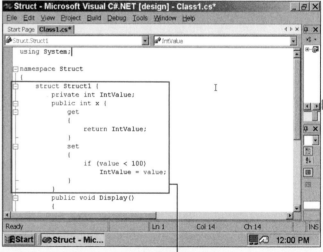

1 Click Start ➪ Programs ➪ Microsoft Visual Studio .NET 7.0 ➪ Microsoft Visual Studio .NET 7.0.

■ The Start page appears.

2 Click New Project.

■ The New Project window appears.

3 Click the Console Application icon in the Templates pane.

4 Type a name for the file.

5 Click OK.

6 Delete all code after the left brace directly below the `namespace Struct` code.

7 Type the struct property values.

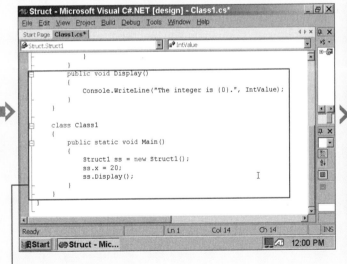

Apply It

The struct attributes mentioned in this task are different from the value type attribute modifiers that determine the accessibility of your struct. You enter the attribute information immediately before you enter the struct declaration, and the attribute appears within closed square brackets ([]).

TYPE THIS:

```
Using System;
[StructLayout(LayoutKind.Union)]
struct Union
{z
// Add struct information here.
}
```

RESULT:

This code establishes a struct that contains the `StructLayout (LayoutKind.Union)` attribute.

8 Type the output code and the `Main` method that contains the struct value.

9 Run the program by pressing the F5 key.

■ The struct value appears on the screen.

10 Save the program as the filename.

ADD AN INDEXER

An indexer gives your class the ability to behave as an array. If you have a class with many elements, then an indexer lets you sort that information so your program can get the element it needs from your class.

C# gives you two methods for adding an indexer to a class or an interface. You can add the indexer directly into your program or, if you add a class to your interface, you can add it using the Add C# Interface Indexer Wizard.

Class and interface index accessors come in two forms: get and set. The get accessor returns the type of the indexer.

The set accessor sets the value of the accessor type. The get and set accessors use the same access modifiers as the indexer declaration itself; the access modifiers for get and set must be as accessible as the indexer itself.

You can add an indexer to an interface through the Add C# Interface Indexer Wizard in the Class View window. The Add C# Interface Indexer Wizard contains fields so you can enter the indexer type, the parameter type, the parameter name, and any comments. After you finish entering data into the wizard, C# will create the skeleton of the indexer for you so you can add the indexer accessors.

ADD AN INDEXER

1 Click Start ➪ Programs ➪ Microsoft Visual Studio .NET 7.0 ➪ Microsoft Visual Studio .NET 7.0.

■ The Start page appears.

2 Click New Project.

■ The New Project window appears.

3 Click the Console Application icon in the Templates pane.

4 Type a name for the file.

5 Click OK.

6 Click the Class View tab.

7 Click the plus sign (⊞) next to the method name.

8 Click the plus sign (⊞) next to the {} method name.

9 Right-click the class name to open the pop-up menu.

10 Click Add.

11 Click Add Indexer.

Apply It

If you declare more than one indexer in the same class or interface, then the signature for each index must be unique.

TYPE THIS:

```
using System;
class Indexer
{
private int [] Array1 = new int[20];
public int this [int Index]
{
get
{
if (index < 0 | | index >= 20)
return 0;
}
set
{
if (!(index < 0 | | index >= 20))
Array1[index] = amount;
}
}
public int [] Array2 = new int[50];
public int this [int Index]
```

RESULT:

You will get an error and your program will not run because you cannot have the same index signature (Index).

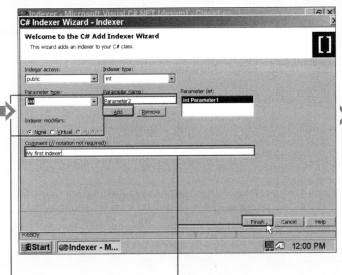

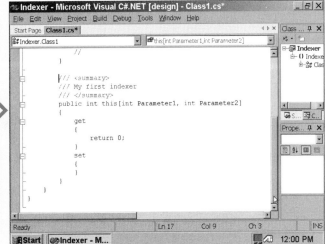

■ The C# Indexer Wizard window appears.

12 Type the indexer parameter name in the Parameter name field.

13 Click Add.

■ The parameter appears in the parameter list field.

14 Add an indexer comment in the Comment field.

15 Click Finish.

■ The indexer skeleton code appears in the parent window.

16 Save the program as the filename.

INCLUDE ENUMERATIONS

Enumerations are value types that assign numerical values to elements in an array. By assigning numerical values to elements, enumerations let you acquire those elements quickly for further processing.

C# assigns the first element in the array the number zero (0) and each successive element in the array receives a successive number. For example, if you enumerate an array with the 12 months of the year, January will receive the number 0 and C# will continue until the end of the array when December gets the number 11.

An enumeration is a special type of array that you declare using the enum keyword. Like an array, you can set

accessibility attributes and access modifiers. The enum elements appear within curly brackets ({}) separated by commas just as array elements do. The key difference between an enumeration and an array is that an enumeration can only be of an integral type, and the default integral type is int. Because enumerations only assign integers to their elements, the only integral type that you cannot include is the char type.

You can change the enumeration value by assigning a number to the first value in the element list, and all successive elements in the list will receive successive numbers. For example, if you give January the number 1, then C# assigns December the number 12.

INCLUDE ENUMERATIONS

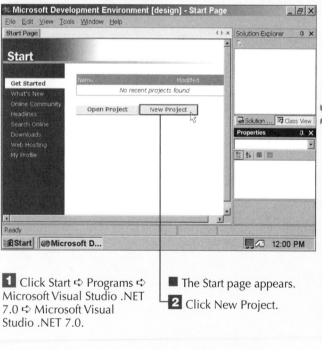

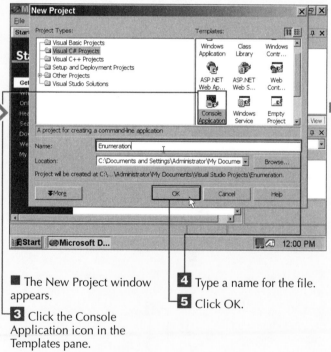

1 Click Start ➪ Programs ➪ Microsoft Visual Studio .NET 7.0 ➪ Microsoft Visual Studio .NET 7.0.

■ The Start page appears.

2 Click New Project.

■ The New Project window appears.

3 Click the Console Application icon in the Templates pane.

4 Type a name for the file.

5 Click OK.

Apply It

You can convert the enumeration type to an integral type — for example, to equate a string in the enumeration with an integer for tracking purposes.

TYPE THIS:

```
using System;
public class Convert;
{
enum SpringMonths {Mar=1, Apr, May, Jun};

public static void Main()
{
int a = (int) SpringMonths.Mar //converts the Mar
value (1) to an integer
Console.WriteLine("March = {0}", a);
}
}
```

RESULT:

```
March = 1
```

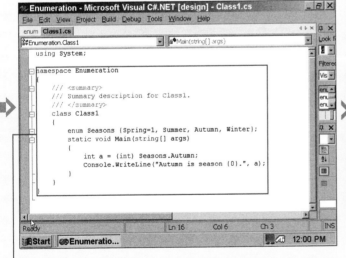

6 Type the code that establishes the enumeration, sets the value, and outputs the value to the screen.

7 Run the program by pressing the F5 key.

■ The enumeration number appears with its proper season.

8 Save the program as the filename.

CREATE STRING LITERALS AND VARIABLES

C reating and manipulating strings is a big part of any programming language. Without programmatic storage of string variables, you cannot create a user interface to your application without difficulty. For example, you need strings for describing entities such as a Client, where a Client has Company Name, Address, City, State, and ZIP Code fields. You cannot represent all these fields by a numeric value. These attributes are instead recognized through a series of characters.

When assigning values to a string variable, you can choose to use a *verbatim* string literal or a *regular* string literal. A verbatim string literal consists of an @ character followed by

zero or more characters inside of double-quote characters; for example, consider @"C:\temp\" a verbatim string literal. This type of assignment interprets the string verbatim. If you leave out the @ character, you are assigning a regular string literal. This assignment will not interpret verbatim, but will evaluate the string for escape sequences as it stores the string. The escape sequences are a backslash followed by a reserved set of single characters. These escape sequences will have an impact on the string that is formatted in the user interface. For example, in the string "First Name\tLast Name" the \t will put a tab between the second and third word in the string.

CREATE STRING LITERALS AND VARIABLES

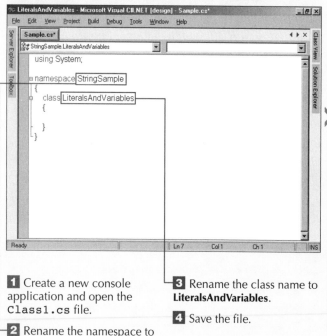

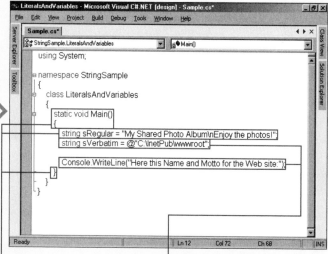

1 Create a new console application and open the `Class1.cs` file.

2 Rename the namespace to **StringSample**.

3 Rename the class name to **LiteralsAndVariables**.

4 Save the file.

5 Add an entry point to the class by adding the `Main` function.

6 Create a regular string to hold the Web site name and motto using `\n` to specify a new line.

7 Create a verbatim string to hold the Web site location by adding the @ symbol before the string value.

8 Write a message about the regular string.

Extra

You can use verbatim strings to avoid having characters interpreted as escape sequences. This is especially important for strings that hold file paths, for example, `string sFilePath = @"c:\temp\myfile.txt"`. The following escape sequences are the only ones allowed:

ESCAPE SEQUENCE	APPLIED FORMATTING
\ '	Single quote
\ "	Double-quote
\ \	Backslash
\ 0	Null
\ a	Alert
\ b	Backspace
\ f	Form feed
\ n	New line
\ r	Carriage return
\ t	Horizontal tab
\ u and \ U	Unicode-escape-sequence *
\ x	Hexadecimal-escape-sequence

* (For example, \u005C is "\")

If any other character follows a backslash in a regular string, a compile-time error occurs. For example, `\z` in a regular string (like `"Brian\zErwin"`) creates a compile-time error because z is not a valid character for an escape sequence.

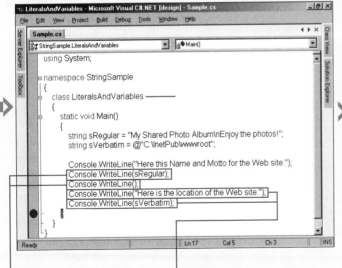

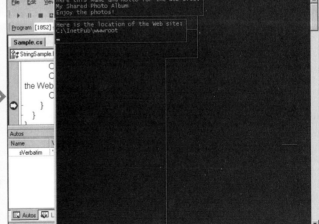

9 Use the `WriteLine` method to output the regular string.

10 Use the `WriteLine` method to output an extra line.

11 Use the `WriteLine` method to output a message about the verbatim string.

12 Use the `WriteLine` method to output the regular string.

13 Set a debug stop at the end of the class.

14 Press F5 to save, build, and run the console application.

■ The regular string appears.

■ The verbatim string appears.

ASSIGN VALUES TO STRINGS

You can assign and reassign literals to string variables, but you can benefit from knowing what goes on behind the scenes.

The `String` class in the .NET Framework is an immutable, fixed-length string of Unicode characters. *Immutable* means that the string cannot change. The `String` is a class and it is not only storage, but it also has capabilities (properties, methods, and fields) that allow manipulation of strings. In the case of changing an existing `String`, when a new value is assigned to an existing `String` you are not updating the object. The updated value is returned in a new instance of a `String` object.

This `String` class implements the `IComparable`, `ICloneable`, `IConvertible`, and `IEnumerable` interfaces. These interfaces, along with the specific implementation in the `String` Class, give `String` objects the ability to do things like: convert `String` objects to other data types, evaluate parts of a string, format a string, and iterate through collections of `String` objects.

Assigning values to a `String` variable is similar to any other type of variable assignment. You can take two approaches, which are allocating a `String` variable and then assigning the value. This requires two separate lines of code. To shorthand this two-step process, you can assign a value to the `String` on the same line.

ASSIGN VALUES TO STRINGS

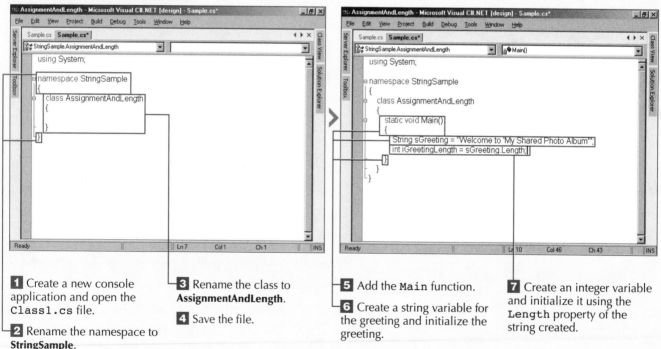

1 Create a new console application and open the `Class1.cs` file.

2 Rename the namespace to **StringSample**.

3 Rename the class to **AssignmentAndLength**.

4 Save the file.

5 Add the **Main** function.

6 Create a string variable for the greeting and initialize the greeting.

7 Create an integer variable and initialize it using the **Length** property of the string created.

Apply It

Spaces do count when assigning strings.

TYPE THIS:

```
using System;
namespace StringSample
{
class AssignmentAndLength
    {
    static void Main()
        {
            String sSpacesCount = "      6789";
            int iSpacesCount = sSpacesCount.Length;

            Console.WriteLine (
            "The greeting: \n{0}\nis {1} characters long.",
                sSpacesCount, iSpacesCount);
        }
    }
}
```

RESULT:

```
C:\>csc AssignStrings_ai.cs
C:\> AssignStrings_ai.exe
The greeting:
      6789
is 9 characters long.
C:\>
```

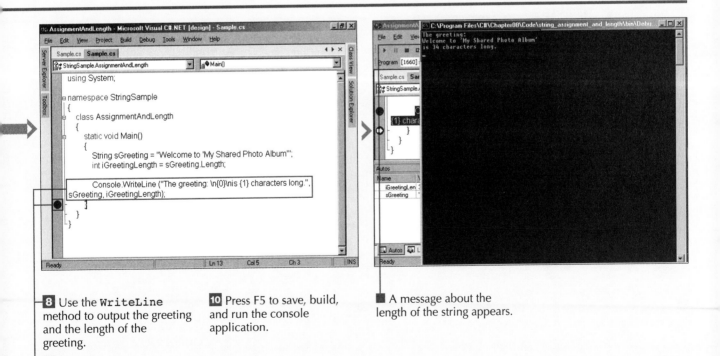

-8 Use the **WriteLine** method to output the greeting and the length of the greeting.

-9 Set a debug stop

10 Press F5 to save, build, and run the console application.

■ A message about the length of the string appears.

CONCATENATE STRINGS

*C*oncatenating, or joining, strings is a common task for building useful strings. Most of the time, you build strings from more than one source. Values for strings can come from a combination of sources (database calls, constants, integer counters, and so on).

To build out a string from multiple sources, you concatenate these strings in a specified sequence. You can accomplish the concatenate of two or more string sources in several ways. You can use the arithmetic operator (+) or the (+=) assignment operator. Use the arithmetic operator (+) to combine strings in the order that they appear in the

expression, or use the assignment operator (+=) to append a string to an existing string. As you append your strings, you have to include the spacing inside the double-quotes of your string.

You can also use the Concat method on the String class to perform concatenation. With this method, you can concatenate one or more String classes together and get a new String returned to you. Another overloaded implementation of the String Class allows you to pass a string array, which is handy if you have many strings to concatenate into one representative string.

CONCATENATE STRINGS

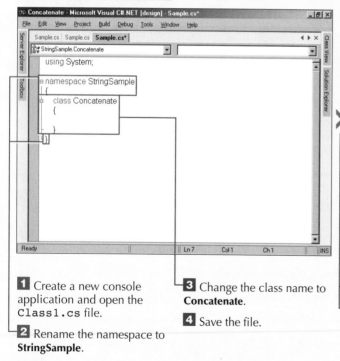

1 Create a new console application and open the `Class1.cs` file.

2 Rename the namespace to **StringSample**.

3 Change the class name to **Concatenate**.

4 Save the file.

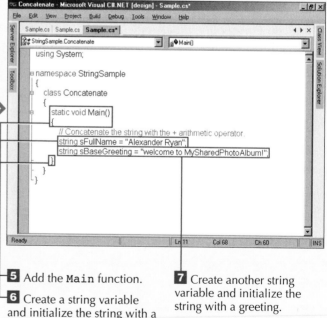

5 Add the **Main** function.

6 Create a string variable and initialize the string with a name.

7 Create another string variable and initialize the string with a greeting.

Knowing that the `String` object is immutable and that it returns a new instance of a `String` object, you may want to explore the `System.Text.StringBuilder` framework class. The `StringBuilder` class lets you concatenate strings without having to create a new object each time you modify the string. The `StringBuilder` class also gives you more flexibility with concatenating, like appending versus inserting.

TYPE THIS:

```
using System;
using System.Text;
namespace StringSample
{
    class Concatenate
    {
        static void Main()
        {
            StringBuilder sbPersonalGreeting =
                new StringBuilder("Hello, how are you today");

            sbPersonalGreeting.Insert(0,"Danny - ");
            sbPersonalGreeting.Append("?");

            Console.WriteLine(sbPersonalGreeting);
        }
    }
}
```

RESULT:

```
C:\> csc ConcatenateStrings_ai.cs
C:\> ConcatenateStrings_ai.exe
Danny - Hello, how are you today?
C:\>
```

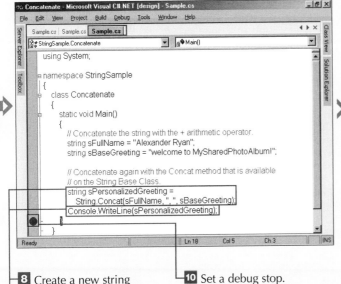

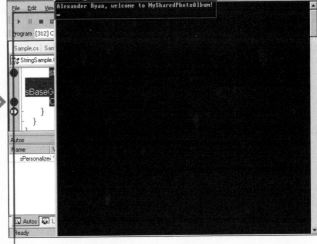

8 Create a new string variable and initialize the variable by using the `String.Concat` function and the two strings previously created.

9 Write the resulting string to the console.

10 Set a debug stop.

11 Press F5 to save, build, and run the console application.

■ A message appears showing the concatenated string.

COMPARE STRINGS

Comparing strings in code is useful when performing logical operations. String comparisons are useful in expressions that are used for an `if` or `switch` statement. For example, you can use a string comparison when someone is logging onto your Web site. You can compare the password that the user entered to the password in the database.

There are several comparison methods for a string, the simplest being two equals signs (`==`), which is the equality operator. This operator checks to see if the two strings hold the same value (length, characters, and sequence of characters).

The `String` class contains some very useful comparison methods — `Compare`, `CompareOrdinal`, `CompareTo`, `StartsWith`, `EndsWith`, `Equals`, `IndexOf`, and `LastIndexOf`. The method you choose depends on if you are looking for a binary response (for example, getting a `true` or `false` for the presence of a substring, or if both strings match based on the method's criteria) or position of where a substring exists.

With the `Compare` method, the comparison is done in the expression of the `if` statement. Note that it returns an integer, which is used in a comparison to zero. If zero is returned, then a match is found.

COMPARE STRINGS

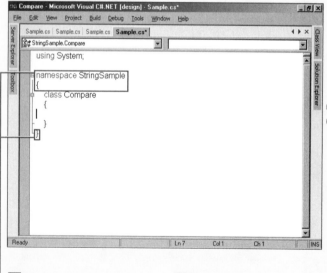

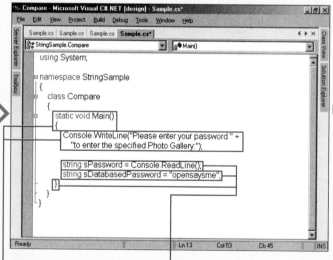

1 Create a new console application and open the `Class1.cs` file.

2 Rename the namespace to **StringSample**.

3 Rename the class name to **Compare**.

4 Save the file.

5 Add the **Main** function.

6 Use the **WriteLine** method to prompt the user for the password.

7 Create a string variable that is initialized with the value that is read from the console.

8 Create a string variable for the password and set the password.

Apply It

Another way to approach string comparisons is to run the `CompareTo` method on the first string variable and give it the second string variable as the parameter to that method.

TYPE THIS:

```
using System;

namespace StringSample
{
    class Compare
    {
        static void Main()
        {
            Console.WriteLine("Please enter your password " +
                "to enter the specified Photo Gallery:");

            string sPassword = Console.ReadLine();
            string sDatabasedPassword = "opensaysme";

            if (sDatabasedPassword.CompareTo(sPassword)==0)
                Console.WriteLine("You can view the photos");
            else
                Console.WriteLine("You do not have permission"
                    + " to view the photos");
        }
    }
}
```

RESULT:

```
C:\>csc CompareStrings.cs
C:\> CompareStrings.exe
Please enter your password to
enter the specified Photo
Gallery.
Opensaysme
You can view the photos.
c:\>
```

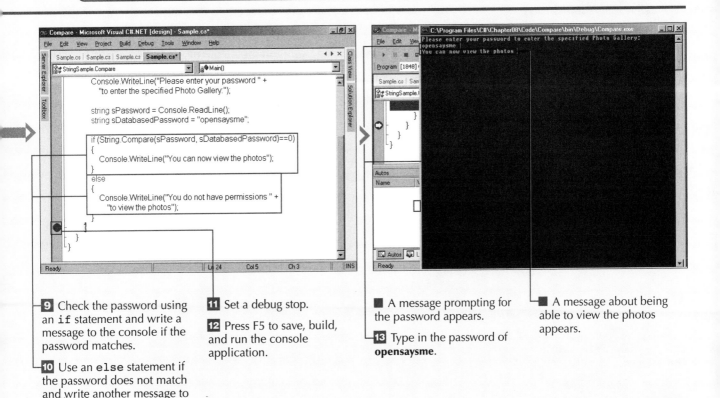

■9 Check the password using an **if** statement and write a message to the console if the password matches.

■10 Use an **else** statement if the password does not match and write another message to the console.

■11 Set a debug stop.

■12 Press F5 to save, build, and run the console application.

■ A message prompting for the password appears.

■13 Type in the password of **opensaysme**.

■ A message about being able to view the photos appears.

SEARCH FOR SUBSTRINGS

When working with filenames that are embedded in a fully qualified file path, it is helpful to have substring searching capabilities. Different parts of that fully qualified path can be useful to your program. For example, you may want to check for the file extension or maybe for a certain directory path. The `String` class provides several methods that assist you in this process.

One way to search for substrings is to use comparision methods. Comparison methods that work with substrings are `StartsWith` and `EndsWith`, which essentially do what the method name indicates (that is, find substrings that start a string and finish off a string). These methods yield a Boolean response that indicates if the substring was found.

If you are just looking for a specific character, you can use the `IndexOf` and `LastIndexOf` method of the `String` class to see what index position contains that character.

Another useful way to find substrings is to use *regular expressions*. This is a more sophisticated way to determine if a substring exists. With regular expressions, you can go further than substrings and look for patterns that exist in the string.

Another handy string-comparison method is the `EndsWith` method. You can use `EndsWith` to identify the extension of a file and determine if code should run or not.

SEARCH FOR SUBSTRINGS

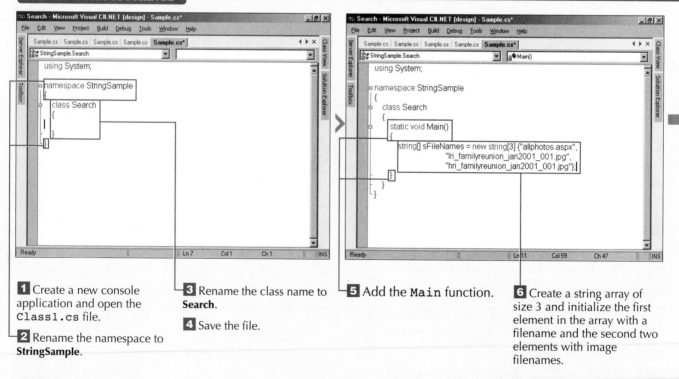

1 Create a new console application and open the `Class1.cs` file.

2 Rename the namespace to **StringSample**.

3 Rename the class name to **Search**.

4 Save the file.

5 Add the **Main** function.

6 Create a string array of size 3 and initialize the first element in the array with a filename and the second two elements with image filenames.

Regular expressions are a very powerful way to find substrings or patterns in a string.
If you are trying to accomplish a complicated search of a string, use regular
expressions.

TYPE THIS:

```
using System;
using System.Text.RegularExpressions;
namespace StringSample
{
    class Search
    {
        static void Main()
        {
            string[] sFileNames = new string[3] {
                "allphotos.aspx",
                "lri_familyreunion_jan2001_001.jpg",
                "hri_familyreunion_jan2001_001.jpg"};
            Regex rePictureFile = new Regex(".jpg");

            foreach (string sFileName in sFileNames)
            {
                if (rePictureFile.Match(sFileName).Success)
                    Console.WriteLine("{0} is a photo file.",
                        sFileName);
            }
        }
    }
}
```

RESULT:

```
C:\>csc SearchSubStrings_ai.cs

C:\> SearchSubStrings_ai.exe

lri_familyreunion_jan2001_001.jpg
    is a photo file.

hri_familyreunion_jan2001_001.jpg
    is a photo file.

C:\>
```

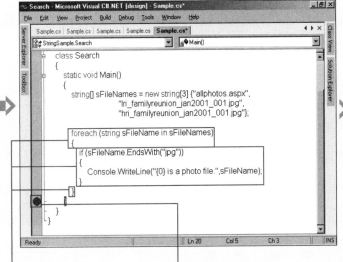

7 Use a `foreach` statement to loop through all the elements in the array.

8 In the `foreach` loop, use the `EndsWith` function to check the element for a `.jpg` extension and write the filename to the console if it is a JPEG file.

9 Set a debug stop.

10 Press F5 to save, build, and run the console application.

■ A message appears displaying the two JPEG filenames.

REPLACE CHARACTERS

I f you need to create a string from replacing characters in an existing string, you can use either the `String` or `StringBuilder` classes to perform this operation. For example, you may want to take a comma-separated file and turn it into a tab-separated file.

On the `String` class, the `Replace` method lets you replace a character in one string with another character. When you use the `String.Replace` method, it will search for all instances of the character in the affected string and replace it with the character you specify. If you do not intend to remove more than one of the same character from your string, your best course of action is to replace your original

string using the `StringBuilder` class discussed earlier in this chapter.

The `StringBuilder.Replace` method is much more flexible with replacing characters within a string. The `StringBuilder.Replace` method gives you four methods for replacing characters: replacing a character string with a new one, replacing all instances of a specified character with another one (just like the `String.Replace` method), replacing all instances of a string within a specified range, and replacing all instances of a character in a specified range with a new character.

REPLACE CHARACTERS

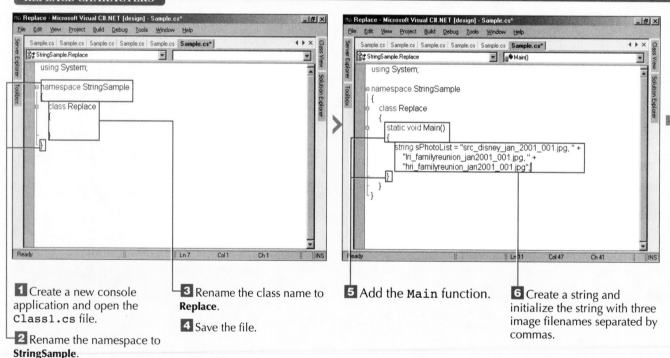

1 Create a new console application and open the `Class1.cs` file.

2 Rename the namespace to **StringSample**.

3 Rename the class name to **Replace**.

4 Save the file.

5 Add the **Main** function.

6 Create a string and initialize the string with three image filenames separated by commas.

Extra

The `String.Replace` method is rather straightforward, but it is also quite limited just like the `String` class it references. If you have a `StringBuilder` class, then you can use the `StringBuilder.Replace` method for changing your original `String` class.

The String.Replace and StringBuilder. Replace methods are both case sensitive, so if you try to replace a character with the lowercase letter t, then Replace function will leave all uppercase T characters alone. If you want to search for all uppercase T characters, then you have to include another String.Replace or String.Builder.Replace method that searches for an uppercase T.

Visual C# returns an `ArgumentNullException` exception if the character that you are trying to replace is a *null value* — the character you are trying to find does not exist or if the string has no characters in it at all.

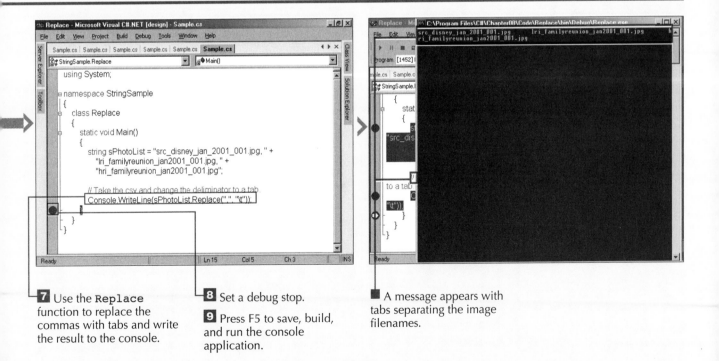

7 Use the **Replace** function to replace the commas with tabs and write the result to the console.

8 Set a debug stop.

9 Press F5 to save, build, and run the console application.

■ A message appears with tabs separating the image filenames.

EXTRACT SUBSTRINGS

String extractions are a very common task in your programs. For example, a source string may contain blank spaces at the beginning or end of a string, and you only want the contents between those blank spaces. Or, you may know the format of the string and want to obtain only a section of that string.

.NET Framework provides methods for extracting substrings that exist as individual characters or as a range of characters in a string. You have a few framework classes that allow string extractions. These classes are `String`, `StringBuilder`, and `RegularExpressions`. The class that you use depends on how sophisticated your extraction needs to be.

The `String` class holds an immutable string of characters. Each of these characters has an *index,* which is the position within the array of characters. The positions are tracked from left to right with the zero index being the first position (*zero-based*). If you know the starting index and (optionally) the length, you can pull out the desired substring.

If you desire to extract a single character, you can reference by the index in the `String` or `StringBuilder` object (for example, `char cThirdChar = sMyString[2];` would extract the third character in the string `sMyString`).

EXTRACT SUBSTRINGS

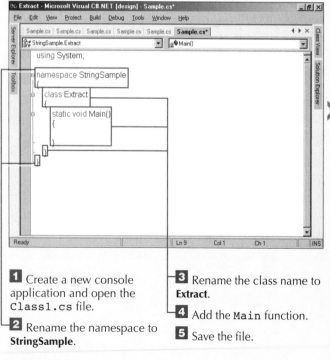

1 Create a new console application and open the `Class1.cs` file.

2 Rename the namespace to **StringSample**.

3 Rename the class name to **Extract**.

4 Add the `Main` function.

5 Save the file.

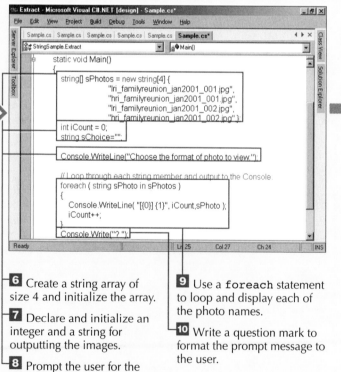

6 Create a string array of size 4 and initialize the array.

7 Declare and initialize an integer and a string for outputting the images.

8 Prompt the user for the format of the photos to view.

9 Use a `foreach` statement to loop and display each of the photo names.

10 Write a question mark to format the prompt message to the user.

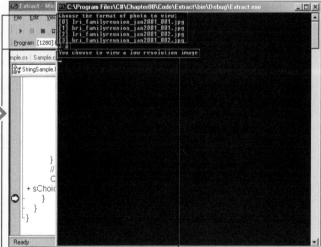

You can use part of one string to build another string.

TYPE THIS:

```
using System;
namespace StringSample
{  class Extract
    {  static void Main(string[] args)
        {  string sPhoto = "src_fmlyreunion_jan2001_001.jpg";
            string sFilePrefix;
            string sBasePhoto =sPhoto.Substring(4);
            Console.WriteLine(sBasePhoto);
            Console.WriteLine("Please choose format to view?");
            Console.WriteLine("[0]Low Resolution");
            Console.WriteLine("[1]High Resolution");
            Console.Write("?: ");

            string sSelection = Console.ReadLine();
            switch (sSelection)
            {  case "0" :
                    sFilePrefix = "lri_"; break;
                case "1" :
                    sFilePrefix = "hri_"; break;
                default :
                    sFilePrefix = "src_"; break;}
            string sFullFile = sFilePrefix + sBasePhoto;
            Console.WriteLine("You will view {0}", sFullFile);
}}}
```

RESULT:

```
C:\>csc ExtractSubstrings_ai.cs
C:\> ExtractSubstrings_ai.exe
fmlyreunion_jan2001_001.jpg
Please choose format to view?
[0]Low Resolution
[1]High Resolution
?: 1
You will view hri_fmlyreunion_
jan2001_001.jpg
C:\>
```

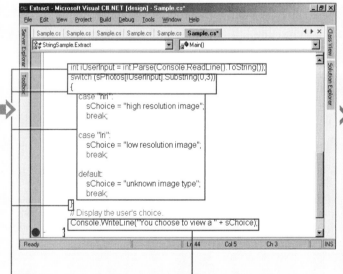

■11 Create an integer variable and initialize the variable.

■12 Use a **switch** statement and the **SubString** function to read the prefix for the filename.

■13 For the case of **hri**, **lri**, and **default**, set the string variable.

■14 Write the message to the console.

■15 Set a debug stop at the end of the class.

■16 Press F5 to save, build, and run the console application.

■ A message appears prompting for image number.

■17 Type a number from **0** to **3** and press Enter.

■ A message appears about the image resolution.

CHANGE THE CHARACTER CASE

You may not always receive a string from the user of your application with the required case to enter the string into your database. For example, you may have user names in your database stored in all caps. The String class helps you change the case of your strings by providing the `String.ToLower` and the `String.ToUpper` methods.

The `String.ToLower` method changes any capital letters in the string to lowercase letters and returns the lowercase string so you can use it in another part of your program. You can add an original string to the method or you can reference another string in your program.

The `String.ToUpper` method is the exact opposite of the `String.ToLower` method. You use the `String.ToUpper`

method for converting any lowercase characters in a string to capital letters. Also like the `String.ToLower` method, you can include either an original string within the method or you can reference another string that references the `String` class.

When you use the `String.ToLower` and `String.ToUpper` methods, Visual C# converts all of the characters in your string to either lower- or uppercase letters and returns a copy of the string but does not change the string itself. If you want to change specific characters in your string, you should use the `String.Replace` method instead.

CHANGE THE CHARACTER CASE

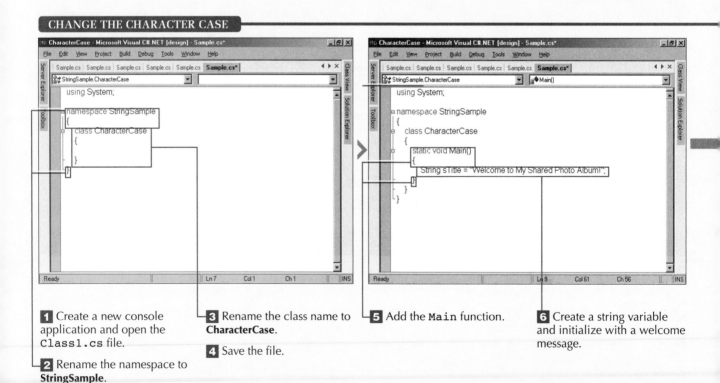

1 Create a new console application and open the `Class1.cs` file.

2 Rename the namespace to **StringSample**.

3 Rename the class name to **CharacterCase**.

4 Save the file.

5 Add the **Main** function.

6 Create a string variable and initialize with a welcome message.

Capitalizing proper nouns, like names, would require
changing the case of the initial character. Here is an example
of doing capitalization on the initial character of a word.

TYPE THIS:

```
using System;
namespace StringSample
{   class InitialCaps
    {   static void Main()
        {   string sFullName = "joE mARkiewiCz";
            string [] sNameParts =
                sFullName.Split(char.Parse(" "));
            string [] sNewParts = new string[2];
            int iCount = 0;

            foreach (string sPart in sNameParts)
            {
                sNewParts[iCount] =
                    sPart[0].ToString().ToUpper() +
                    sPart.Substring(
                        1,(sPart.Length - 1)).ToLower();
                iCount++;
            }
            string sNewFullName = String.Join(" ",sNewParts);

            Console.WriteLine("Applying the custom intitial "
                + "caps formatting on '{0}' give the following "
                + "result: {1}", sFullName, sNewFullName);
}}}
```

RESULT:

```
C:\>csc
ChangeCase_ai.cs

C:\>
ChangeCase_ai.exe

Applying the custom
intitial caps
formatting on 'joE
mARkiewiCz'

gives the following
result: Joe
Markiewicz

C:\>
```

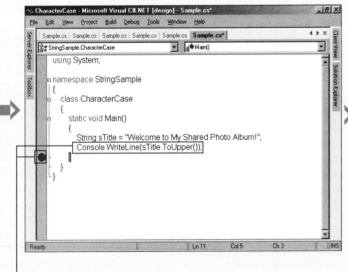

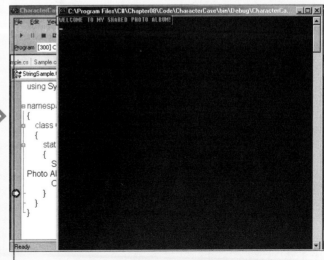

7 Use the **ToUpper**
function to convert the
message to uppercase and
output the message to the
console.

8 Set a debug stop.

9 Press F5 to save, build,
and run the console
application.

■ A welcome message
appears in upper case.

TRIM SPACES

When you have a string that contains unwanted white space in the beginning or end of a string, you can resolve this with using the trimming capabilities built into the `String` class. Visual C# provides three options for creating a copy of your string and trimming the white spaces from them: `String.Trim`, `String.TrimEnd`, and `String.TrimStart`.

The `String.Trim`, `String.TrimEnd`, and `String.TrimStart` methods determine what white space is and what is not by using the `Char.IsWhiteSpace` method. The `Char.IsWhiteSpace` method indicates whether the specified Unicode character is categorized as white space.

The `String.Trim` method trims both ends of the string. If only the end or beginning white space characters need to be trimmed, you can use the `String.TrimEnd` and `String.TrimStart` methods respectively. These trim methods also have overloaded implementations that allow specified character(s) to be included as nondesirable characters to be trimmed off of the extremes of the string. To include additional characters, you would provide an array of characters in the parameter list of the desired trim method. This character list does not have to be specified in any order. It uses all members of the array as it trims characters off of the string.

TRIM SPACES

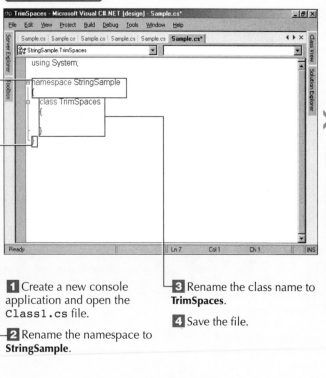

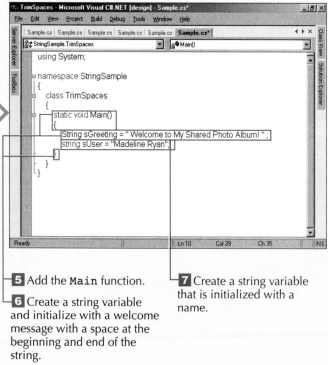

1 Create a new console application and open the `Class1.cs` file.

2 Rename the namespace to **StringSample**.

3 Rename the class name to **TrimSpaces**.

4 Save the file.

5 Add the **Main** function.

6 Create a string variable and initialize with a welcome message with a space at the beginning and end of the string.

7 Create a string variable that is initialized with a name.

Apply It

Trimming strings for more than white space can enable you to strip any other unwanted characters like punctuation.

TYPE THIS:

```
using System;

namespace StringSample
{
    /// <summary>
    /// The Trim can accept an array of unicode chars that
    /// will be used to trim from either end of the string.
    /// Note that it does not matter what order the chars
    /// are set.
    /// </summary>
    class TrimSpaces
    {
        static void Main()
        {
            String sGreeting =
                " Welcome to My Shared Photo Album! " ;

            Console.Write(sGreeting.Trim(
                char.Parse(" "), char.Parse("!")));
        }
    }
}
```

RESULT:

```
C:\>csc TrimSpaces_ai.cs
C:\> TrimSpaces_ai.exe
Welcome to My Shared Photo Album
C:\>
```

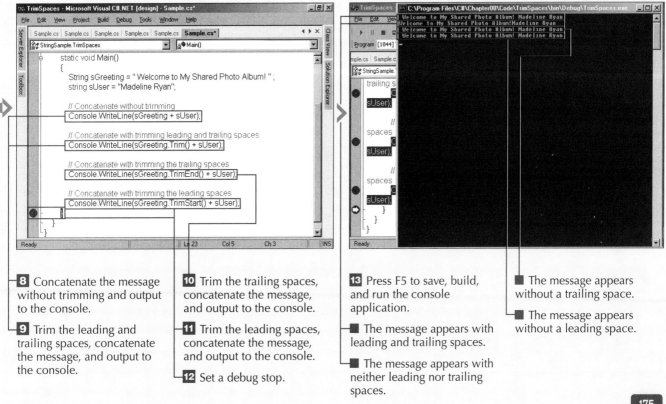

8 Concatenate the message without trimming and output to the console.

9 Trim the leading and trailing spaces, concatenate the message, and output to the console.

10 Trim the trailing spaces, concatenate the message, and output to the console.

11 Trim the leading spaces, concatenate the message, and output to the console.

12 Set a debug stop.

13 Press F5 to save, build, and run the console application.

■ The message appears with leading and trailing spaces.

■ The message appears with neither leading nor trailing spaces.

■ The message appears without a trailing space.

■ The message appears without a leading space.

REMOVE CHARACTERS

You can clean up your string of unwanted characters with members of the .NET Framework `String` class. The `String` class contains members that can remove unwanted characters from the extremes of a string or throughout the string.

To trim characters from the extremes (start and end), you can refer to the "Trim Spaces" task in this chapter. To remove characters from anywhere in the string, you can use the `String.Remove` method. The `String.Remove` method requires two parameters for execution. The first parameter, `startIndex`, is an integer that indicates the

starting position for deleting characters. The second parameter, `count`, is an integer that indicates the number of characters to delete from the `startIndex`.

When using the `Remove` method, you will most likely determine the `startIndex` and `count` programmatically. For example, you may know a list of characters that are in data file from a mainframe. You can search for the characters in the string for their position. You can use the `IndexOf` and `LastIndexOf` methods of the `String` class to see what index position contains that character. This position can be used as the `startIndex`, and you can give a `count` of 1.

REMOVE CHARACTERS

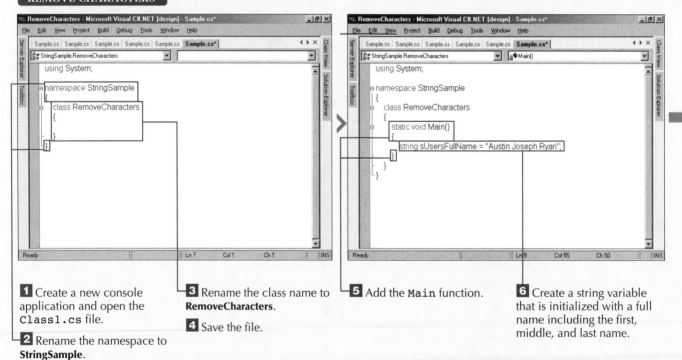

1 Create a new console application and open the `Class1.cs` file.

2 Rename the namespace to **StringSample**.

3 Rename the class name to **RemoveCharacters**.

4 Save the file.

5 Add the **Main** function.

6 Create a string variable that is initialized with a full name including the first, middle, and last name.

Apply It

This example takes this section's example one step further and programatically determines the values for the `startIndex` and `count` parameters.

TYPE THIS:

```
using System;

namespace StringSample
{
    class RemoveCharacters
    {
        static void Main(string[] args)
        {
            string sUsersFullName = "Austin Joseph Ryan";

            string[] sNameParts = sUsersFullName.Split(
                char.Parse(" "));

            if (sNameParts.GetUpperBound(0)==2)
            {
                string sShortName =
                    sUsersFullName.Remove(sNameParts[0].Length,
                        sNameParts[1].Length + 1);
                Console.WriteLine(sShortName);
            }
        }
    }
}
```

RESULT:

```
C:\>csc RemoveCharacters_ai.cs
C:\> RemoveCharacters_ai.exe
Austin Ryan
C:\>
```

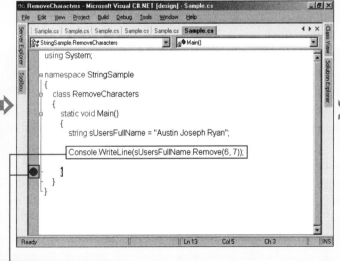

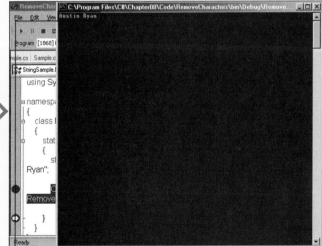

7 Use the **Remove** function to remove the middle name from the string.

8 Set a debug stop.

9 Press F5 to save, build, and run the console application.

■ A message appears with just the first and last name.

SPLIT A STRING

Splitting strings into multiple strings is useful when you are trying to manually parse a large string. The .NET String class can divide strings into a set of substrings with the Split method.

Ideally when it comes to splitting strings, your string contains a subset of strings that are separated by a common character or escape sequence used as a delimiter between each of the substrings. If you have a common character that is used as a delimiter, you can use the String.Split method to create a string array that contains each logical substring.

The String.Split method takes in an array of Unicode characters that delimit the substrings, and a string array is returned. Optionally, you can provide a second parameter, count, that limits the number of substrings to be added to the resulting string array. If you provide the count parameter you will get the last part of the string in the last element of the array, including the delimiter(s). Also, you need to make sure that the count parameter is positive. If you enter a negative number, the method returns an ArgumentOutofRange exception. Lastly, if you provide a zero for count, you will get an array with no elements.

SPLIT A STRING

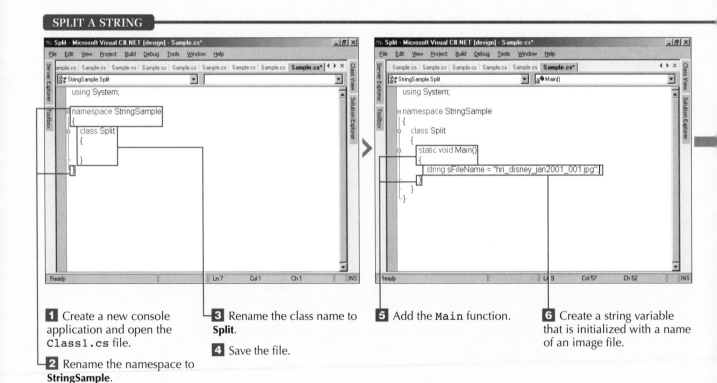

1 Create a new console application and open the `Class1.cs` file.

2 Rename the namespace to **StringSample**.

3 Rename the class name to **Split**.

4 Save the file.

5 Add the **Main** function.

6 Create a string variable that is initialized with a name of an image file.

Apply It

If you format files with a standard naming convention, you can split the filename into logical substrings that can be used later in your programming logic.

TYPE THIS (INTO YOUR CLASS):

```csharp
static void Main()  {
    string sFileName = "hri_disney_jan2001_001.jpg";
    string[] sFileParts = new string[4];
    char [] cDelim = new char[1] {char.Parse("_")};
    sFileParts = sFileName.Split(cDelim,4);

    string sPhotoType;  string sPhotoEvent = sFileParts[1];
    string sPhotoDate = sFileParts[2];
    string sPhotoIndex = sFileParts[3].Remove(3,4);

    switch (sFileParts[0]) {
        case "hri" :
            sPhotoType = "high resolution image"; break;
        case "tni" :
            sPhotoType = "thumbnail image"; break;
        default :
            sPhotoType = "unknown image type"; break;
        }
    Console.WriteLine("The " + sPhotoType + " selected was "
        + "index " + sPhotoIndex + " of pictures at "
        + sPhotoEvent + " which was taken "
        + sPhotoDate + ".");
}
```

RESULT:

```
C:\>csc SplitString_ai.cs

C:\> SplitString_ai.exe

The high resolution image selected
    was index 001 of pictures at
    disney which was taken jan2001.

C:\>
```

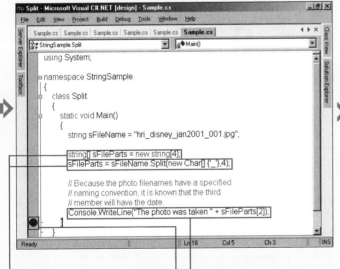

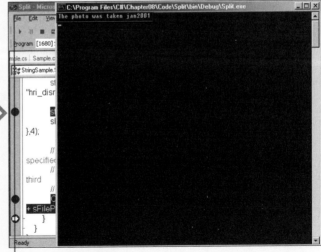

7 Create a **string** array of size 4.

8 Add the **Split** function to split the image file up into four elements using the underscore (_) character for the delimiter.

9 Write the date that the picture was taken by accessing the second element.

10 Set a debug stop.

11 Press F5 to save, build, and run the console application.

■ A message appears, showing the date the image was taken.

179

JOIN STRINGS

The `String` class provides methods for joining several strings and merging them into one continuous string. The `String.Join` method lets you join the strings with separators you specify between each string.

Joining strings together is common when interacting with relational databases. For example, when you build a string that contains the full address for a customer, you should not store this entire string in the database. For more efficient use of your database, you will normalize the storage of the address into separate fields and/or tables. Because the address will be in separate fields, when you pull the data from the database and display it on a user interface, you will need to join the strings together.

You can implement the `String.Join` in two ways. The simplest implementation requires two parameters. The first parameter is a string that designates the separator used between each substring. The second parameter is an array of strings. Most likely, you will have a `String` array before calling this method, but you can give the array list nested in the parameter (for example, `new string[]{"a","b","c"}`).

The other implementation includes the same parameters as the other with two additional parameters. These parameters are `startIndex`, which sets the first array element used in the join, and `count`, which limits the number of elements used in the join.

JOIN STRINGS

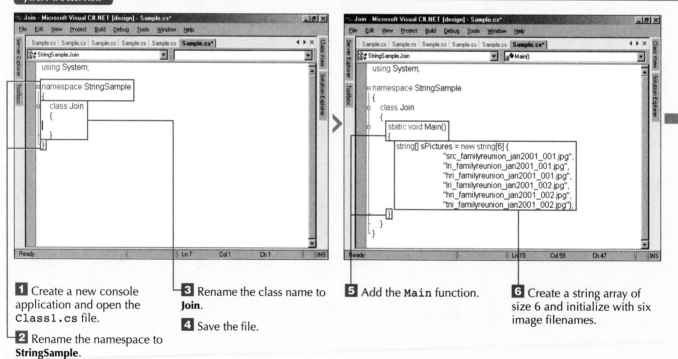

1 Create a new console application and open the `Class1.cs` file.

2 Rename the namespace to **StringSample**.

3 Rename the class name to **Join**.

4 Save the file.

5 Add the **Main** function.

6 Create a string array of size 6 and initialize with six image filenames.

Apply It

You can pull data from enumerations to populate a string array and with that array you can join the members into one string.

TYPE THIS:

```
using System;
using System.Globalization;

namespace StringSample
{
    class WeekDays
    {
        static void Main()
        {
            string [] sDaysOfTheWeek = new string[7];
            DateTimeFormatInfo dtfInfo =
                new DateTimeFormatInfo();
            sDaysOfTheWeek = dtfInfo.DayNames;
            string sWeekDays = String.Join
                (", ",sDaysOfTheWeek,1,5 );
            Console.WriteLine
                ("The week days are: " + sWeekDays);
        }
    }
}
```

RESULT:

```
C:\>csc JoinStrings_ai.cs

C:\> JoinStrings_ai.exe

The week days are: Monday, Tuesday,
    Wednesday, Thursday, Friday

C:\>
```

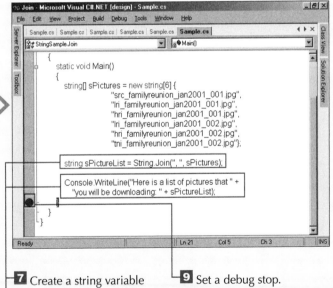

7 Create a string variable and initialize the variable using the `Join` function to join the elements of the string array together.

8 Format a message and write the message to the console.

9 Set a debug stop.

10 Press F5 to save, build, and run the console application.

■ A message appears that shows all of the filenames.

PAD STRINGS

You may sometimes need to have your strings appear a certain way on your screen. For example, you may want a string of numbers right-aligned so that the numbers can be read more easily. The String Class enables you to left- and right-align strings by using the String.PadRight and String.PadLeft methods, respectively.

You can left-align strings by using the String.PadRight method. The String.PadRight method adds spaces on the right for a specific total length of your string. When you use the String.PadRight method, you specify how long the string needs to be with a totalWidth argument. This width value minus the number of characters in your string

determines how many white spaces the method should add to the end of the string. If you do not want white spaces, you can replace the white space by providing a width and a padding character.

The String.PadLeft method is a mirror image of the String.PadRight method. In the case of the String.PadLeft method, you can enter the width of the string and the method will add the number of white spaces by subtracting the string width from the length of the string. You can also pad your flush-right string with characters instead of white spaces by adding the char argument and the padding character.

PAD STRINGS

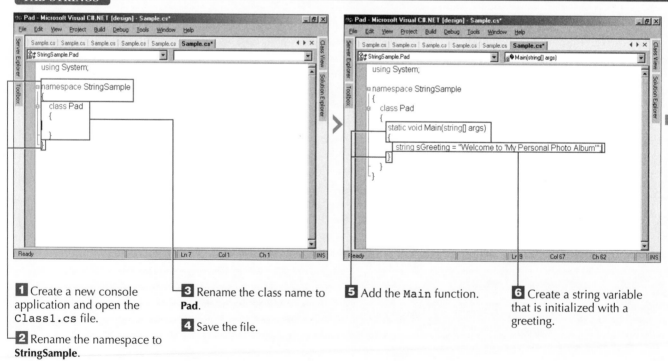

1 Create a new console application and open the Class1.cs file.

2 Rename the namespace to **StringSample**.

3 Rename the class name to **Pad**.

4 Save the file.

5 Add the **Main** function.

6 Create a string variable that is initialized with a greeting.

Apply It

You can pad with other characters besides white space.

TYPE THIS:

```
using System;

namespace StringSample
{
    /// <summary>
    /// Take the same Greeting and pad with a '-' instead of
    /// a space.  Do this with taking the string length plus
    /// padding amount.
    /// </summary>
    class Pad {
        static void Main()
        {   string sGreeting =
                "Welcome to 'My Personal Photo Album'";
            string sGreetingPadded;

            sGreetingPadded = sGreeting.PadLeft
                ((sGreeting.Length + 5),char.Parse("-"));
            sGreetingPadded = sGreetingPadded.PadRight
                ((sGreetingPadded.Length + 5),char.Parse("-"));

            Console.WriteLine(sGreetingPadded);
        }
    }
}
```

RESULT:

```
C:\>csc PadStrings_ai.cs
C:\> PadStrings_ai.exe
---Welcome to 'My Personal
   Photo Album'---
C:\>
```

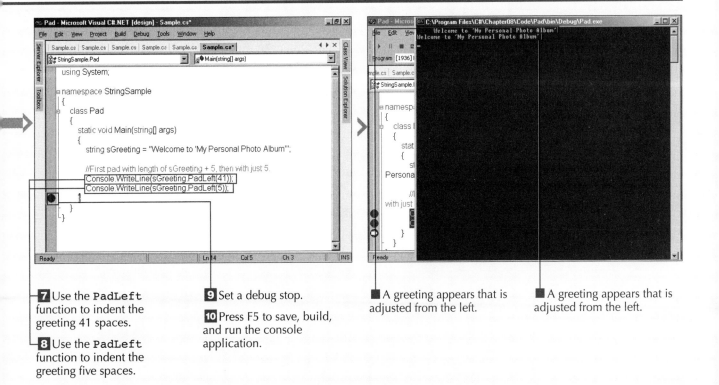

7 Use the **PadLeft** function to indent the greeting 41 spaces.

8 Use the **PadLeft** function to indent the greeting five spaces.

9 Set a debug stop.

10 Press F5 to save, build, and run the console application.

■ A greeting appears that is adjusted from the left.

■ A greeting appears that is adjusted from the left.

183

VIEW INFORMATION ABOUT PROPERTIES

A *property* provides access to the attribute of a struct or a class such as the length of a string or the name of a contact. Properties are members of classes, structs, and interfaces.

Properties contain *accessors* that specify the statements to execute in your class, struct, or interface. For example, if you write a program that converts Fahrenheit temperatures into Celsius temperatures, you can include a Fahrenheit that retrieves the Fahrenheit temperature from the user so your class can convert that value into its Celsius.

The declaration structure of a property is very similar to other types of declarations you have already learned about. The structure includes any optional attributes and modifiers, one of the four types of access modifiers (public, private, protected, or internal), and the property name. After you enter the property name, you enter the accessor information and any interface type, both of which are described later in this chapter.

A property is very similar to a field except that C# does not classify the property as a variable as it does with a field. The property instead reads and writes variables to objects that accesses your class, struct, or interface.

VIEW INFORMATION ABOUT PROPERTIES

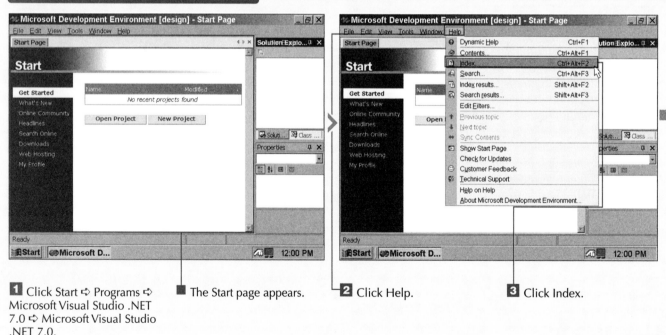

1 Click Start ➪ Programs ➪ Microsoft Visual Studio .NET 7.0 ➪ Microsoft Visual Studio .NET 7.0.

■ The Start page appears.

2 Click Help.

3 Click Index.

Extra

You should remain cognizant of accessibility issues with properties. That is, the property must be as accessible as another property or another type. For example, if you have two properties A and B, property A must be as accessible in all areas of your program where property B is accessible.

To take this example further, suppose that property A does not have an accessibility modifier (thus the default accessibility is protected) and property B has the public accessibility modifier. Property B appears within subclass B, and subclass B inherits from parent class A. Parent class A contains property A.

Because property B and property A do not have the same accessibility types, the MDE window will catch this error and you will not be able to compile your program until you change one or both of the properties so they have the same accessibility type.

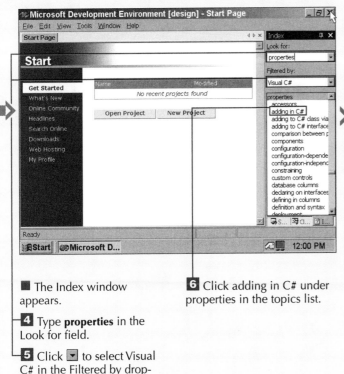

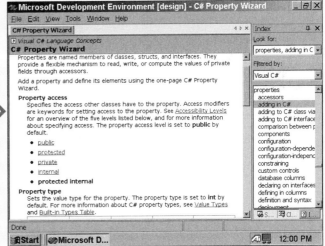

■ The Index window appears.

4 Type **properties** in the Look for field.

5 Click ▾ to select Visual C# in the Filtered by drop-down list.

6 Click adding in C# under properties in the topics list.

■ The C# Property Wizard page appears so you can load sample array files and see how they work.

COMPARE PROPERTIES AND INDEXERS

On the surface it may seem like properties and indexers (indeed, properties and many other C# features) have many similarities, and to some degree that is true. After all, it makes little sense to reinvent the wheel for every C# feature. However, properties and indexers do have some important differences.

Both properties and indexers use the get and set arguments. The get argument reads and returns a value of the property type. The get value can also compute a value (such as converting Fahrenheit to Celsius) and return the computed value.

The set argument writes the property received from the get argument and appears after the get argument. The

set argument is similar to a method that returns void because it writes the value of the property type and does not return the value.

In the case of the get and set accessors, indexers contain the same formal parameters as the indexer does but properties do not contain any parameters at all. Otherwise, property accessors have some greater flexibility than indexers: A property is identified by its name instead of its signature, you can access a property through a simple name or access through a class, struct, or interface member, and the property is a static or instance member.

COMPARE PROPERTIES AND INDEXERS

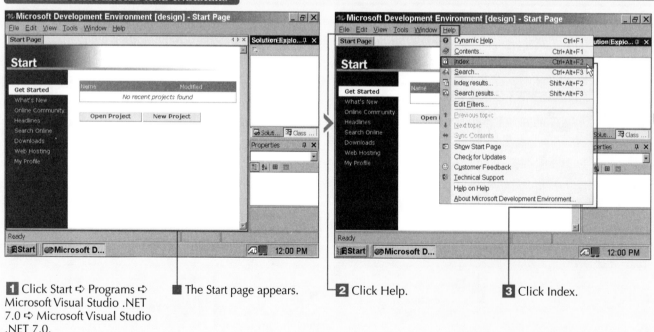

1 Click Start ➪ Programs ➪ Microsoft Visual Studio .NET 7.0 ➪ Microsoft Visual Studio .NET 7.0.

■ The Start page appears.

2 Click Help.

3 Click Index.

Extra

Properties contain some limitations that you should know about so you can avoid confusing property abilities with other features such as indexers and classes.

- Because C# does not classify properties as variables, you cannot pass a property with the `ref` or `out` parameters. The `ref` and `out` parameters cause a method to refer to the same variable that the method acquired.

- C# automatically classifies the property as an instance property unless you specifically add the static modifier in the argument. Your program cannot reference a static property through an instance but only through the type name.

- If you declare a property as a static property, then you cannot use the this keyword or the virtual, abstract, or override modifiers.

If you want more information about properties and how they work differently from indexers, the MDE window online help contains downloadable examples of using properties in their properties tutorial. After you search for and access the properties tutorial page, you can access the samples by clicking the "Properties Sample" link on the page.

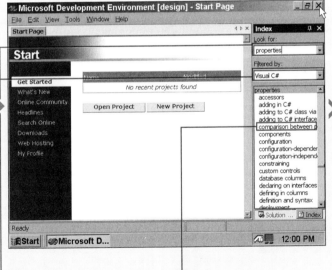

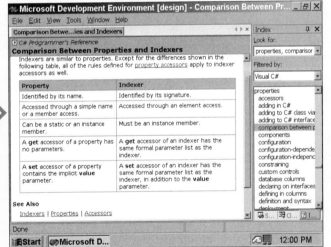

■ The Index window appears.

4 Type **properties** in the Look for field.

5 Click ▼ to select Visual C# in the Filtered by drop-down list.

6 Click comparison between properties and accessors under properties in the topics list.

■ The Comparison Between Properties and Indexersv help file appears in the parent window.

PROGRAM PROPERTY ACCESSORS

The get and set keywords comprise the property accessors. The get keyword reads information into the property, and the set keyword writes property information into your class, struct, or interface for further processing in your program.

Any property includes the token get and/or set accessors, but if you want to do anything with your property, you must add the accessor body. The get accessor effectively reads the value of a field — either a value that you enter into the program itself or that the user enters during runtime.

After the get accessor retrieves the value, it must return the value with the return or throw statement. All return

statements in the get accessor must specify an expression, such as a string name, that can be converted to the property type. Unless another portion of your class, struct, or interface references a property as part of an expression, the get accessor computes the value of the property.

The set accessor acts much like a method with the void return type. The body of a set accessor provides a new value for the property. A set accessor must include a return type, but unlike the get accessor, that return type must not include an expression.

PROGRAM PROPERTY ACCESSORS

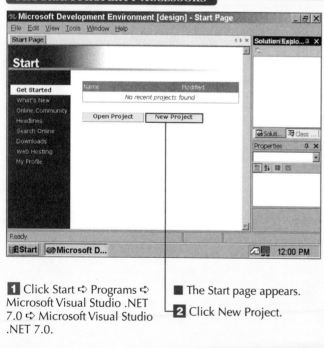

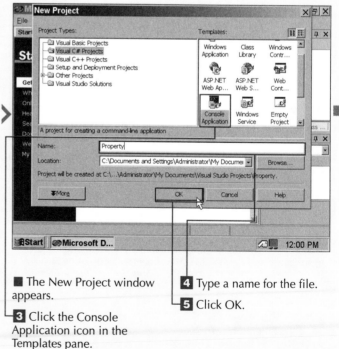

1 Click Start ➪ Programs ➪ Microsoft Visual Studio .NET 7.0 ➪ Microsoft Visual Studio .NET 7.0.

■ The Start page appears.

2 Click New Project.

■ The New Project window appears.

3 Click the Console Application icon in the Templates pane.

4 Type a name for the file.

5 Click OK.

Apply It

You can override a property accessor in one property
with an accessor from another property.

TYPE THIS:

```
using System;
class Test;
{
    abstract int Area
    {get;
     set;
    }
class Cube: Area
{
    public int side;
    public Cube(int s)
    {side = x;
    }
    public override int Area
    {get
        {
            return side * side;
        }
        set
        {side = Math.Sqrt(value);
        }}}
```

RESULT:

This code overrides the
abstract Area property
with the code for
returning the cube side
value.

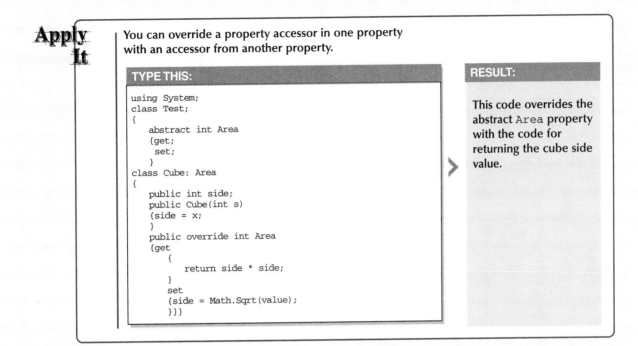

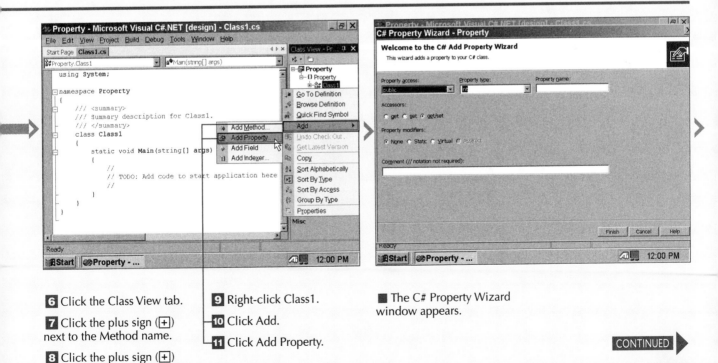

6 Click the Class View tab.

7 Click the plus sign (⊞)
next to the Method name.

8 Click the plus sign (⊞)
next to the {} Method name.

9 Right-click Class1.

10 Click Add.

11 Click Add Property.

■ The C# Property Wizard
window appears.

CONTINUED

PROGRAM PROPERTY ACCESSORS

C# provides two different approaches for adding property accessors. First, you can enter the accessors entirely in code. Second, you can have C# provide you with the skeleton property information by adding the property in the C# Property Wizard.

You can access the C# Property Wizard via the Class View window. The Property Wizard contains all the basic building blocks of a property including the get and set accessors. When you finish entering the accessors and all other property information in the Property Wizard, the basic get and/or set accessor skeletons appear so that you can add arguments into the skeletons.

After you add the accessor information, you add property values into the accessor bodies. The get accessor must adhere to the same rules as value-returning methods. Because the return type of a method that is not void must specify an expression that has the same type as the method, the get accessor must specify an expression that has the same property type.

The set accessor must also adhere to rules — in this case, the rules for void methods. Both set accessors and void methods require that any return statement does not specify an expression. If the set accessor completes normally, the accessor writes the property value and returns that value to the property caller.

PROGRAM PROPERTY ACCESSORS (CONTINUED)

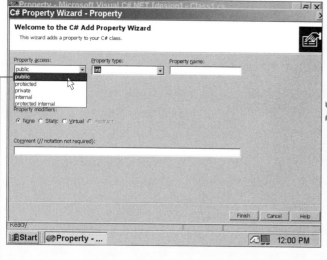

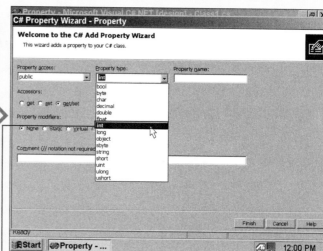

12 Click ▼ to select a property access modifier from the drop-down list.

13 Click ▼ to select property type from the drop-down list.

Apply It

The `get` accessor must end with a `return` or `throw` statement just as a method does. If you do not include a `return` or `throw` statement, your program will not compile.

TYPE THIS:

```
using System;
class Return;
private string name;
public string Name
{
    get
    {
    }
}
```

RESULT:

This code will return an error because there is no return or throw type within the `get` argument.

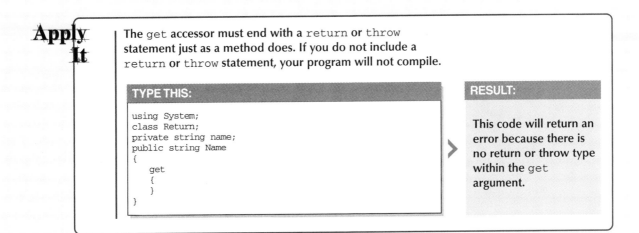

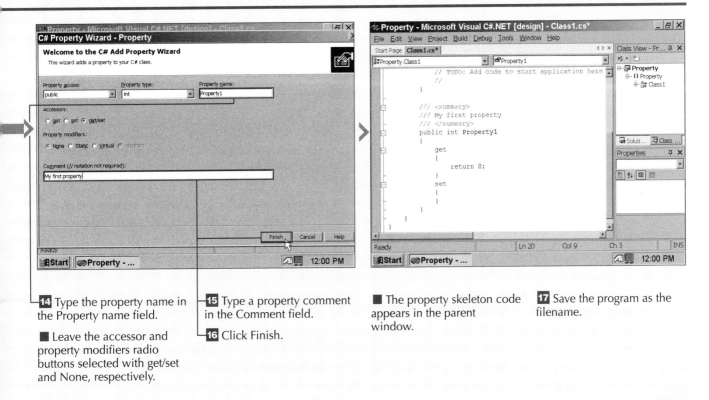

■14 Type the property name in the Property name field.

■ Leave the accessor and property modifiers radio buttons selected with get/set and None, respectively.

■15 Type a property comment in the Comment field.

■16 Click Finish.

■ The property skeleton code appears in the parent window.

■17 Save the program as the filename.

DECLARE ABSTRACT PROPERTIES

Abstract properties are properties that you can place in abstract classes. If you remember, an abstract class acts as the base class for inheriting classes. The same is true for inheriting and base interfaces. So, abstract properties are base class properties so properties in inheriting classes or interfaces can access them.

Like a class, you have to declare an abstract property by using the abstract keyword. An abstract property automatically comes with the virtual modifier just as a class does. The virtual modifier tells your program to check for overriding properties in inheriting classes automatically.

An abstract property does not declare any accessors. Instead, the abstract property provides only basic

information about properties that properties in inheriting classes can use. When the inheriting property combines its accessors with the abstract property information, the program creates a complete property that you can then use for computing property values.

Because the abstract property does not include any specific information — it merely "sets the table" for an inheriting property to perform its duty — the only text in the body of an abstract property is a semicolon after the get and set accessors. If you try to enter any other information, the MDE window will report the error and your program will not compile.

DECLARE ABSTRACT PROPERTIES

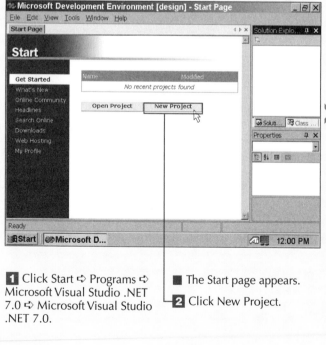

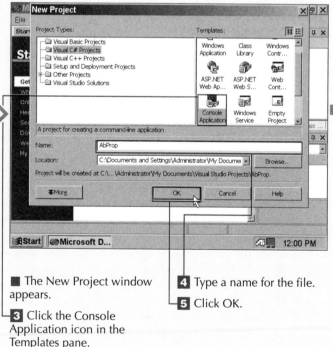

1 Click Start ➪ Programs ➪ Microsoft Visual Studio .NET 7.0 ➪ Microsoft Visual Studio .NET 7.0.

■ The Start page appears.

2 Click New Project.

■ The New Project window appears.

3 Click the Console Application icon in the Templates pane.

4 Type a name for the file.

5 Click OK.

Extra

As with an abstract class or interface, there are restrictions that you must be aware of.

One restriction is that you cannot add any modifiers to an abstract property because C# automatically designates the abstract property as virtual. That means that you cannot add any of the other modifiers including `static`, `override`, or `new`. That also includes the virtual modifier. As long as you enter `abstract` as the property modifier and that abstract property resides in an abstract class or interface, you will have no problems.

Another restriction is that you cannot use the `base` keyword for retrieving property information from an abstract property. For example, if you declare an abstract property with an integer value of `A` and try to enter `return base.A` for returning the value of `A`, you will not be able to do so. The MDE window will catch your mistake if you attempt this maneuver.

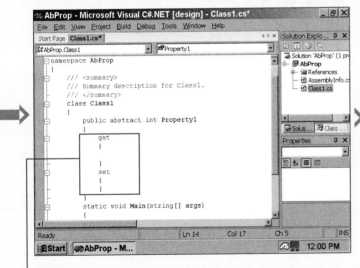

6 Type the abstract property code.

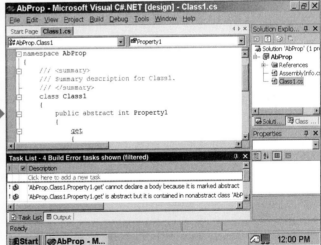

7 Run the program by pressing F5.

■ Because the abstract property cannot take a body, the MDE window registers the error.

8 Save the program as the filename.

INCLUDE PROPERTIES ON INTERFACES

You can declare properties not only on classes but also on interfaces. When you have classes that process an interface, those classes take the properties from those interfaces for further processing. Properties on an interface have a slightly different form than properties on a class.

You declare a property on an interface by using the new keyword. You can preface the keyword with attributes that C# uses to denote certain conditions; for example, you can tell your program that the property is obsolete and is no longer used.

After the new keyword, you can add the access type, which is the same as it is on class properties, classes, methods, and

other C# components. After you add the access type, you can enter the name of your interface property.

The interface accessors appear next enclosed in curly braces ({}). Neither the set and get accessors contain any other information in their bodies except for a semicolon. Like an abstract property, the interface property acquires information from other component properties (such as the one in a class) instead of processing properties itself. The get and set accessors serve only to determine whether the property is read-only (get), write-only (set), or read-write (get and set).

INCLUDE PROPERTIES ON INTERFACES

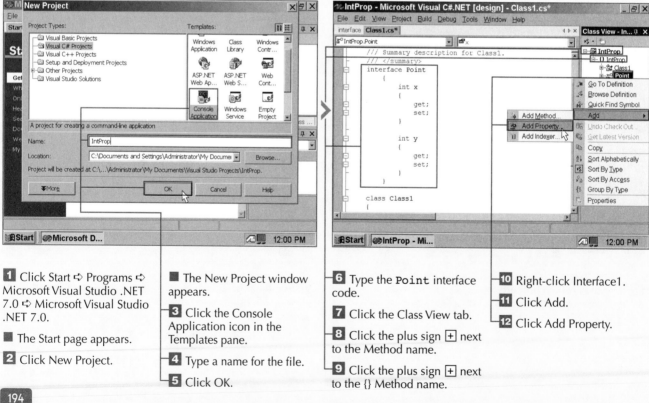

1 Click Start ➪ Programs ➪ Microsoft Visual Studio .NET 7.0 ➪ Microsoft Visual Studio .NET 7.0.

■ The Start page appears.

2 Click New Project.

■ The New Project window appears.

3 Click the Console Application icon in the Templates pane.

4 Type a name for the file.

5 Click OK.

6 Type the Point interface code.

7 Click the Class View tab.

8 Click the plus sign ⊞ next to the Method name.

9 Click the plus sign ⊞ next to the {} Method name.

10 Right-click Interface1.

11 Click Add.

12 Click Add Property.

Apply it

When a class or struct implements an interface, you can write your class or struct property to declare explicit interface member implementations. This is useful if you need to have an internal interface for performing tasks without passing it on to other parts of your program (and perhaps as output).

TYPE THIS:

```
interface Clones
{
    object Clone();
}
interface Compare
{
    int CompareTo(object template);
}
class Assembly: Clones, Compare
{
    int Compare.CompareTo(object template);
}
```

RESULT:

The above example declares Compare. CompareTo as an explicit interface member implementation.

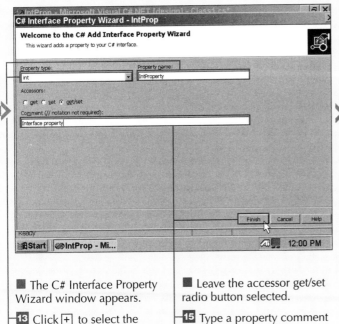

■ The C# Interface Property Wizard window appears.

-13 Click ⊞ to select the property type from the drop-down list.

-14 Type the property name in the property name field.

■ Leave the accessor get/set radio button selected.

-15 Type a property comment in the Comment field.

-16 Click Finish.

■ The interface property code appears in the parent window.

17 Save the program as the filename.

VIEW INFORMATION ABOUT WINDOWS FORMS

S oon after Microsoft introduced Windows 3.0, it also released a new version of Basic called Visual Basic. Both the operating system and the programming language became instant hits; Visual Basic became so popular because you can create a Windows program interface by dragging and dropping interface elements. C# continues this tradition by letting you create forms as an interface for users to enter information.

A *form* is an area on your screen that presents information to the user of your program so that the user can receive and enter information. Forms can take on several different guises including your standard windows, multiple document

interface, windows, dialog boxes, and surfaces so you can place different objects such as a graphic.

You can add objects such as buttons, controls, and fields into a form by dragging and dropping those elements from a default set of element templates. The form is an instance of a class, and this approach lets you create forms that can inherit from other forms because a class can inherit from another class. The form can inherit from the Form class template or from another form; inheriting from another form gives your form the extensibility it needs to add new features and functionality.

VIEW INFORMATION ABOUT WINDOWS FORMS

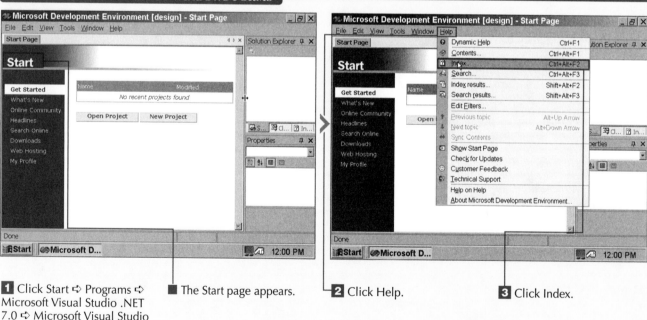

1 Click Start ➪ Programs ➪ Microsoft Visual Studio .NET 7.0 ➪ Microsoft Visual Studio .NET 7.0.

■ The Start page appears.

2 Click Help.

3 Click Index.

Extra

Microsoft added its form capability that it perfected in Visual Basic into C# as another tool that sets it apart from Visual C++ and Java. (Some Java development tools contain form creation capabilities, however.) Forms are not contained to C# and Visual Basic but are part of the Visual Studio .NET framework so you can import forms from one Visual Studio .NET programming language to another.

Forms act as the user interface for your program so users can interact with your program, the program database, the computer file system, and even the Windows registry. You can write forms in code, but the Windows Forms Designer makes it so easy that you do not have to worry about coding elements in your form.

If you used forms in Visual Basic 6 and want to use the same forms in C#, Visual Studio .NET handles forms differently. The MDE window online help contains a page with a comparison of form changes from Visual Basic 6 to Visual Studio .NET. If you have upgraded to Visual Studio .NET from a version of Visual Studio older than version 6, you can still compare forms in both versions by consulting the comparison help page along with your old Visual Studio documentation.

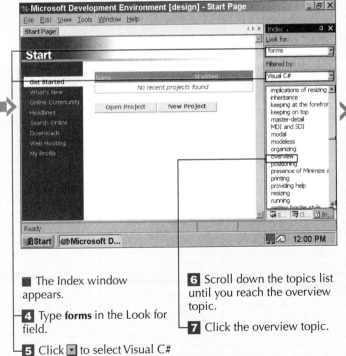

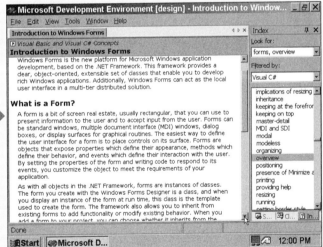

■ The Index window appears.

4 Type **forms** in the Look for field.

5 Click ▼ to select Visual C# in the Filtered by drop-down list.

6 Scroll down the topics list until you reach the overview topic.

7 Click the overview topic.

■ The Introduction to Windows Forms page appears so you can read more information about Windows forms.

ADD A WINDOWS FORM IN THE WINDOWS FORM DESIGNER

You add Visual Studio .NET forms — what Microsoft terms Windows forms — in C# by using the Windows Form Designer. In many cases you do not have to create a Windows form from scratch because C# creates one for you automatically when you open a new project, thus saving you time.

The form appears in the parent window so you can edit its properties and add information to the form. Form properties appear in the Properties window. If you add a new form in the Windows Form Designer, then the new form will appear in its own window with its own name.

When you view the form for the first time, you will notice that the form has dots throughout the form. These dots represent the grid, and you can use these dots as boundaries for objects that you add to the form. The gridlines help ensure that all the objects in your form look pleasing to the eye and that form objects do not interlap.

A box comprised of dashed lines appears around the perimeter of the form. This selection box lets you know that the current form is selected. The white boxes that appear within the selection box are the form handles. You can use these handles for resizing your form until it is the size you want.

ADD A WINDOWS FORM

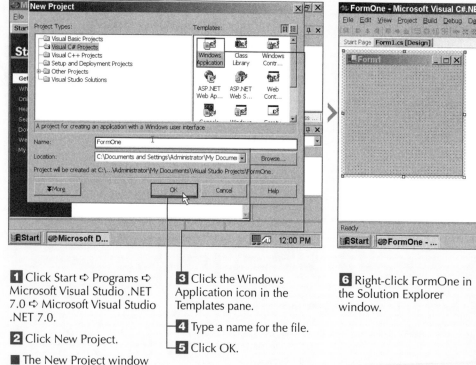

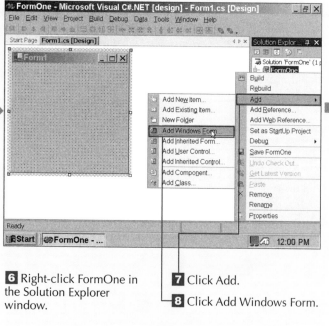

1 Click Start ➪ Programs ➪ Microsoft Visual Studio .NET 7.0 ➪ Microsoft Visual Studio .NET 7.0.

2 Click New Project.

■ The New Project window appears.

3 Click the Windows Application icon in the Templates pane.

4 Type a name for the file.

5 Click OK.

6 Right-click FormOne in the Solution Explorer window.

7 Click Add.

8 Click Add Windows Form.

Extra

Your new form already contains all the standard elements of a Windows form including a title bar. From left to right, the title bar contains a multicolored logo for performing window functions. This built-in function makes it easier for you to program your form and gives the user a familiar, standard interface for your program.

You can program in code if you want to, but if you are uncertain about how to proceed, you can create a form and then view the underlying code to see the nuts and bolts of your form. In the Solution Explorer window, you can click the form with your right mouse button. In the pop-up menu that appears, click View Code. A new window appears that contains the code for your form. You can go back to the designer by clicking the form tab with the [Design] label after the form name.

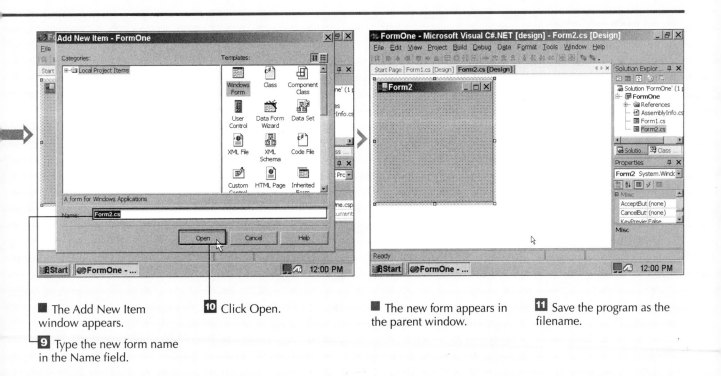

■ The Add New Item window appears.

⑨ Type the new form name in the Name field.

⑩ Click Open.

■ The new form appears in the parent window.

⑪ Save the program as the filename.

SET THE FORM TYPE

When you open a new Windows application, C# opens a new Windows form. This form inherits information from the Windows form template that automatically appears when you open a new Windows application so you do not have to create a form from scratch. You can also set up an inheriting form that inherits from another form in your C# project.

A Windows form looks very much like the standard window that you see in Windows. C# builds Windows forms around the Windows framework so you can access various Windows features including the files on the user's computer and the Windows registry. Windows forms also let you create graphics in your form with code using the Visual Studio .NET GDI classes.

You use Windows forms for developing Windows applications where the client computer and the user enters information into your program. Programs that use Windows forms rely on the computer the program runs on as well as a network for processing power and accessing data.

Inherited forms let you obtain features from another form so you do not have to add form elements repeatedly. Inheriting also promotes consistency between forms. Before you can inherit a form, the inherited form must already have been compiled into an executable file and a reference to the namespace must have been added into the class that inherits the form.

SET THE FORM TYPE

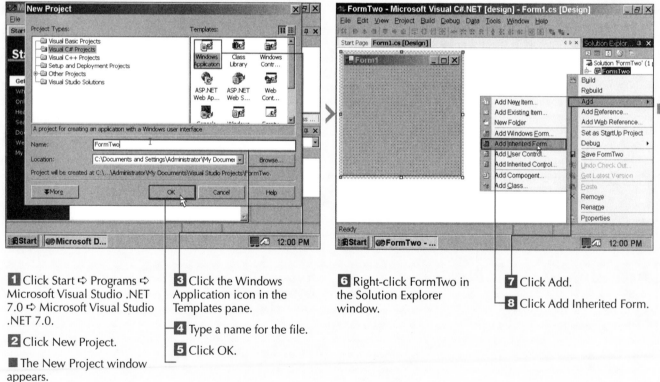

■ 1 Click Start ➪ Programs ➪ Microsoft Visual Studio .NET 7.0 ➪ Microsoft Visual Studio .NET 7.0.

■ 2 Click New Project.

■ The New Project window appears.

■ 3 Click the Windows Application icon in the Templates pane.

■ 4 Type a name for the file.

■ 5 Click OK.

■ 6 Right-click FormTwo in the Solution Explorer window.

■ 7 Click Add.

■ 8 Click Add Inherited Form.

Apply It

You can inherit a form in code rather than add a form from the Solution Explorer window.

TYPE THIS:

```
using System;
using System.Drawing;
using System.Collections;
using System.ComponentModel;
using System.Windows.Forms;
using System.Data;

namespace MyFormProgram
{
public class Form1 : System.Windows.Forms.Form
    // Enter rest of your form here.
```

RESULT:

Entering a form in code means that you must add six System names, the name of your program in the namespace argument, and finally the class name and type. This is a lot of typing, and it is usually a good idea to create a Windows application and let the MDE window do the work for you.

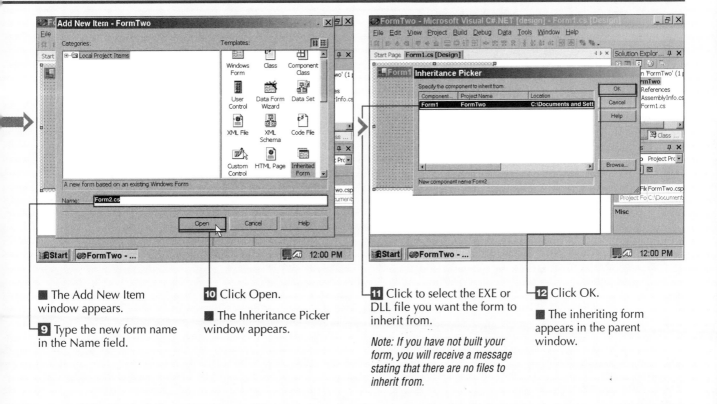

■ The Add New Item window appears.

9 Type the new form name in the Name field.

10 Click Open.

■ The Inheritance Picker window appears.

11 Click to select the EXE or DLL file you want the form to inherit from.

Note: If you have not built your form, you will receive a message stating that there are no files to inherit from.

12 Click OK.

■ The inheriting form appears in the parent window.

CHOOSE THE STARTUP WINDOWS FORM

A Windows form does not automatically start when you start your program. You must tell your program what form you want it to display when your program first launches. You can do this by setting the properties of your form in the Solution Explorer window.

The Properties pages contain information about the common and configuration properties in your program, but the General tab contains the information you need to know. Specifically, the Startup Object information lets you select the class in your project that you want to start first when the user starts your program.

Because a Windows form is a class, you determine what class you want to take precedence over any other class in your form. Each class has a main method that starts the class, but with so many different classes, C# will not start any of these form classes ahead of any others until you set the Startup Object property in the Property Pages window.

After you choose the startup Windows form for your program and compile it, the form will appear in the location that you specify in the MDE Properties window. If you do not specify a location, then the form will appear in the upper-left corner of the screen.

CHOOSE THE STARTUP WINDOWS FORM

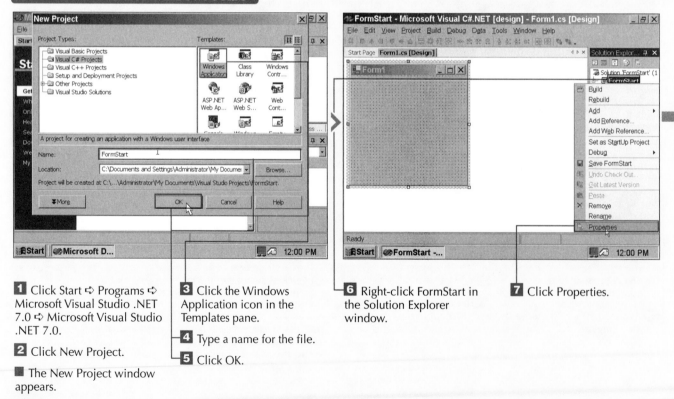

1 Click Start ➪ Programs ➪ Microsoft Visual Studio .NET 7.0 ➪ Microsoft Visual Studio .NET 7.0.

2 Click New Project.

■ The New Project window appears.

3 Click the Windows Application icon in the Templates pane.

4 Type a name for the file.

5 Click OK.

6 Right-click FormStart in the Solution Explorer window.

7 Click Properties.

Apply It

If you prefer to compile your C# classes from the command line instead of from the MDE window, you can specify the form class that you want to start in the command-line arguments.

C# uses the `csc` command for compiling your C# classes from the command line, and you can compile multiple classes on the same line. However, if you compile multiple form classes, then you must specify the class that will appear first by using the `/main` argument. The `/main` argument specifies the class with the `Main` method that appears when the user first starts the program. The `/main` argument includes the argument itself, a colon, and the class name.

TYPE THIS:

```
csc class1.cs class2.cs /main:Class2
```

RESULT:

The command line above tells C# to compile the `class1.cs` and `class2.cs` filenames and open `Class2` (the class that contains the form) when the program runs.

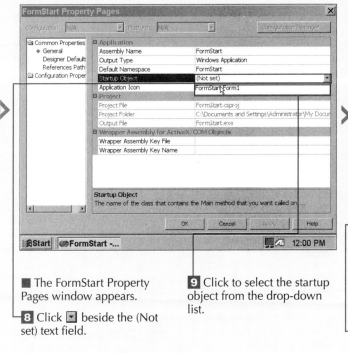

■ The FormStart Property Pages window appears.

8 Click ▼ beside the (Not set) text field.

9 Click to select the startup object from the drop-down list.

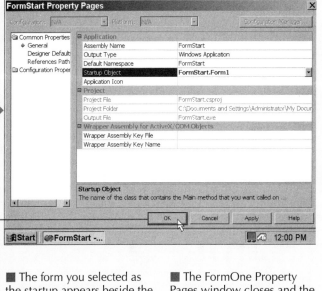

■ The form you selected as the startup appears beside the Startup Object field.

10 Click OK.

■ The FormOne Property Pages window closes and the MDE window reappears with the form in the parent window.

CREATE A MODAL FORM

C# places forms in two categories: modal and modeless. The mode status of your form lets you tailor the behavior of your form so when your form runs it gives you the results you want. A modeless form is the default form type.

A modal form, also known as a dialog box, must be closed before you can continue working with the program. For example, you probably have encountered dialog boxes that will not let you work with any other part of the program until you provide some direction such as clicking the OK or Cancel button. A modeless form lets you move between the form and other windows without requiring the user to give the form direction about what to do first.

C# lets you create your own dialog boxes within the Windows Form Designer by setting the appropriate form properties. When you set the properties you also disable some of them so the user will only be able to close the dialog box until the user presses a button, for example, the OK button.

The Form.Show method tells your form that it is modeless. When your program runs and the program encounters the Form.Show method, it will execute code that appears after the method.

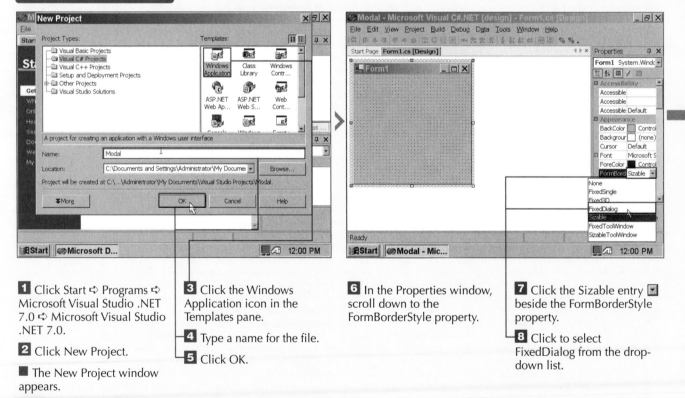

1 Click Start ➪ Programs ➪ Microsoft Visual Studio .NET 7.0 ➪ Microsoft Visual Studio .NET 7.0.

2 Click New Project.

■ The New Project window appears.

3 Click the Windows Application icon in the Templates pane.

4 Type a name for the file.

5 Click OK.

6 In the Properties window, scroll down to the FormBorderStyle property.

7 Click the Sizable entry beside the FormBorderStyle property.

8 Click to select FixedDialog from the drop-down list.

Extra

You should use modal forms when you have a form or dialog box that contains important information or information that you need direction from the user on before the program can proceed. Modeless forms are good for non-important information or for such items as toolboxes that contain buttons for use with other parts of your program.

The `Form.ShowDialog` method contains the optional owner argument that lets you determine which form in your program is the main form. Then, if you have any child forms that inherit from that main form, the owner argument will let the child forms know that they should take on the modal properties of the main form.

TYPE THIS:

```
frmAbout MyForm = new frmAbout();
MyForm.ShowDialog( this );
```

RESULT:

The this **keyword in the** Form. ShowDialog **method argument tells your program that** MyForm **is the main form.**

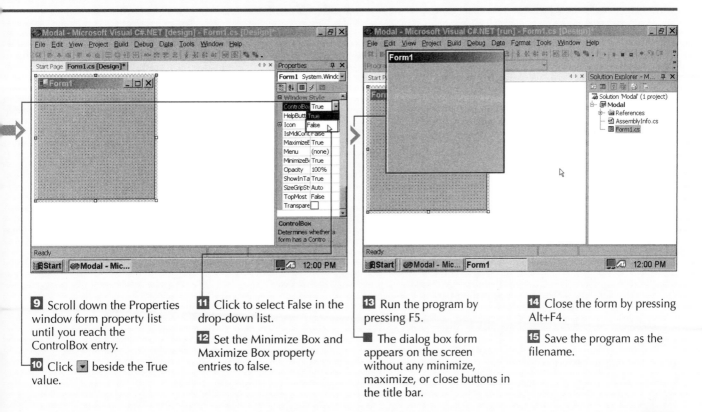

9 Scroll down the Properties window form property list until you reach the ControlBox entry.

10 Click ▼ beside the True value.

11 Click to select False in the drop-down list.

12 Set the Minimize Box and Maximize Box property entries to false.

13 Run the program by pressing F5.

■ The dialog box form appears on the screen without any minimize, maximize, or close buttons in the title bar.

14 Close the form by pressing Alt+F4.

15 Save the program as the filename.

LAYOUT A FORM

The Windows Form Designer in C# lets you design forms that will meet the needs of your users. C# provides three different interface styles that your form can take: the single-document interface (SDI), the multiple-document interface, and the Explorer-style interface.

The single-document interface lets you open only one document at a time. For example, you can have only one copy of Notepad open in your computer at any one time. If you want another Notepad document open you must open a second Notepad window.

The multiple-document interface displays a parent window so you can open many windows within that parent window.

An example of an MDI includes a program like Microsoft Word where you can open the Word window and open up several document windows within it.

The Explorer-style interface splits a window into two different panes or regions on the page. The left-pane contains directory information in a tree or other hierarchy and the right-hand pane contains file information from the selected directory or object in the left-pane. Windows Explorer is the most obvious example of this interface but it can also be used with other windows where you have to navigate through a large number of objects such as data files of a certain type.

LAYOUT A FORM

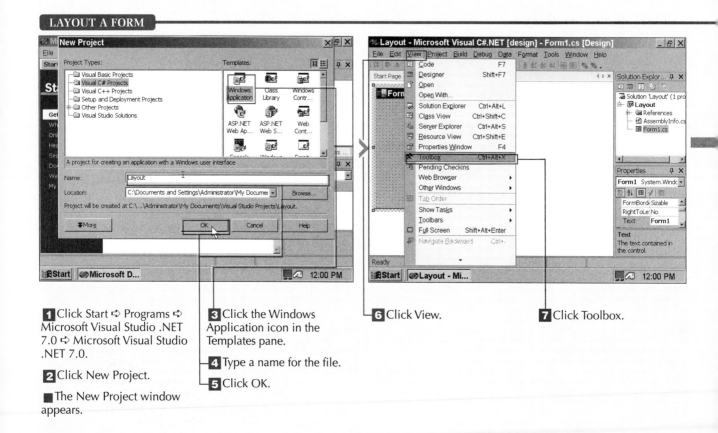

1 Click Start ➪ Programs ➪ Microsoft Visual Studio .NET 7.0 ➪ Microsoft Visual Studio .NET 7.0.

2 Click New Project.

■ The New Project window appears.

3 Click the Windows Application icon in the Templates pane.

4 Type a name for the file.

5 Click OK.

6 Click View.

7 Click Toolbox.

Extra

The program you design determines the type of window that you want to create. For example, if you have a program that requires working on more than one piece of data at a time (such as an online form), you may want to let the user work with more than one window. Then you can use the MDI style. A calculator application is better suited to an SDI style because you usually do not have to open up more than one calculator at a time.

The MDE window online help contains more detailed information about creating and designing MDI forms. There are several design aspects to be aware of when you design an MDI form including:

- •Creating an MDI parent form

- • Creating one or more MDI child forms that appear within the parent form

- • Arranging MDI child forms within a parent form

- • Determining the active MDI child form

- • Sending data to the active MDI child form

This is design information that is beyond the scope of this book, but you can search for MDI in online help for more information.

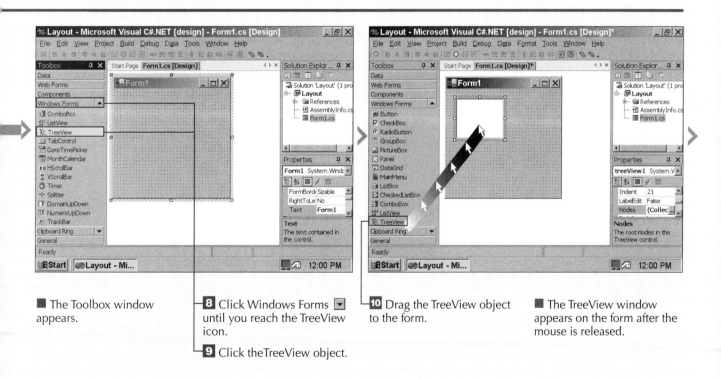

■ The Toolbox window appears.

-8 Click Windows Forms ▾ until you reach the TreeView icon.

-9 Click theTreeView object.

-10 Drag the TreeView object to the form.

■ The TreeView window appears on the form after the mouse is released.

CONTINUED ▶

LAYOUT A FORM

When you design your form you can add various controls from the Toolbox. Controls are buttons, text boxes, checkboxes, radio buttons, and other features that let the user manipulate data in the form and send that data back to the program.

After you determine the organization of your form windows — SDI, MDI, or Explorer-style — you can move on to issues about form design. The Windows Form Designer also lets you change the appearance of the form by letting you set the form size, colors, and other information.

When your Windows form appears, eight small boxes, or handles, appear around the perimeter of the form. You can move your mouse pointer to one of these handles, click and

hold down your left mouse button, and move the form accordingly. The mouse pointer turns from an arrow into a two-sided arrow when you resize it. For example, if you move the bottom center handle you can raise the height of the form. If you have controls, such as buttons, then they will resize automatically when you resize your form.

The dots in the form represent the form grid that acts as a guide for placing your controls. No matter where you place the controls on the form, the button will move the control to the nearest grid point.

LAYOUT A FORM (CONTINUED)

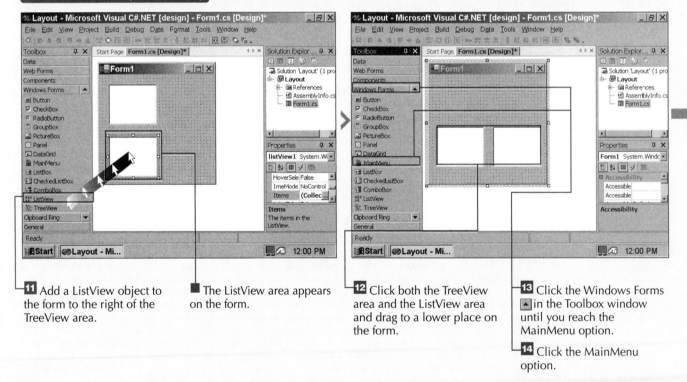

◼ 11 Add a ListView object to the form to the right of the TreeView area.

◼ The ListView area appears on the form.

◼ 12 Click both the TreeView area and the ListView area and drag to a lower place on the form.

◼ 13 Click the Windows Forms ▲ in the Toolbox window until you reach the MainMenu option.

◼ 14 Click the MainMenu option.

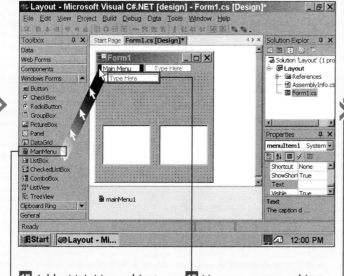

Apply It

You can change the size of the form as well as the title of the form in code. The argument `private void InitializeComponent()` in the code contains the form size and name. You can create your own form from scratch by typing the following code block within your form class. Type the following code within the public class `Form:System.Windows.Forms.Form class`.

TYPE THIS:

```
private void InitializeComponent()
{
    this.components = new System.ComponentModel.Container()
    this.Size = new System.Drawing.Size(100,100);
    this.Text = "MyForm";
}
```

RESULT:

This code creates a new form with the size of 100 pixels wide and 100 pixels high.

---

15 Add a MainMenu object to the form.

■ The MainMenu object appears at the top of the form and the object name appears in a window directly beneath the form.

16 Name your menu object by clicking the object in the form and typing in a new label.

17 Scroll up the WinForms list and add a Label object to your form below the MainMenu object.

■ The label appears. You can change the label text in the Properties window.

18 Save the program as the filename.

SET A FORM LOCATION

As you design your form in the Windows Form Designer, one important consideration is where a form can appear either on the screen or, in the case of an MDI form, where child forms appear within parent forms. You can set the location of the form by using the Properties window. C# uses two properties for setting the form location: Location and StartPosition.

The Location property specifies the location of the upper-left corner of the form in terms of the x pixel and y pixel. For example, if you have a form location with the x and y pixels at 10, 10, then the top left corner of the form will appear 10 pixels from the left and 10 pixels from the top of the screen, respectively.

When you open a new Windows application in C#, the StartPosition setting is at WindowsDefaultLocation, which computes the best location for the form based on the video resolution the user has.

You can change the StartPosition to four other locations including the center of the screen, in the center of the parent window, within the bounds specified by the version of Windows the user is running, or you can set the location manually. You must set StartPosition to Manual so you can set the actual location in the Location property.

SET A FORM LOCATION

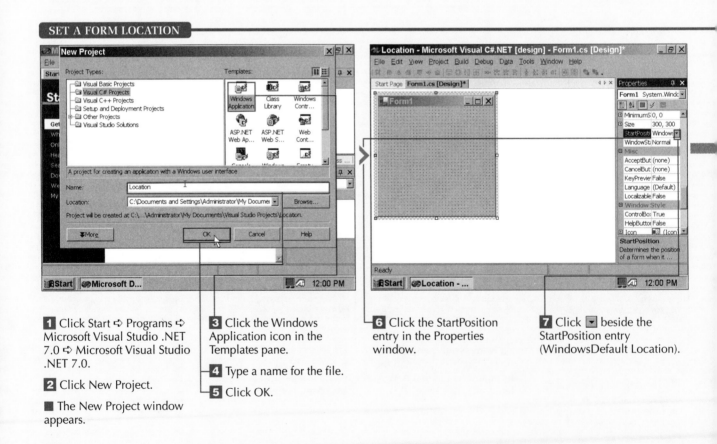

1 Click Start ➪ Programs ➪ Microsoft Visual Studio .NET 7.0 ➪ Microsoft Visual Studio .NET 7.0.

2 Click New Project.

■ The New Project window appears.

3 Click the Windows Application icon in the Templates pane.

4 Type a name for the file.

5 Click OK.

6 Click the StartPosition entry in the Properties window.

7 Click ▾ beside the StartPosition entry (WindowsDefault Location).

Apply It

You can position your form in code if it is more convenient for you to do so. You position your form in code by entering the `this.Location` argument that includes the built-in Point structure. The Point structure identifies the x and y values of the upper corner of your form. Type the following code within the public class `Form:System.Windows.Forms.Form` class.

TYPE THIS:

```
private void InitializeComponent()
{
this.components = new System.ComponentModel.Container()
this.Size = new System.Drawing.Size(100,100);
this.Text = "MyForm";
this.Location = new System.Drawing.Point(15,15);
}
```

RESULT:

The upper-left corner of the form is placed at 15 pixels from the left and 15 pixels from the top of the screen, respectively.

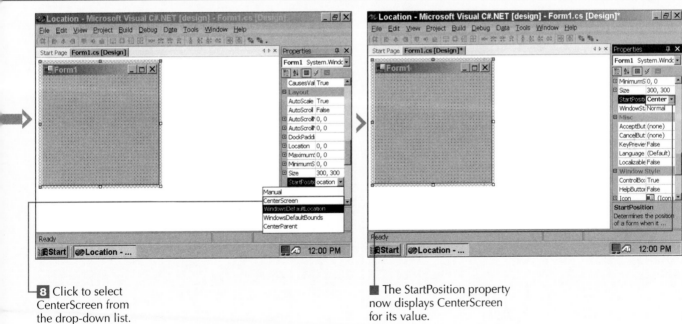

■8 Click to select CenterScreen from the drop-down list.

■ The StartPosition property now displays CenterScreen for its value.

CHANGE FORM PROPERTIES

When you create a new form, the Properties window contains a list of properties in a table that you can use to change the form properties. Changing form properties let you customize the form to your liking.

If you add a control or other feature to a form and click that control or feature, then the Properties window will display the properties for that control or feature. The Properties window displays all sorts of information that you can either change or view depending on the property.

The Properties window organizes the information into various categories, such as Appearance for different

appearance attributes such as background color. Those category names can open and close if you click the small expansion/retraction button to the left of the category name just as you do when you open directory information in Windows Explorer.

Some attributes contain expansion buttons that indicate that you can set attributes within that attribute. When you click the expansion button, the subattributes will appear in the table. When you click one of the attributes, you can select from a drop-down menu list or enter the value in the table. After you enter the value, the table will reflect your changes.

CHANGE FORM PROPERTIES

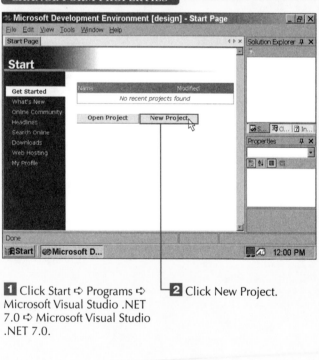

1 Click Start ➪ Programs ➪ Microsoft Visual Studio .NET 7.0 ➪ Microsoft Visual Studio .NET 7.0.

2 Click New Project.

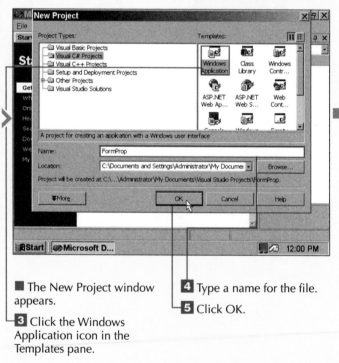

■ The New Project window appears.

3 Click the Windows Application icon in the Templates pane.

4 Type a name for the file.

5 Click OK.

Apply It

You can set the maximum and minimum sizes of your form so when the user shrinks or enlarges the form it will only shrink and enlarge to a certain size. For example, you may want the user to shrink a form only to the width of its widest text box. Type the following code with the public class Form:System.Windows.Forms.Form.

TYPE THIS:

```
private void InitializeComponent()
{
    this.components = new System.ComponentModel.Container()
    this.Size = new System.Drawing.Size(100,100);
    this.Text = "MyForm";
    this.MaximumSize = new System.Drawing.Size(400,400);
}
```

RESULT:

This code can maximize the form size to as high as 400 pixels wide by 400 pixels high.

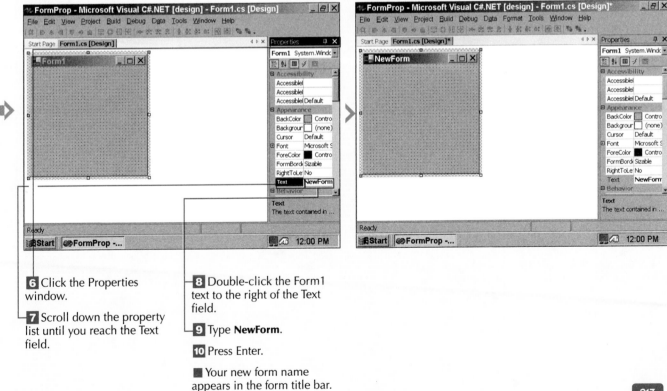

6 Click the Properties window.

7 Scroll down the property list until you reach the Text field.

8 Double-click the Form1 text to the right of the Text field.

9 Type **NewForm**.

10 Press Enter.

■ Your new form name appears in the form title bar.

CREATE A TRANSPARENT FORM

I f you design a C# program for use with Windows 2000 Server or Professional, then you can control the opacity of the form. Windows 2000 lets you determine how transparent or how solid the form appears on your screen.

A less opaque, or solid, form on your screen is very useful if you want to have a form that is not currently selected in the background so users will know that they cannot use that form. You may also want to keep a form completely transparent to the user so you can keep the form within that space so other elements do not infringe upon that space.

You set the form opacity level by setting the Opacity property in the Properties window. The opacity level ranges from 0% completely transparent to 100% completely opaque. The two digits after the decimal point represent the percentage of form opacity. After you set the opacity property, the form becomes more or less opaque depending on your setting. The default opacity setting is 100%.

If your program users do not use a version of Windows 2000, then the Opacity property will not apply, and the form will appear on the user's screen as completely opaque.

CREATE A TRANSPARENT FORM

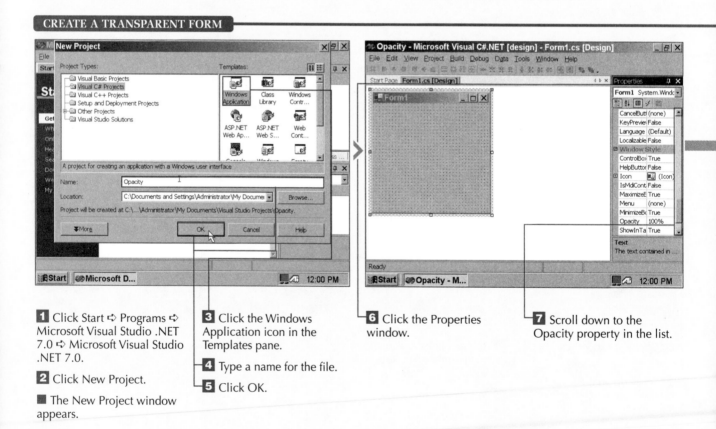

1 Click Start ➪ Programs ➪ Microsoft Visual Studio .NET 7.0 ➪ Microsoft Visual Studio .NET 7.0.

2 Click New Project.

■ The New Project window appears.

3 Click the Windows Application icon in the Templates pane.

4 Type a name for the file.

5 Click OK.

6 Click the Properties window.

7 Scroll down to the Opacity property in the list.

If your run you program on a computer running Windows 2000 or later, you can set the opacity of your form to make the form more transparent. Making your form less opaque can let the user know that the form is inactive, or you can hide the form from the user by making the form completely transparent. Type the following code with the public class `Form:System.Windows.Forms.Form`.

TYPE THIS:

```
private void InitializeComponent()
{
    this.components = new System.ComponentModel.Container()
    this.Size = new System.Drawing.Size(100,100);
    this.Text = "MyForm";
    this.Opacity = 0.8;
}
```

RESULT:

The form opacity is set to 80 percent — a 100 percent opacity level is 1 — which results in a somewhat faded form on the screen.

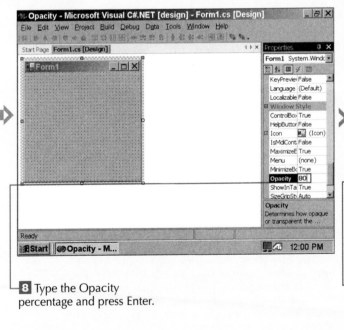

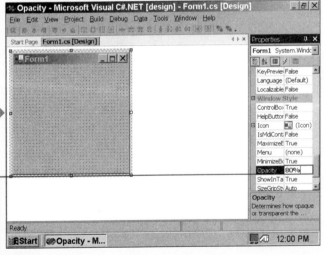

■8 Type the Opacity percentage and press Enter.

■ The new Opacity percentage appears in bold type.

■ If you run your program in Windows 2000, the form appears at 80 percent opacity.

■9 Save the program as the filename.

AN INTRODUCTION TO WEB FORMS AND CONTROLS

The Net Platform

The .NET platform provides the ASP.NET Framework for building user interfaces for Web applications. Even though ASP.NET is a totally new framework, you may find ASP.NET applications easy to develop due to many of the transferable skills that come from development with ASP applications. ASP.NET runs on the same platform that ASP applications run on today, Windows 2000 and Internet Information Server (IIS) 5.0. ASP.NET applications uses *Web Forms* as the primary file type, which have an extension of `.aspx`. IIS processes this

file type through a special Internet Server Application Program Interface (ISAPI) filter that handles the requested Web Form. Web Forms are a close relative to ASP (Active Server Page) pages. The server-side processing in ASP.NET applications exposes to you a vast amount of information that ASP hides and makes available only if you program in C++ for ISAPI extensions and filters. Even though the information is exposed, you are able to use some of the shortcuts that are available with ASP applications.

Web Form Controls

When building Web Forms, you choose from two classifications of controls: The Web Server Controls, which resides in the `System.Web.UI.WebControls` namespace, and the HTML Controls, which are in the namespace `System.Web.UI.HtmlControls`. The HTML Controls directly map to standard HTML tags, which all browsers support. For example, the `HTMLButton` class maps to a button html tag. The Web Server Controls are more abstract classes whose object model does not necessarily reflect HTML syntax. They include most standard HTML tags and extend them with controls that implement the use of multiple HTML tags to render the control. For example, the DataGrid Class can generate table tags, anchor tags, and/or button tags, depending on how it is configured in design time. Using Web Server Controls requires you to use the `asp` namespace inside of the Web Form. For example, the Button Web server control has the following syntax inside of the Web Form: `<ASP:BUTTON ID="cmdContinue" TEXT="Continue" onClick="Button_OnClick" RUNAT="Server"/>`. Compare this to the definition

the equivalent HTML control has as well as to the equivalent standard HTML tag:

```
HTML Control: <input type=submit
value="Enter"ID="cmd Continue
OnServerClick="Submit_Click"
runat=server>.
```

```
Standard HTML tag: <input type=submit
value="Enter" ID="cmdContinue
OnServerClick="Submit_Click">.
```

The main difference between the Web Server and HTML Controls is that the element on the Web Form has a `runat="server"` attribute. This attribute allows for capabilities that are present in server-side code. The main difference between the Web Server Controls and HTML Controls is the namespace provided for the Web Server Controls (`asp:`).

This chapter gives you a quick overview of ASP.NET programming. You can read the book *ASP.NET: Your visual blueprint for creating Web applications on the .NET framework* (Hungry Minds, Inc., 2001), if you want to dig into further details of Web development with ASP.NET.

Separation of User Interface and User Services

ASP.NET applications give you the ability to separate user interface code and your user services code. The user interface code, which is your HTML tags, typically requires different skills than a developer that is responsible for user services code, the code that supports your user interface and runs on the Web server. This separation of code is a welcomed change to development of Web applications on the Microsoft platform; having this code seperation promotes more of the service-based model that Microsoft supports. This code separation also yields a programming style in ASP.NET applications that is better-structured code compared to the ASP style of programming.

The standard type of page that you develop on an ASP.NET application is a Web Form. Web Forms in ASP.NET applications consist of two files. One file holds the HTML, or presentation, and has the .aspx extension. The other file, which contains the user services code, is the code-behind page. If you program in C# for the code-behind page, your page has an extension of .cs (but if you are developing in Visual Studio .NET, the extension is aspx.cs). This code-behind page holds the code that needs to run on the Web server or application server. The language that runs in the code-behind page needs to be a compliant .NET language, such as C#. The following page directive at the top of the .aspx page associates these two pages, where WebFormName is the name of the .aspx page and ApplicationName is the name of the virtual directory:

```
<%@ Page language="c#"
Codebehind=" WebFormName.aspx.cs"
AutoEventWireup="false"
Inherits="ApplicationName.WebFormName" %>
```

The code in a code-behind page follows object-oriented programming (OOP) concepts, where code is implemented within an event handler and the code within this handler accesses objects through their properties, fields, and methods. These objects can be elements on the Web Form or class libraries. In ASP code, programmers are responsible for all of this, except the event handling is not there. With the absence of event handling, the style of server-side ASP was procedural coding versus OOP.

In current ASP development, you are limited to VBScript and JScript for server-side code. Using these scripting languages for server-side code has its limitations (such as error handling, data types, and event handling). Having first-class languages such as VB and C#, as the server-side code for an .aspx page yields more programming power and better structured code. To interact with the .aspx page, you can inherit the Page class of the System.Web.UI namespace on the code-behind page. The Page class exposes some familiar objects that are common in ASP development today (such as Response, Request, Application, Session, and Server) and implements some common events that VB programmers are accustomed to using (such as Page_Load, Page_Unload, and Page_Init).

Web Forms

Web Forms are the primary file type used in ASP.NET to create Web pages. Web Forms have an extension of .aspx. These pages are the next generation pages to ASP pages that are created in ASP applications. Web Forms are more sophisticated than the earlier asp pages found in ASP applications. Web Forms offer new capabilities such as separation of code from presentaion, the availability of a vast array of controls that are provided by the framework, and the capability of creating your own controls.

CREATE AN ASP.NET WEB SITE

A SP.NET applications can run on the same platform as ASP applications. ASP.NET applications are supported on the IIS Web server. ASP.NET pages require preprocessing by the aspnet_iaspi.dll.

Similar to creating an ASP site, when you create a Web site for ASP.NET, you need a virtual directory configured as an application. ASP.NET applications are supported on Windows 2000 and Windows NT 4 with Service Pack 6a, with the exception of using Web Services. Web Services are supported on all platforms supported by the Microsoft .NET Framework SDK, except Windows 95. The Microsoft .NET Framework SDK is supported on Windows 2000,

Windows NT 4 with Service Pack 6a, Windows Me, Windows 98, Windows 98 SE, and Windows 95.

All ASP.NET applications that you configure in a virtual directory have a special icon that is assigned in the IIS Microsoft Management Console, or MMC. This icon is different than the standard icon for a virtual directory that is not an application or just a subdirectory of the root Web site. An icon that is configured as a virtual directory looks like an open package versus a standard folder icon that you see in Windows Explorer. You can go into the IIS MMC to configure the site or just let VS .NET take care of this for you.

CREATE AN ASP.NET WEB SITE

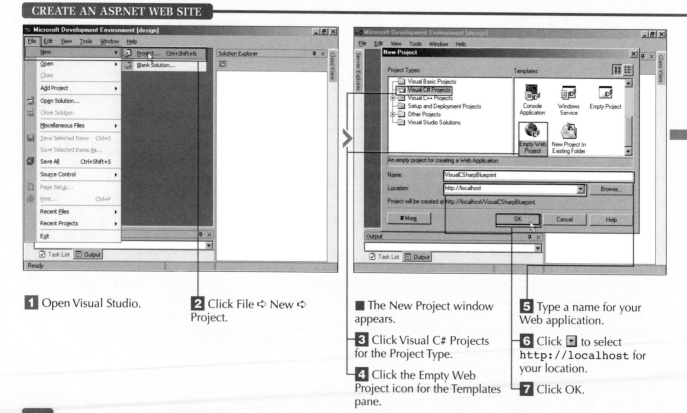

1 Open Visual Studio.

2 Click File ➪ New ➪ Project.

■ The New Project window appears.

3 Click Visual C# Projects for the Project Type.

4 Click the Empty Web Project icon for the Templates pane.

5 Type a name for your Web application.

6 Click ▣ to select http://localhost for your location.

7 Click OK.

Apply It

You can easily trace the execution of code in ASP.NET by placing the `Trace` attribute in the `@Page` directive. If you desire to trace the entire application, you can change the web.config file. You search for the trace tag in the web.config file. Make sure both enabled and `pageOutput` attributes are set to true. The output tracing gives details on the page request, execution time for page process, control sequence, cookie information, headers, and server variables.

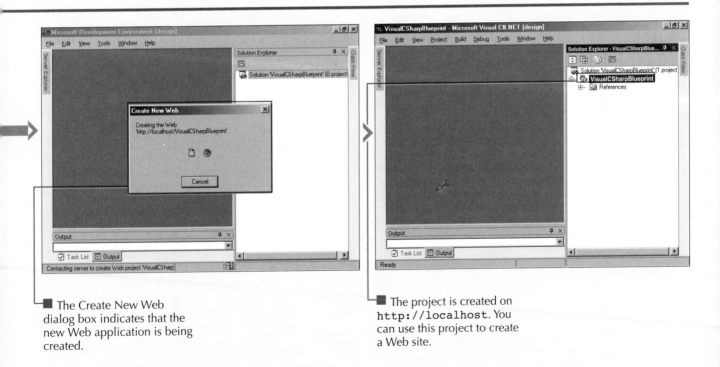

■ The Create New Web dialog box indicates that the new Web application is being created.

■ The project is created on `http://localhost`. You can use this project to create a Web site.

CREATE A WEB FORM

The majority of your ASP.NET application consists of Web Forms and their corresponding code-behind files. Web Forms give you the flexibility of separating code from presentation, which promotes better structured code that is easier to develop and maintain.

To create a Web Form, you add an .aspx page to an existing site. See page 218 for details on creating a new Web site. When you implement server-side code for the .aspx page, you create an aspx.cs page to house the *code-behind* page. The extension of this file ends with .cs, which indicates that you programmed the code in the code-behind page in C#. If you implemented the page with

Visual Basic, the extension is aspx.vb. Note that the aspx part of the extension is optional.

Implementing the server-side code that supports your Web page can be done either with <script> blocks in your HTML or with code-behind pages. Using code-behind pages allows for cleaner separation of code. Either way, you will create event handlers that contain the implementation of the code necessary to make your page functional. For example, you can use the Page_Load event to initialize controls on your Web Form. This is similar to the Form_Load event that is used in VB forms development.

CREATE A WEB FORM

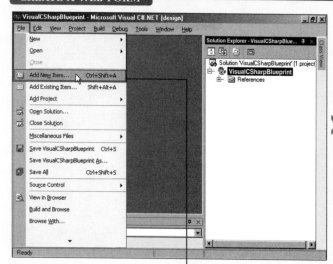

1 Open a new Web project.

2 Add an ASP.NET Web page by clicking File ➪ Add New Item from the Visual Studio Menu.

3 Click Web Project Items to select a Category.

4 Click Web Form to select a Template.

5 Type a name for the Web Form with an **.aspx** extension.

6 Click Open.

■ A Web page with a Web Form appears in Design mode.

Extra

When developing Web Forms, you can implement server-side code in two ways. The first implementation, well supported in VS .NET, involves creating an additional code-behind page containing an extension of `.cs`. The second implementation is embedding a server-side `<script>` tag.

Example:

```
<html>
<script language="C#" runat="server">
void Submit_Click(object sender, EventArgs e) {
    if (txtName.Value == "RobertPhillips" &
        txtPwd.Value == "pharmacist")
        spnMessage.InnerHtml = "You are authenticated!";
    else
        spnMessage.InnerHtml = "Login Failed!";
}
</script>
<body> <form method=post runat=server>
<h3>Enter Name: <input id="txtName" type=text size=40 runat=server>
<h3>Enter Password: <input id="txtPwd" type=password size=40 runat=server>
<input type=submit value="Enter" OnServerClick="Submit_Click" runat=server>
<h1><span id="spnMessage" runat=server> </span></h1>
</form></body></html>
```

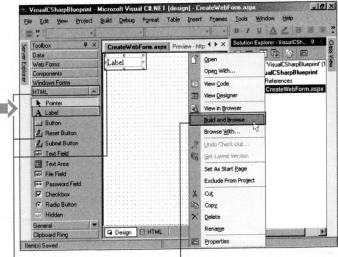

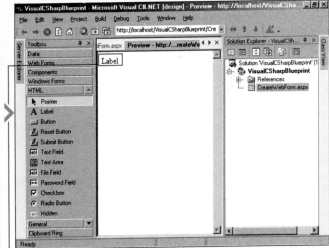

■7 Click View ➪ Toolbox to open the Toolbox panel.

■8 Click the HTML tab to display the HTML controls.

■9 Double-click the Label button in the Toolbox.

■ A label control appears.

■ If your Solution Explorer panel is not open, click View ➪ Solution Explorer to open it.

■10 Right-click the filename in the Solutions Explorer window and choose Build and Browse.

■ The Web page appears with a label control in the Preview window.

ADD SERVER CONTROLS TO A WEB FORM

The power of Web Forms comes into play when you start leveraging the built-in capabilities of server controls. Server controls have rich capabilities that are typically available only in Win32-based applications or what would be available in ActiveX controls.

For rich user interfaces, you can either write very complicated DHTML or use ActiveX controls. Natively, only Internet Explorer is an ActiveX container; therefore, it is not widely accepted in Web development, leaving a wide gap in capabilities between the user interface richness in Win32 applications versus Web applications. To address this gap, ASP.NET applications provide *Web server controls*. Server controls send standard HTML to the client versus an

embedded object that requires special browser or operating system runtime capabilities to host the object. You can configure server controls through their attributes or server-side code.

After you add a server control to a Web Form, you have several ways to configure the control. With the simplest standard input controls — for example, the TextBox, Button, and CheckBox — you use the Properties window typically docked in the lower-right hand side of your VS integrated development environment (IDE). For more sophisticated server-side controls, you can configure advanced options in the Property Builder or Auto Format dialog boxes.

ADD SERVER CONTROLS TO A WEB FORM

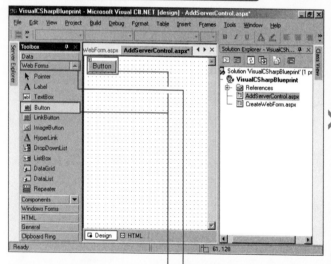

1 Add a new Web Form to your Web project.

Note: See page 220 for more information on adding a Web Form.

2 Click View ➪ Toolbox to view the Toolbox panel.

3 Click the Web Forms tab to display the server controls.

4 Double-click Button in the Toolbox.

■ A button appears on the form.

5 Right-click the Button control and select Properties.

The following example demonstrates the use of the Panel Web server control, which is useful for pages that view different content based on the state of the page. To get the full code sample, see the companion CD-ROM.

TYPE THIS:

```
<SCRIPT LANGUAGE="C#" RUNAT="Server">
    void cmdDescription_Click(object Source, EventArgs e)
    {
        if (pnlDescription.Visible == true)
        {
            pnlDescription.Visible = false;
            cmdDescription.Text = "Show Photo Description";
        }
        else
        {
            pnlDescription.Visible = true;
            cmdDescription.Text = "Hide Photo Description";
        }
    }
</SCRIPT>
```

RESULT:

The resulting panel that is show is rendered in the following <div> tag:

```
<div id="pnlDescription"
style="background-
color:SkyBlue;height:
50px;width:300px;">
```

Here is where the description displays:

```
</div>
```

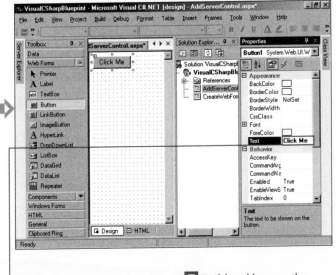

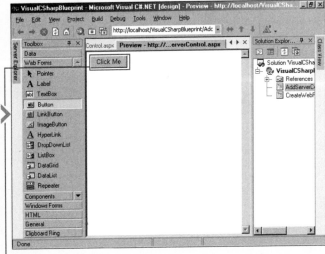

■ The Properties window appears.

6 Change the **Text** value for the button to **Click Me**.

7 Build and browse the Web page.

Note: See page 220 for more information on building and browsing a Web page.

■ The Web page appears with the Button server control in the Preview window.

RESPOND TO AN EVENT IN SERVER-SIDE CONTROLS

You can implement event handlers to respond to user interaction with your Web Form. Some common events available to program are mouse clicks on buttons, or the mouse moving over text. Using event handlers, a common object-oriented programming practice, creates a more efficient programming model. This model only executes code when the corresponding event fires for the handler. Without this model, you must use procedural style coding, which evaluates code from top to bottom and requires you to run code to determine if you should call a procedure.

You can implement event handlers in the code-behind pages. To create an event handler in the code-behind page, you need to assign a programmatic id to the server-side control. You do this giving a value for the id attribute on the HTML tag for the server-side control.

ASP.NET uses the id for the control with the event name to construct the event handler. For example, a server control with id = "cmdTest" needs an event handler called cmdTest_Click() to respond to a user clicking a Button server control. Inside this handler or procedure, you implement code that needs to run in response to the event firing.

RESPOND TO AN EVENT IN SERVER-SIDE CONTROLS

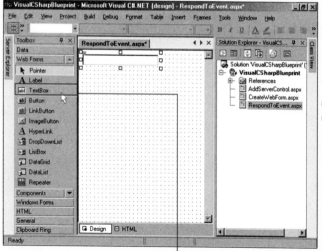

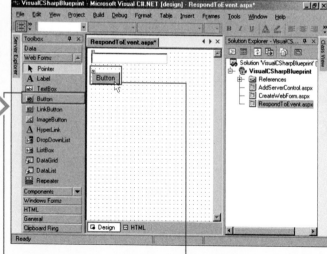

1 Add a new Web Form to your Web project.

Note: See page 220 for more information on adding a Web Form.

2 Add a TextBox control to the Web page.

Note: See page 222 for more information on adding server controls to a Web Form.

3 Add a Button control to the Web page.

4 Double-click the Button server control.

Apply It

You can create a code-behind page that responds to an event using the following bare bones of implementation. This is hand-crafted code and not the automatically generated code that comes from the VS .NET environment. You first create the `.aspx` page `RespondToEvent_ai.aspx` with the first block of code. Next, you create the supporting code-behind page, `RespondToEvent_ai.aspx.cs`. You then place both of these files into an existing ASP.NET site to receive the results into the Web page.

TYPE THIS:

```
<%@ Page Inherits="RespondToEvent_ai" Src="RespondToEvent_ai.aspx.cs" %>
<html>
<head>
</head>
<body>
<form runat="Server">
<P/>
<asp:labelID="lblGreeting" runat="Server" />
</form>
</body>
</html>
```

RESULT:

A page that displays the following:

Welcome to MySharePhotoAlbum.com

TYPE THIS:

```
using System;
using System.Web.UI;
using System.Web.UI.WebControls;
public class RespondToEvent_ai : Page {
    public Label lblGreeting;
    public void Page_Load(object Source, EventArgs e) {
        lblGreeting.Text="Welcome to MySharePhotoAlbum.com";
    }
}
```

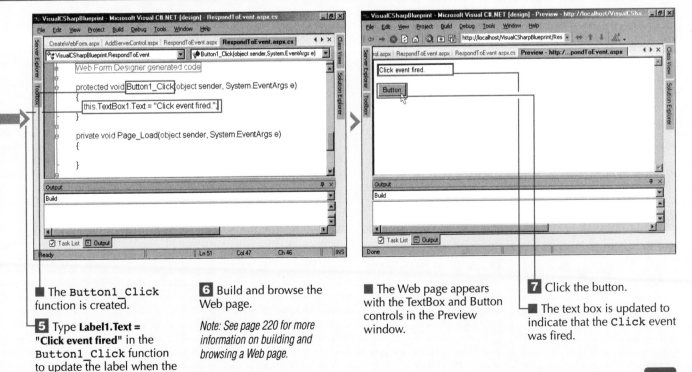

■ The `Button1_Click` function is created.

5 Type **Label1.Text = "Click event fired"** in the `Button1_Click` function to update the label when the button is clicked.

6 Build and browse the Web page.

Note: See page 220 for more information on building and browsing a Web page.

■ The Web page appears with the TextBox and Button controls in the Preview window.

7 Click the button.

■ The text box is updated to indicate that the `Click` event was fired.

225

READ AND CHANGE PROPERTIES FROM OBJECTS ON A WEB FORM

To make a Web Form interactive, you must take input from a user and send a custom response back to the user based on their interaction. To create custom responses on Web Forms, you can write code that produces a response based on accessing the properties of the controls on your Web Form. To construct code that leverages object properties, you need an event handler. See page 224 for how to create event handlers. Inside that procedure, you have the ability to read and write to an object property that is in the scope of the event hander procedure.

Use of a property requires knowing the id of the tag that describes the control. For example, a server-side button

control's tag may look like `<asp:TextBox id= "txtFirstName" runat="server"></asp:TextBox>`. For this server-side control, you must program with the id set to `"txtFirstName"`. To write to a property on this control, you create an expression with the form `object.property = value;`. For example, you can set a value for what displays in the text box with the expression `txtFirstName.Value = "Donna";`.

To read a property from a control, you use the form `string sFirstName = txtFirstName.Value;`. Note, however, that `sFirstName` is a variable that holds the value of the `Value` property of the TextBox control.

READ AND CHANGE PROPERTIES FROM OBJECTS ON A WEB FORM

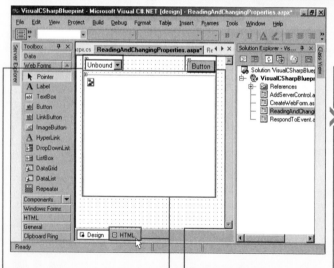

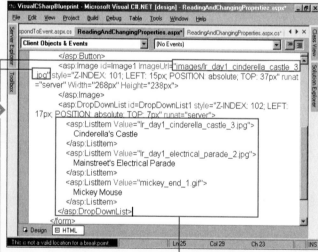

1 Add a new Web Form to your Web project.

Note: See page 220 for more information on adding a Web Form.

2 Add a DropDownList control to the Web page.

3 Add a Button control to the Web page.

4 Add an image control to the Web page.

Note: See page 222 for more information on adding server controls to a Web Form.

5 Click the HTML page tab to view the HTML.

6 Add the **ImageUrl** attribute to the **Image** control and set the attribute equal to the picture you want to initially display.

Note: You may need to copy the images directory from the CD-ROM to the working directory.

7 Add several `<ListItem>` tags to add options for the DropDownList control.

8 In Design view, double-click the Button control.

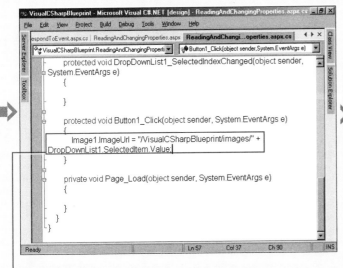

Apply It

You can read properties on one control to determine what the value on another control should be. This code reads the Checked property on a radio button to determine what the `SelectionMode` property should be on a calendar Web server control. To get the full code sample, see the companion CD-ROM.

TYPE THIS:

```
<SCRIPT LANGUAGE="C#" RUNAT="Server">
void SubmitBtn_Click(Object Sender, EventArgs e)
{
    if (Day.Checked) {
        calPhoto.SelectionMode = CalendarSelectionMode.Day;}
    else if (DayWeek.Checked) {
        calPhoto.SelectionMode = CalendarSelectionMode.DayWeek; }
    else if (DayWeekMonth.Checked) {
        calPhoto.SelectionMode = CalendarSelectionMode.DayWeekMonth; }
    else if (None.Checked) {
        calPhoto.SelectionMode = CalendarSelectionMode.None; }
}
</SCRIPT>
```

RESULT:

> A calendar control that you can change the selection mode with, making the desired selection and resubmitting the page.

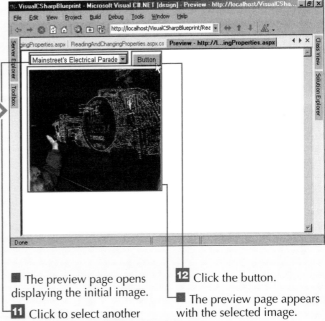

■ The `Click` event handler for the button is created for you.

9 Set the `ImageUrl` property for image control to the selected item's value in the drop-down list box.

Note: Server.MapPath is used here to translate the physical path to the images directory (for example, c:\inetpub\wwwroot\VisualCSharp Blueprint\images\).

10 Build and browse the Web page.

■ The preview page opens displaying the initial image.

11 Click to select another image from the drop-down list.

12 Click the button.

■ The preview page appears with the selected image.

USING SERVER-SIDE COMPONENTS ON WEB FORMS

Sever-side components can provide solutions to common programing problems that are needed to enable your ASP.NET applications. If you do not leverage the server-side components, you will either write your own custom server-side components or buy a third-party component.

Server-side components enable you to extend the capabilities of ASP.NET Web Forms to utilize any services that run on the .NET platform. These services can include asynchronous messaging (System.Messaging), file sytem I/O and browsing (System.IO), using and creating XML documents (System.XML), accessing data (System.Data), and troubleshooting your application (System.Diagnostics). This list only gives a few

capabilities of the .NET Framework Class Library, which contains hundreds of classes.

To leverage a server-side component that is part of the .NET Framework, you need to access the namespace that contains the .NET Framework class. For example, the Framework class that allows file access is Sytem.IO. To programmatically access this, you place the following at the top of the code-behind page: using System.IO;. After you import this namespace, you can create objects from classes that are part of this namespace. For example, you can create a DirectoryInfo object with the code DirectoryInfo dir = new DirectoryInfo(".."); and retrieve a list of all files in a specified directory using the GetFiles method.

USING SERVER-SIDE COMPONENTS ON WEB FORMS

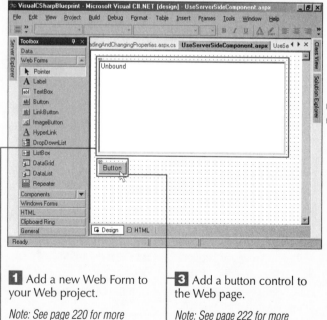

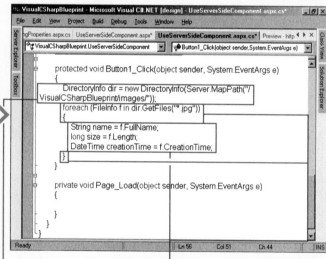

1 Add a new Web Form to your Web project.

Note: See page 220 for more information on adding a Web Form.

2 Add a ListBox control to the Web page.

3 Add a button control to the Web page.

Note: See page 222 for more information on adding server controls to a Web Form.

4 Double-click the Button server control.

■ The **Click** event handler for the button is created for you.

5 Create a variable of **DirectoryInfo** type and initialize it with the location of the images directory.

Note: You may need to copy the images directory from the CD-ROM to the working directory.

6 Use a **foreach** loop to loop through all of the JPEG files.

7 Read the name, size, and creation time properties of the file into variables.

Apply It

You can use the HTTPRequest object from ASP.NET's Framework to get to information from a user request.

TYPE THIS:

```
<%@ Page language="c#"%>
<html>
    <head>
    </head>
    <body>
        <form method="post" runat="server">
            <%
            HttpRequest oRequest;
            oRequest = this.Request;

            foreach (string sRequest in oRequest.ServerVariables)
            {
                Response.Write(sRequest + " = " +
                    oRequest.ServerVariables[sRequest] + "<br>");
            }
            %>
        </form>
    </body>
</html>
```

RESULT:

A page lists all the details of the Server Variables in the HTTPRequest object.

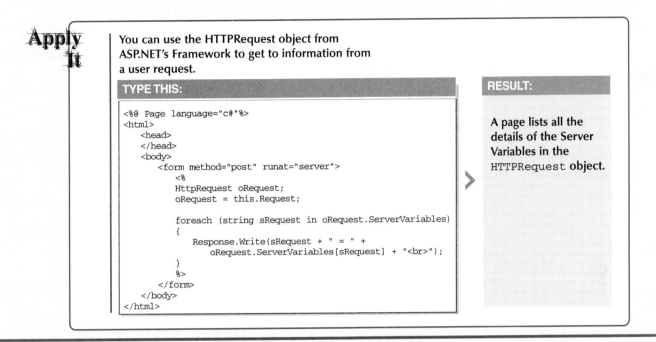

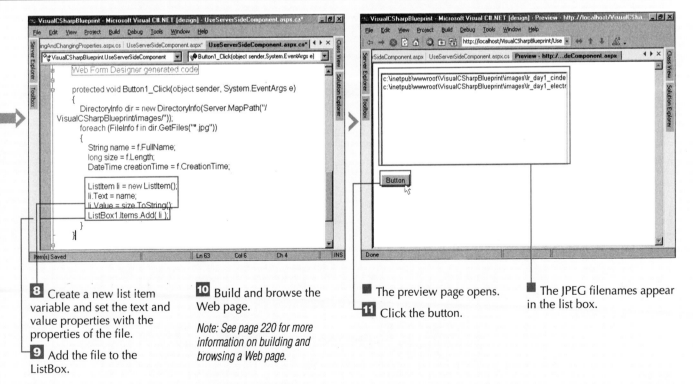

8 Create a new list item variable and set the text and value properties with the properties of the file.

9 Add the file to the ListBox.

10 Build and browse the Web page.

Note: See page 220 for more information on building and browsing a Web page.

■ The preview page opens.

11 Click the button.

■ The JPEG filenames appear in the list box.

INTRODUCING DATA ACCESS WITH ADO.NET

Most production-grade applications need some form of data access. Data access in the .NET Framework is simplified for you through the ADO.NET Framework classes. These classes are found in `System.Data` namespace, which has two major namespaces: one for SQL Server data stores and another for data stores that can be accessed through OLE DB.

The SQL Server .NET Data Provider classes come from the `System.Data.SqlClient` namespace. The SQL Server .NET Data Provider uses its own protocol to communicate with SQL Server. The provider is lightweight and performs well, accessing a SQL Server data source directly without adding an OLE DB or Open Database Connectivity (ODBC) layer. When you need to work with other database besides Microsoft SQL Server, you should use the OLE DB .NET Data Provider, which you can find in the `System.Data.OleDb` namespace.

If you are familiar with ADO, you may notice some similarities when accessing data in C# with ADO.NET. The `Connection` and `Command` objects, for example, have almost identical properties and methods. The brand new part in ADO.NET is in the area of reading and persisting records of data. In the days of ADO, Recordsets transported returned data from a SQL database; however, in ADO.NET, the Recordset is gone, replaced by things like the `DataSet`, `DataReader`, `DataTables`, and `DataViews`.

To orient you to ADO.NET's new object model, these pages outline a few key members of the ADO.NET classes (`System.Data` namespace). Because both the `System.Data.SqlClient` and `System.Data.OleDb` implement most of the same base classes, the examples reflect the perspective of only one of the providers, `SqlClient`.

CONNECTION

Connections are the starting point to your data access and determine how you connect to the data store. You need to set properties, like `ConnectionString`, to establish communications to your data store.

SQLCONNECTION KEY PROPERTIES AND METHODS	
PROPERTY	**DESCRIPTION**
ConnectionString	(read/write) string used to open a SQL Server database
ConnectionTimeout	(read) maximum time allowed for a connection attempt
Database	(read) name of the current (or soon to be) connected database
DataSource	(read) name of SQL Server instance to connect to
ServerVersion	(read) string that identifies version of the connected SQL Server instance
State	(read) current state of the connection
METHOD	**DESCRIPTION**
BeginTransaction	(overloaded) begins a database transaction
ChangeDatabase	changes the current database for an open `SqlConnection`
Close	closes the connection to the database
CreateCommand	creates and returns a `SqlCommand` object associated with the `SqlConnection`
Open	opens a database connection with the property settings specified by the `ConnectionString`

ADO.NET commands are important for stored procedures and running SQL Statements.

SQLCOMMAND KEY PROPERTIES AND METHODS	
PROPERTY	DESCRIPTION
CommandText	(read/write) the T-SQL statement or stored procedure to execute at the data source
CommandTimeout	(read/write) maximum time allowed for a command execution attempt
CommandType	(read/write) a value indicating how the CommandText property is to be interpreted
Connection	(read/write) the SqlConnection used by this instance of the SqlCommand
Parameters	(read) the SqlParameterCollection
Transaction	(read/write) the transaction in which the SqlCommand executes
METHOD	DESCRIPTION
Cancel	cancels the execution of a SqlCommand
CreateParameter	creates a new instance of a SqlParameter object
ExecuteNonQuery	executes a T-SQL statement against the connection and returns the number of rows affected
ExecuteReader	(overloaded) sends the CommandText to the connection and builds a SqlDataReader
ExecuteScalar	executes the query, and returns the first column of the first row in the resultset returned by the query
ExecuteXmlReader	sends the CommandText to the connection and builds an XmlReader object
Prepare	creates a prepared version of the command on an instance of SQL Server

A DataAdapter is the object that bridges between the source data and the DataSet object so retrieve and updates can occur.

DATAADAPTER KEY PROPERTIES AND METHODS	
PROPERTY	DESCRIPTION
AcceptChangesDuringFill	(read/write) a value indicating whether AcceptChanges is called on a DataRow after it is added to the DataTable
TableMappings	(read) a collection that provides the master mapping between a source table and a DataTable
METHOD	DESCRIPTION
Fill	adds or refreshes rows in the DataSet to match those in the data source using the DataSet name, and creates a DataTable named "Table"
FillSchema	adds a DataTable named "Table" to the specified DataSet and configures the schema to match that in the data source based on the specified SchemaType
GetFillParameters	retrieves the parameters set by the user when executing a SQL select statement
Update	Calls the respective insert, update, or delete statements for respective action in the specified DataSet from a DataTable named "Table"

DISPLAY DATA WITH THE DATAGRID CONTROL

You can use the DataGrid Web Server Control to build tables containing data. One of the advantages of using the DataGrid Web Server Control is not having to manually construct the table. Because you will bind DataGrid control to data, you do not have to programmatically loop through DataSets and other data structure types, nor write out table tags, formatting, and data field values as you hit each record in the data storage.

The process of binding to a DataGrid is quite simple. First you must retrieve a data source. Then you assign that data source to the DataSource property of the DataGrid control. Lastly, you call the DataBind method of the DataGrid control.

The data source for the DataGrid control will most likely be a database, but the control is not restricted to binding to only traditional database stores. For example, ADO.NET data structures can be built from other providers like Exchange, WebDav, and Active Directory. Also, any lists derived from ICollection can also be used as a data source.

DISPLAY DATA WITH THE DATAGRID CONTROL

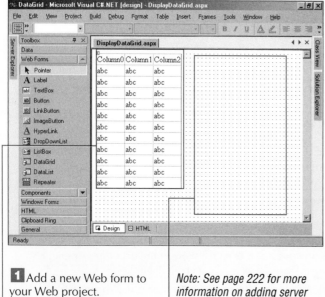

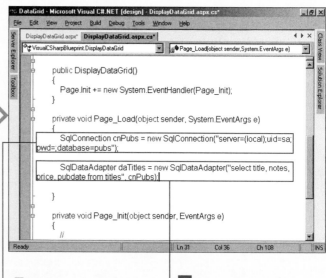

1 Add a new Web form to your Web project.

Note: See page 220 for more information on adding a Web form.

2 Add a DataGrid control to the Web page.

Note: See page 222 for more information on adding server controls to a Web form.

3 Double-click on the page.

■ The form's code-behind page appears with the **Page_Load** event handler.

4 Add a **SqlConnection** variable and initialize with a valid connection string to your database.

5 Add a **SqlDataAdapter** variable and initialize with a valid **select** statement.

Apply It

The `DataGrid` Web Server Control has paging capabilities that are used to display a result into multiple navigable pages. When the page index changes, the `CurrentPageIndex` attribute on the `DataGrid` needs to be set.

TYPE THIS:

```
<SCRIPT language="C#" runat="server">
    void Page_Load(object sender, System.EventArgs e){
        if (!IsPostBack)
            BindData(); }
    void Grid_Change(Object sender,
        DataGridPageChangedEventArgs e){
        dgdTitles.CurrentPageIndex = e.NewPageIndex;
        BindData(); }
    void BindData() {
        SqlConnection cnPubs = new SqlConnection(
            "server=(local);uid=sa;pwd=;database=pubs");
        SqlDataAdapter daTitles = new SqlDataAdapter(
            "select title, notes, price, pubdate "
            + "from titles", cnPubs);
        DataSet dsTitles = new DataSet();
        daTitles.Fill(dsTitles, "titles");
        dgdTitles.DataSource=
            dsTitles.Tables["titles"].DefaultView;
        dgdTitles.DataBind(); }
</SCRIPT>
```

RESULT:

An HTML page with an HTML table containing all rows in the `titles` table for the specified columns.

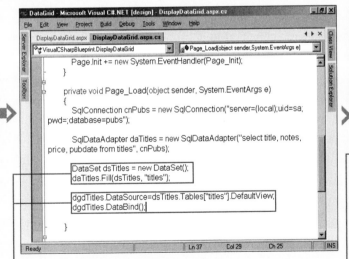

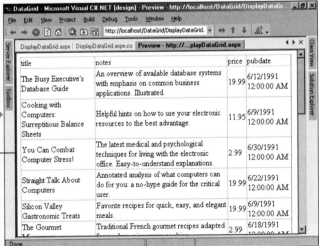

6 Add a `DataSet` variable and use the `Fill` method of the `DataAdapter` to populate the `DataSet`.

7 Set the `DataSource` property for the data grid to the `DataSet` created and use the `DataBind` method to bind the `DataGrid`.

8 Build and browse the Web page.

Note: See page 220 for more information on building and browsing a Web page.

■ The data returned from the `select` statement is displayed in the `DataGrid`.

CONFIGURE THE DATAGRID CONTROL

The DataGrid control is one of the richest Web Server Controls that you have available in the ASP.NET framework.

To access the majority of the DataGrid control's features, open the Property Builder dialog box. You can choose from among five views: General, Columns, Paging, Format, and Borders. The Property Builder dialog box is essentially a fancy user interface to the Properties dialog box, which is used for configuring all controls. Due to the DataGrid control having so many built-in features, the Property Builder dialog box comes in handy for quick configurations.

Another way you can configure the DataGrid control is the AutoFormat dialog box. The AutoFormat dialog window is very similar to the auto format capabilities found for tables in Microsoft Word and Excel. The AutoFormat dialog box is a very quick way to format the grid, but you are stuck with a predetermined list of styles.

Both the Property Builder and Auto Format dialog boxes are available in the pop-up menu for the DataGrid; you can access the pop-up menu by right-clicking the DataGrid. To familiarize yourself with the DataGrid control's capabilities, use both of these dialog boxes and make changes to the settings provided. After you make these changes, go to the HTML for the Web form and notice the changes made to the asp:DataGrid element in your Web form.

CONFIGURE THE DATAGRID CONTROL

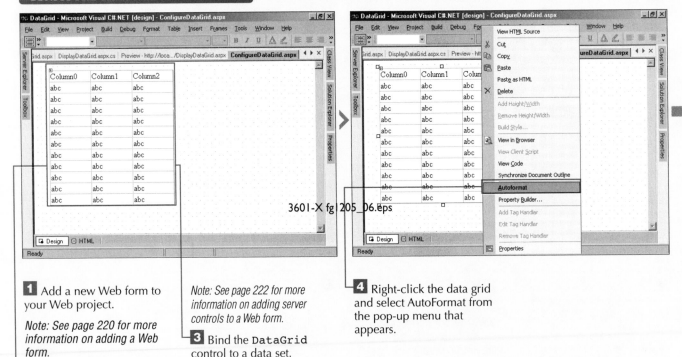

3601-X fg1205_06.eps

1 Add a new Web form to your Web project.

Note: See page 220 for more information on adding a Web form.

2 Add a DataGrid control to the Web page.

Note: See page 222 for more information on adding server controls to a Web form.

3 Bind the DataGrid control to a data set.

Note: See page 232 for more information on binding a data grid to a data set.

4 Right-click the data grid and select AutoFormat from the pop-up menu that appears.

Extra

You can take the code from the Apply It on page 233 one step further by adding sorting to the columns. To implement sorting, set the `AllowSorting` attribute on the `DataGrid` tag equal to `true` and map the `OnSortCommand` to an event handler. When a sort request is made, a page level variable (`SortExpression`) is updated based on the column that was selected.

Example:

```
string SortExpression = "";
void Grid_Change(Object sender,
    DataGridPageChangedEventArgs e) {
    dgdTitles.CurrentPageIndex = e.NewPageIndex;
    BindData(); }
void Sort_Grid(Object sender,
    DataGridSortCommandEventArgs e) {
    SortExpression = e.SortExpression.ToString();
    BindData(); }
void BindData() {
    if (SortExpression == "")
        SortExpression = "title";
    SqlConnection cnPubs = new SqlConnection(

"server=(local);uid=sa;pwd=;database=pubs");
    SqlDataAdapter daTitles = new SqlDataAdapter(
        "select title, notes, price, pubdate from "
        + "titles order by " + SortExpression,
cnPubs);
    // Use this Data Adapter for rebinding. }
```

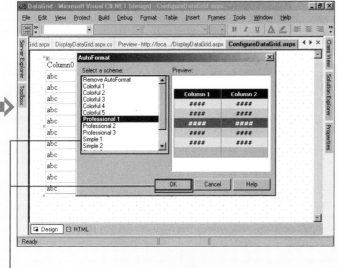

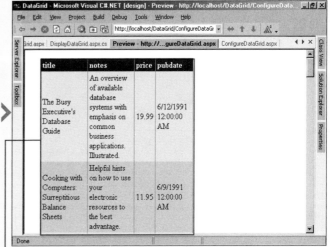

■ The AutoFormat dialog box appears.

5 Click to select a scheme for your data grid.

6 Click the OK button.

7 Build and browse the Web page.

Note: See page 220 for more information on building and browsing a Web page.

■ The data grid appears in the preview window formatted with the scheme selected.

INSERT DATA INTO A SQL DATABASE

For .NET applications, you can use the `System.Data` namespace for inserting data into SQL databases. Using the `System.Data` namespace allows you to insert into any database with the same basic code. Switching to another database usually only requires changing the `ConnectionString` property on the database connection.

A simple way to get new data persisted into a SQL database is by running a SQL `insert` statement. SQL `insert` statements allow you to populate a database table with a new row of data that is provided by your application. You can collect new data from the user and dynamically build out a SQL `insert`.

The basic process of running an `insert` statement is to first acquire a `Connection` object so that you can communicate to the database. The key to obtaining a `Connection` object is to build a connection string that contains the authentication, server, and data catalog information (with other optional information). After a connection is obtained, you can use the connection to obtain a `Command` object. With the `Command` object, you can set the `CommandText` property equal to the `insert` statement. Then, you can execute the `insert` statement using one of several execution options. The most likely option to use is the `ExecuteNonQuery`.

INSERT DATA INTO A SQL DATABASE

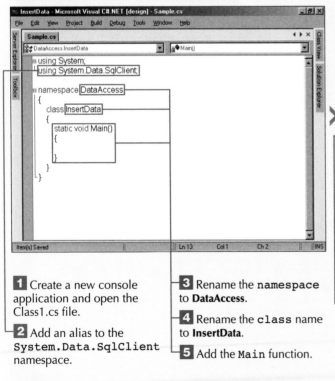

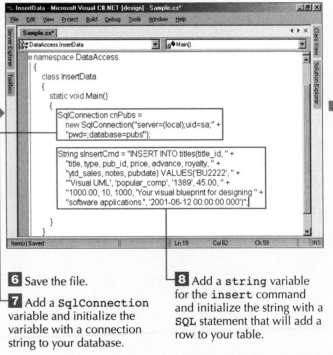

1 Create a new console application and open the Class1.cs file.

2 Add an alias to the `System.Data.SqlClient` namespace.

3 Rename the **namespace** to **DataAccess**.

4 Rename the **class** name to **InsertData**.

5 Add the `Main` function.

6 Save the file.

7 Add a `SqlConnection` variable and initialize the variable with a connection string to your database.

8 Add a `string` variable for the `insert` command and initialize the string with a SQL statement that will add a row to your table.

Extra

If you insert data with the same primary key more than once, you will violate a constraint in the pubs database. If you are running a sample without proper error handling, you will halt/kill the application. To degrade gracefully you should implement exception-handling code in the try/catch/finally **blocks.**

Example:

```
// In the if block change the code to the following
// (to capture exceptions like the primary key already
// exists, which will be the case if you run this
// sample more than once).

SqlCommand cmdTitles = new SqlCommand(sInsertCmd, cnPubs);

try
{
    cmdTitles.Connection.Open();
    cmdTitles.ExecuteNonQuery();
}
catch (Exception e)
{
    Console.WriteLine(e.Message);
}
finally
{
    cmdTitles.Connection.Close();
}
```

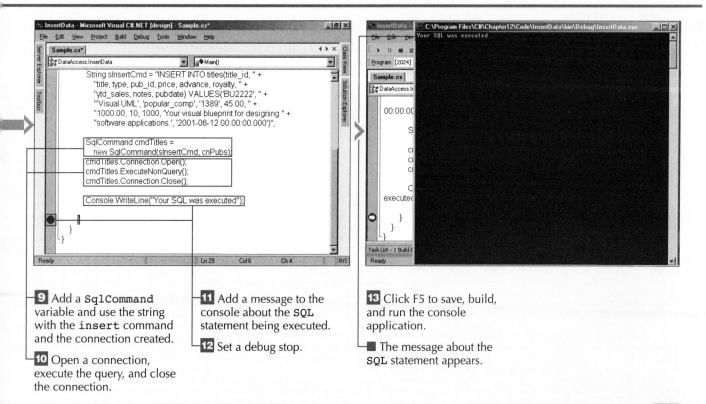

9 Add a `SqlCommand` variable and use the string with the `insert` command and the connection created.

10 Open a connection, execute the query, and close the connection.

11 Add a message to the console about the `SQL` statement being executed.

12 Set a debug stop.

13 Click F5 to save, build, and run the console application.

■ The message about the `SQL` statement appears.

UPDATE DATA FROM A SQL DATABASE

For .NET applications, you can use the `System.Data` namespace to update data in SQL databases. Using the `System.Data` namespace puts a layer of abstraction between your code and the data store's API (Application Programming Interface).

One way of updating data is by executing SQL `update` statements. SQL `update` statements are typically built from information the user provides. The current data that is in the SQL database is retrieved and displayed to the user. The user changes the values that need to be updated and then submits the information for updating.

A basic `update` statement contains the destination table, sets expressions, and includes an optional conditional

statement. The dynamic portions are the set expressions and the conditional statement. The set expression specifies which columns to update. The conditional statement determines which rows in the table need to be updated. Also, the conditional statement is typically based on the primary key(s) of the table.

The steps of running an `update` statement are very similar to running an `insert` statement, requiring a `Connection` object and a `Command` object. Within the `Command` object you set the `CommandText` property equal to the `update` statement. At this point, you can execute the `update` statement using `ExecuteNonQuery`. See page 240 for further details on `ExecuteNonQuery`.

UPDATE DATA FROM A SQL DATABASE

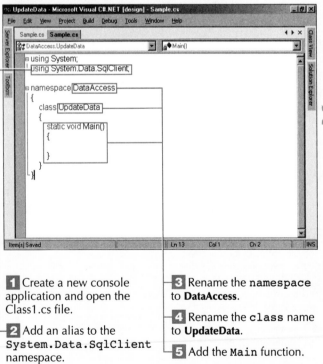

1 Create a new console application and open the Class1.cs file.

2 Add an alias to the `System.Data.SqlClient` namespace.

3 Rename the **namespace** to **DataAccess**.

4 Rename the **class** name to **UpdateData**.

5 Add the **Main** function.

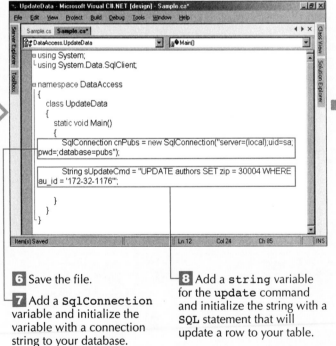

6 Save the file.

7 Add a `SqlConnection` variable and initialize the variable with a connection string to your database.

8 Add a **string** variable for the **update** command and initialize the string with a SQL statement that will update a row to your table.

Apply It

This console application does the same work as the code displayed in the screenshots of this section, but wraps it inside a database transaction.

TYPE THIS:

```
SqlTransaction txPubs = cnPubs.BeginTransaction();
cmdTitles.Transaction = txPubs;
cmdTitles.ExecuteNonQuery();
Console.WriteLine("You ran the following:");
Console.WriteLine(sUpdateCmd);
Console.Write("Commit change? [Y/N] ");
char cCommitResponse = (char) Console.Read();
if (cCommitResponse == char.Parse("Y"))
    txPubs.Commit();
else
    txPubs.Rollback();
```

RESULT:

```
C:\>csc UpdateData_ai.cs

C:\> UpdateData_ai.exe

You ran the following SQL Statement:

UPDATE authors SET zip = 30004 WHERE
au_id = '172-32-1176'

Do you want to commit the change?
[Y/N] Y

C:\>
```

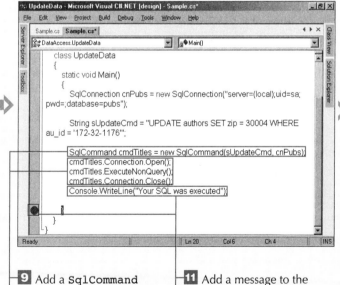

9 Add a `SqlCommand` variable and use the string with the **update** command and the connection created.

10 Open a connection, execute the query, and close the connection.

11 Add a message to the console about the SQL statement being executed.

12 Set a debug stop.

13 Click F5 to save, build, and run the console application.

■ The message about the SQL statement appears.

DELETE DATA FROM A SQL DATABASE

For .NET applications, you can use the System.Data namespace for deleting data from SQL databases. If you learn how to delete data with the System.Data namespace for your current database, you can reuse this knowledge to delete data on your next database choice.

Running a SQL delete statement is a simple way to remove rows from a table in a SQL database. Similar to inserting data, you can dynamically build out a SQL delete statement based on user input to the application.

A basic delete statement contains the requested table and a condition statement that indicates which row or rows in that table need to be deleted. The dynamic portion of the delete statement typically is in the condition statement, but in some cases the table may be dynamically determined.

The basic process of running a SQL delete statement is very similar to running an insert statement. You need a Connection object and a Command object. Within the Command object, set the CommandText property equal to the delete statement. At this point, you can execute the delete statement with the ExecuteNonQuery method. The ExecuteNonQuery method runs SQL statements that do not need to return data, but instead return only the rows affected.

DELETE DATA FROM A SQL DATABASE

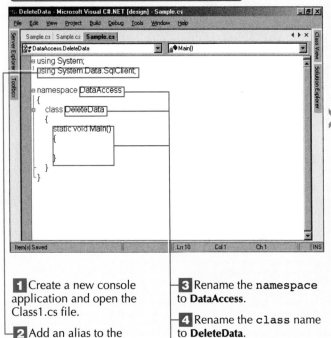

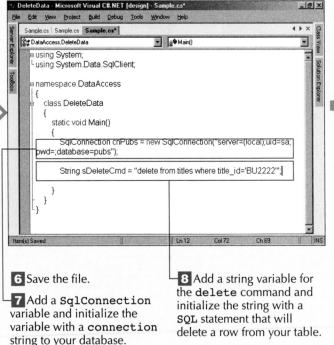

1 Create a new console application and open the Class1.cs file.

2 Add an alias to the System.Data.SqlClient namespace.

3 Rename the **namespace** to **DataAccess**.

4 Rename the **class** name to **DeleteData**.

5 Add the **Main** function.

6 Save the file.

7 Add a **SqlConnection** variable and initialize the variable with a **connection** string to your database.

8 Add a string variable for the **delete** command and initialize the string with a **SQL** statement that will delete a row from your table.

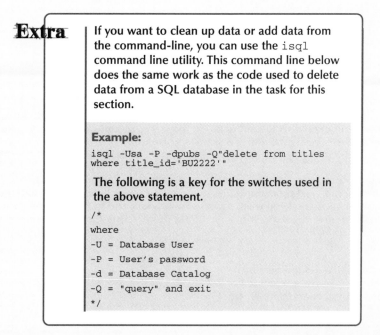

Extra

If you want to clean up data or add data from the command-line, you can use the `isql` command line utility. This command line below does the same work as the code used to delete data from a SQL database in the task for this section.

Example:
```
isql -Usa -P -dpubs -Q"delete from titles
where title_id='BU2222'"
```

The following is a key for the switches used in the above statement.

```
/*
where
-U = Database User
-P = User's password
-d = Database Catalog
-Q = "query" and exit
*/
```

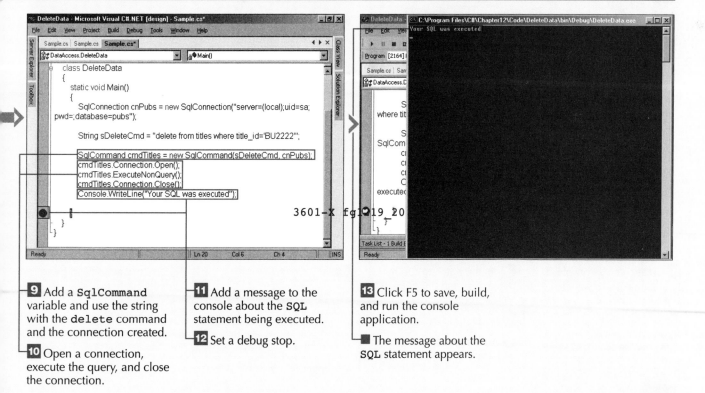

9 Add a `SqlCommand` variable and use the string with the **delete** command and the connection created.

10 Open a connection, execute the query, and close the connection.

11 Add a message to the console about the **SQL** statement being executed.

12 Set a debug stop.

13 Click F5 to save, build, and run the console application.

■ The message about the **SQL** statement appears.

EXECUTE A STORED PROCEDURE IN A SQL DATABASE

You can build secure, performance-driven applications by implementing stored procedures for accessing data. Using stored procedures allows you to wrap your data access into precompiled procedures. These procedures can be secured, giving rights to only the users that need access.

If all your data access is put into stored procedures, you can remove direct access to your tables. Stored procedures give you known entry points to your data. If you keep read, update, and delete access enabled on your tables, you cannot protect your data from harmful modification, whether intentional or unintentional.

To implement stored procedures, first determine which provider you want to use, the SQLClient namespace or the OleDb namespace, depending on your database. No

matter which namespace you choose, you need a connection to the data source and a Command object to prepare, execute, and evaluate results of a stored procedure.

The key part of the Command object is collection of parameters. Parameters are used to pass in data that is needed to execute the SQL statements inside the stored procedure and to hold information that the program needs to inspect after the procedure has completed its execution. These output or return parameters may have records of data or just a single value that indicates the result of the execution.

EXECUTE A STORED PROCEDURE IN A SQL DATABASE

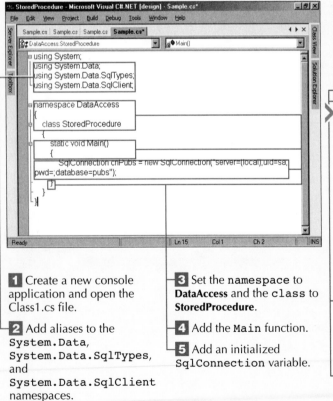

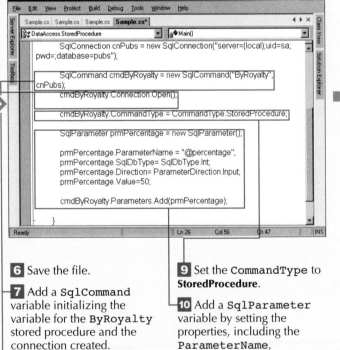

1 Create a new console application and open the Class1.cs file.

2 Add aliases to the System.Data, System.Data.SqlTypes, and System.Data.SqlClient namespaces.

3 Set the namespace to **DataAccess** and the class to **StoredProcedure**.

4 Add the Main function.

5 Add an initialized SqlConnection variable.

6 Save the file.

7 Add a SqlCommand variable initializing the variable for the ByRoyalty stored procedure and the connection created.

8 Open the connection.

9 Set the CommandType to **StoredProcedure**.

10 Add a SqlParameter variable by setting the properties, including the ParameterName, SqlDbType, Direction, and Value.

Extra

You can shorthand the five lines that are required to prepare and set a parameter into a single line of code. In terms of code execution time, most likely both of these implementations would precompile down to the same Intermediate Language (IL). Which implementation to choose is a matter of style. The more verbose style is typically chosen because it is easier to troubleshoot.

The line of code for adding a parameter

```
cmdByRoyalty.Parameters.Add("@percentage",SqlDbType.Int, 15).Value=50;
```

can replace the following lines in the code used in the screenshots in this section

```
SqlParameter prmPercentage = new SqlParameter();
prmPercentage.ParameterName = "@percentage";
prmPercentage.SqlDbType= SqlDbType.Int;
prmPercentage.Direction=
ParameterDirection.Input;
prmPercentage.Value=50;

cmdByRoyalty.Parameters.Add(prmPercentage);
```

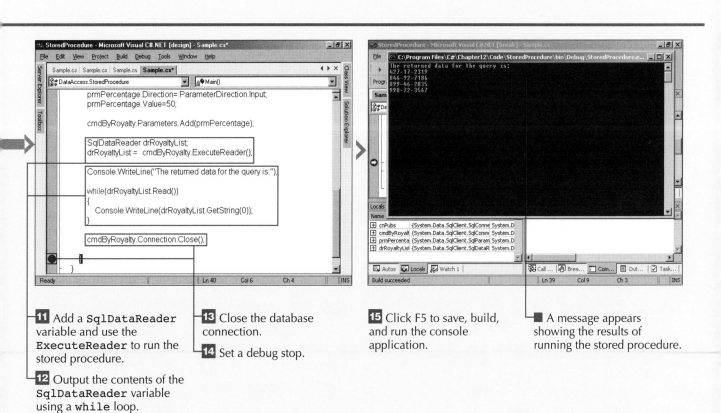

11 Add a `SqlDataReader` variable and use the `ExecuteReader` to run the stored procedure.

12 Output the contents of the `SqlDataReader` variable using a `while` loop.

13 Close the database connection.

14 Set a debug stop.

15 Click F5 to save, build, and run the console application.

■ A message appears showing the results of running the stored procedure.

READ XML FROM A FILE

XML is a great lightweight storage of data for your applications. If you are using Microsoft SQL 2000, you can retrieve queries in the form of XML. You will sometimes need to pull XML data from files.

To read XML files, you can use an implementation of the XMLReader class. The XMLReader class is an abstract base class that provides noncached, forward-only, read-only access. Because it is an abstract class, you need to use one of the current implementations in the System.XML namespace which are XMLTextReader, XMLValidatingReader, and XMLNodeReader classes.

Typically, you use the XMLTextReader if you need to access the XML as raw data. After you load the XMLTextReader, you will iterate through XML data by using the Read method, sequentially retrieving the next record from the document. The Read method returns false if no more records exist. To process the XML data, each record has a node type that can be determined from the NodeType property. This NodeType property will help you determine how to process the node. The XMLTextReader class will enforce the XML rules but does not provide data validation.

READ XML FROM A FILE

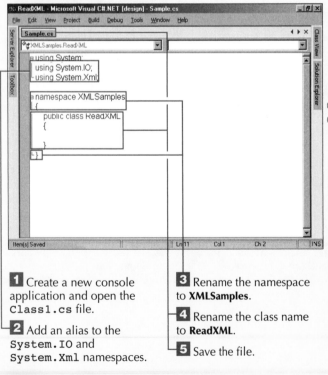

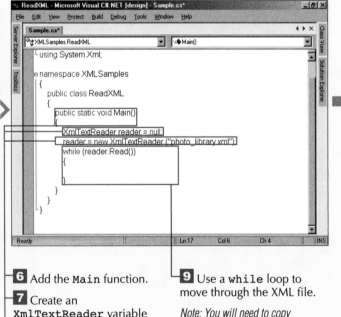

1 Create a new console application and open the Class1.cs file.

2 Add an alias to the System.IO and System.Xml namespaces.

3 Rename the namespace to **XMLSamples**.

4 Rename the class name to **ReadXML**.

5 Save the file.

6 Add the Main function.

7 Create an XmlTextReader variable and initialize with null.

8 Create a new XmlTextReader variable and initialize with the name of the XML file.

9 Use a while loop to move through the XML file.

Note: You will need to copy photo_library.xml from the CD-ROM to the working directory.

Extra

The following is an example that reads the XML with a `StringReader` and evaluates several node types. The output documents the nodes that are detected and writes out the node name, type, and value.

Example:
```
while (reader.Read() {
    switch (reader.NodeType) {
        case XmlNodeType.ProcessingInstruction:
            OutputXML (reader, "ProcessingInstruction"); break;
        case XmlNodeType.DocumentType:
            OutputXML (reader, "DocumentType"); break;
        case XmlNodeType.Comment:
            OutputXML (reader, "Comment"); break;
        case XmlNodeType.Element:
            OutputXML (reader, "Element");
            while(reader.MoveToNextAttribute())
                OutputXML (reader, "Attribute");
            break;
        case XmlNodeType.Text:
            OutputXML (reader, "Text"); break;
        case XmlNodeType.Whitespace:
            break;
}}
```

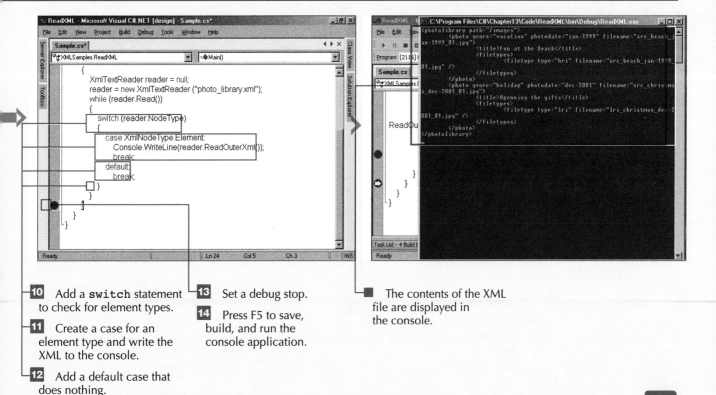

■10 Add a **switch** statement to check for element types.

■11 Create a case for an element type and write the XML to the console.

■12 Add a default case that does nothing.

■13 Set a debug stop.

■14 Press F5 to save, build, and run the console application.

■ The contents of the XML file are displayed in the console.

SAVE XML TO A FILE

You will sometimes need to persist data as XML. In ADO.NET, the persistence mechanism for DataSets is XML. XML provides an excellent way to save and retrieve data without a database server.

One of the fastest ways to write data is by using the XMLTextWriter class that is part of the System.Xml namespace. This writer provides a fast, forward-only way of generating XML and helps you to build XML documents that conform to the W3C Extensible Markup Language (XML) 1.0 and the Namespaces in XML specifications. You can find the latest XML specification at www.w3c.org.

The XMLTextWriter is an implementation of the XMLWriter abstract class. You can write your own

implementation of this abstract class, but if the XMLTextWriter has what you need, you use this .NET Framework class. Typically, you use an XMLTextWriter if you need to quickly write XML to file, stream, or a TextWriter, and do not need to use the Document Object Model (DOM).

The XMLTextWriter has formatting capabilities to assist in giving a file with nice indentions that are handy when reading the documents in a text viewer. When you construct your XML, you use one of several Write methods, depending on what part of the XML document you are constructing (element, attribute, or comment).

SAVE XML TO A FILE

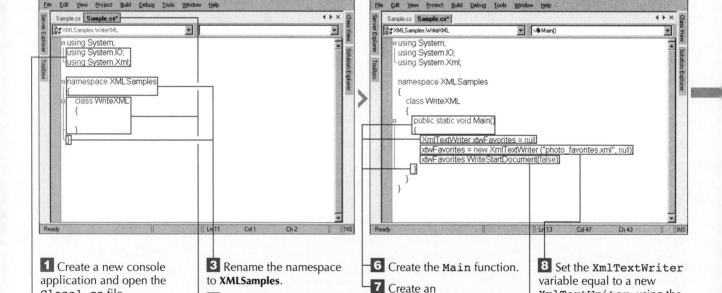

1 Create a new console application and open the **Class1.cs** file.

2 Add an alias to the **System.IO** and **System.Xml** namespaces.

3 Rename the namespace to **XMLSamples**.

4 Rename the class name to **WriteXML**.

5 Save the file.

6 Create the **Main** function.

7 Create an **XmlTextWriter** variable and initialize the variable to **null**.

8 Set the **XmlTextWriter** variable equal to a new **XmlTextWriter**, using the location of the XML file.

9 Begin the XML document using the **WriteStartDocument** method.

Apply It

You can use verbatim strings to handcraft XML and set the indention in your code. Remember that you will have to double up your quotes inside of the string.

TYPE THIS:

```
using System; using System.IO; using System.Xml;
public class Sample
{   public static void Main()
    {   XmlDocument doc = new XmlDocument();
        string sXML =
@""<?xml version=""1.0"" standalone=""no""?>
<!—This file represents a list of favorite photos—>
<photofavorites owner=""Frank Ryan"">
 <photo cat=""vacation"" date=""2000"">
  <title>Maddie with Minnie</title>
 </photo>
</photofavorites>";   // end of string
        doc.LoadXml(sXML);
        doc.Save("data.xml");
}}
```

RESULT:

XML document created in the internals of the class and echoed out to the console.

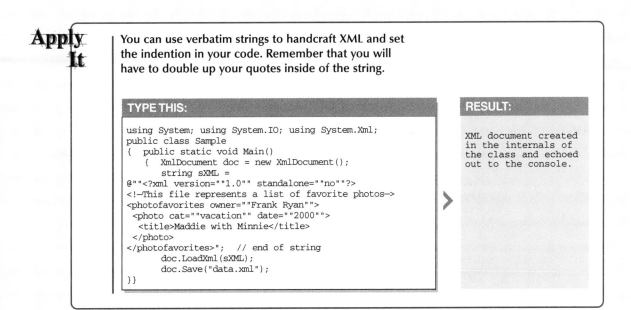

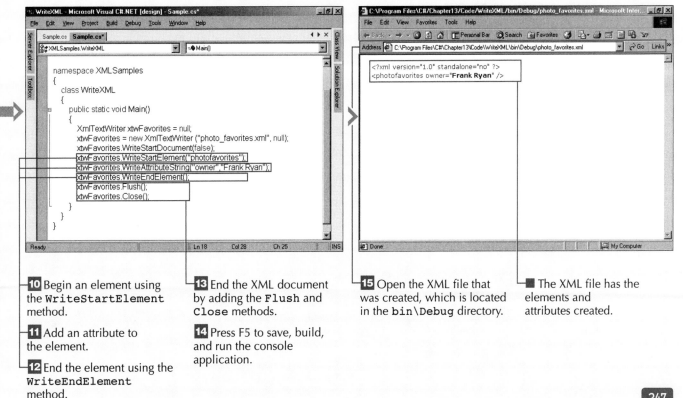

⒑ Begin an element using the **WriteStartElement** method.

⒒ Add an attribute to the element.

⒓ End the element using the **WriteEndElement** method.

⒔ End the XML document by adding the **Flush** and **Close** methods.

⒕ Press F5 to save, build, and run the console application.

⒖ Open the XML file that was created, which is located in the **bin\Debug** directory.

■ The XML file has the elements and attributes created.

QUERY XML WITH XPATH

XML is great for portable data. If you want a quick way to query XML documents for pieces of data relevant to your application, XPath is a high-performance mechanism to get this done. XPath is specified by W3C and is a general query language specification for extracting information from XML documents. XPath functionality has its own namespace in the .NET Framework. The System.Xml.XPath namespace has four classes that work together to provide efficient XML data searches.

The classes provided by System.Xml.XPath are: XPathDocument, XPathExpression, XPathNavigator, and XPathNodeIterator. XPathDocument is used to cache your XML document in a high-performance oriented cache for XSLT processing. To query this cache, you will

need an XPath expression. This can be done with just a string that contains an XPath expression or you can use the XPathExpression class. If you want performance, you will use the XPathExpression class because it compiles once and can be rerun without requiring subsequent compiles. The XPath expression is provided to a select method on the XPathNavigator class. The XPathNavigator object will return an XPathNodeIterator object from executing the Select method. After calling this method, the XPathNodeIterator returned represents the set of selected nodes. You can use MoveNext on the XPathNodeIterator to walk the selected node set.

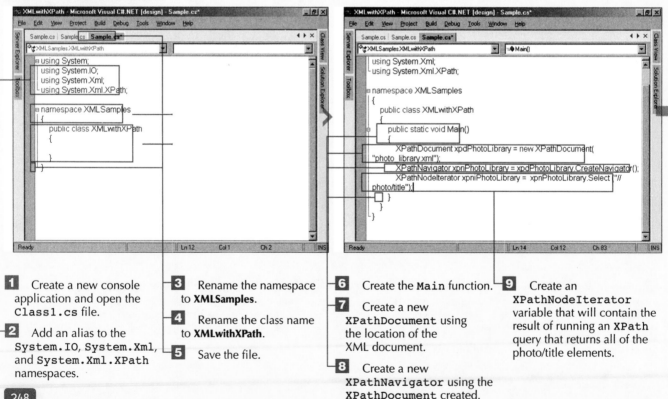

1 Create a new console application and open the Class1.cs file.

2 Add an alias to the System.IO, System.Xml, and System.Xml.XPath namespaces.

3 Rename the namespace to **XMLSamples**.

4 Rename the class name to **XMLwithXPath**.

5 Save the file.

6 Create the Main function.

7 Create a new XPathDocument using the location of the XML document.

8 Create a new XPathNavigator using the XPathDocument created.

9 Create an XPathNodeIterator variable that will contain the result of running an XPath query that returns all of the photo/title elements.

Apply It

You can use the recursive decent operator to search for an element at any depth. Make sure that the source XML document, `photo_library.xml`, is in the working directory of the EXE file.

TYPE THIS:

```
using System; using System.IO; using System.Xml; using System.Xml.XPath;
namespace XMLSamples {
public class XMLwithXPath {
    private const String sXMLDocument = "photo_library.xml";
    public static void Main() {
        Console.WriteLine ("XPath query results are:");
        XPathDocument xpdPhotoLibrary = new XPathDocument(sXMLDocument);
        XPathNavigator xpnPhotoLibrary = xpdPhotoLibrary.CreateNavigator();
        XPathNodeIterator xpniPhotoLibrary =
            xpnPhotoLibrary.Select ("//photo/title");
        while (xpniPhotoLibrary.MoveNext())
            Console.WriteLine(xpniPhotoLibrary.Current.Name
                + " = " + xpniPhotoLibrary.Current.Value);
}}}
```

RESULT:

```
XPath query results are:
title = Fun at the Beach
title = Opening the gifts
```

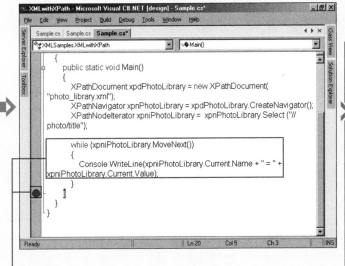

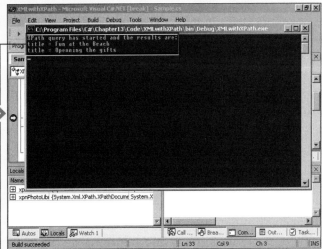

-10- Add a `while` loop to output the name and the value of the node to the console.

-11- Set a debug stop.

-12- Press F5 to save, build, and run the console application.

■ A message appears that shows the name and the value for the two elements that match the **XPath** query.

APPLY XSL TO XML

XML documents are a good choice for transportable data, but may contain more data than is necessary for your application. To retrieve only a portion of the XML data, you can transform a source XML document into another XML document by using an *XSLT transformation*. The resulting document does not always have to be XML. In some cases, you use XSLT transformations to create HTML documents.

XSLT is a language for transforming source XML documents into other document formats using XPath or XSLT as the query language. You can use the XslTransform class, which is part of the System.Xml.Xsl namespace to

orchestrate XSLT transformations. To build well-performing XSLT transformations, you can use an XPathDocument as the XSLT data store. If you are working with a DataSet, you can use XmlDataDocument as your source file in a transformation.

To map the XslTransform class to an XSLT style sheet, you can use the Load method. When you execute the Transform method of the XslTransform class, there are several overload options. In the steps that follow, the Transform method writes the XML to a file.

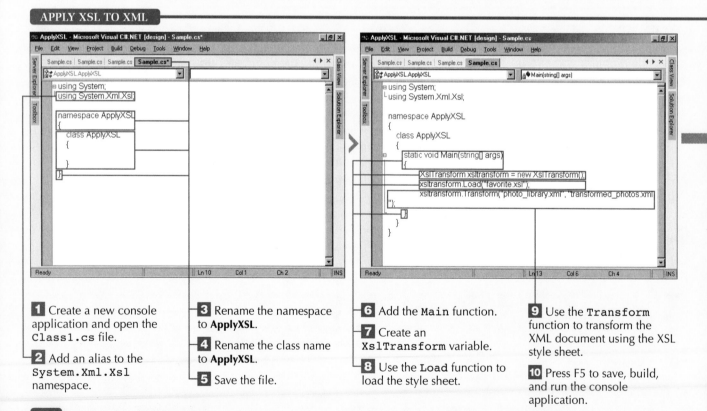

1 Create a new console application and open the Class1.cs file.

2 Add an alias to the System.Xml.Xsl namespace.

3 Rename the namespace to **ApplyXSL**.

4 Rename the class name to **ApplyXSL**.

5 Save the file.

6 Add the Main function.

7 Create an XslTransform variable.

8 Use the Load function to load the style sheet.

9 Use the Transform function to transform the XML document using the XSL style sheet.

10 Press F5 to save, build, and run the console application.

Apply It

For faster transformations, load your XML into an XPathDocument. To run this sample, you need to put the XML and XSL source documents in the working directory of your EXE file.

TYPE THIS:

```
using System; using System.Xml; using System.Xml.Xsl; using System.Xml.XPath;
namespace ApplyXSL{
class ApplyXSL {
    static void Main(){
        XPathDocument xpdLibrary =  new XPathDocument ("photo_library.xml");
        XslTransform xsltFavorites = new XslTransform();
        xsltFavorites.Load("favorite.xsl");
        XmlReader reader = xsltFavorites.Transform(xpdLibrary, null);
        while (reader.Read()) {
            // With each node write to the console. (Look at cd for full code.)
            }
}}}
```

RESULT:

```
C:\>csc ApplyXSL_ai.cs
C:\> ApplyXSL_ai.exe
"Screen will echo out the nodes in the document.
Including the type node, name, and contents."
C:\>
```

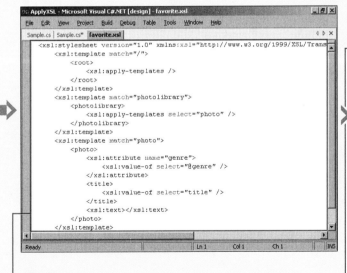

11 Open the style sheet and review the contents of the style sheet.

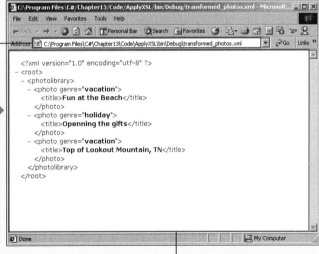

12 Open the XML document that was created from the transform.

■ The resulting XML document appears.

INTRODUCTION TO DISTRIBUTED APPLICATIONS

The .NET Framework is Microsoft's new computing platform designed to simplify application development in the highly distributed environment of the Internet. Microsoft has put a major effort in revamping the architecture for their component-based solutions. When you create applications on the .NET platform, you find component development tightly integrated with the solutions you build.

Most application development solutions benefit from creating component-based solutions. The .NET platform enables you to take a very simple approach to distributed component-based solutions by using *private assemblies*.

By using private assemblies, you can reap the benefits of component programming without the headaches of dealing with versions that are not backward-compatible. Also, it is easier to control your component and how those components get versioned into existing deployed applications.

With highly reuseable components, you can create shared assemblies. Shared assemblies give you more control with your components, but for a price. Shared assemblies enable you to share components across applications, to version your component, and to localize components, among other capabilities.

EVOLUTION OF COM AND DCOM TO .NET

Applications that use components have proven to be an effective way to build applications. For Microsoft, the open standard for component development started in 1993 with the introduction of the *Component Object Model,* or COM. Microsoft further enhanced COM into a distributed model with DCOM, Distributed COM, in 1996. Used on more than 150 million systems worldwide today, COM is widely accepted and heavily leveraged in enterprise application for many Fortune 500 companies. The most recent version that is integral to Windows 2000 is COM+. COM+ was an integration of Microsoft Transaction Server (MTS) and COM.

COM/COM+ is the backbone for Microsoft's Distributed interNet Applications (DNA) platform.

Despite Microsoft's success with DNA, they are evolving to a new framework. With a mature framework, like DNA via COM, there are issues that cannot be properly addressed due to preserving compatability with earlier versions of COM. .NET takes the issues of what COM+ has today and addresses them based on the best of the COM+ runtime and what other competitive component runtimes have to offer.

DLL HELL

The .NET platform addresses one of the major issues of DNA applications, DLL Hell. This refers to the problems that occur when multiple applications attempt to share a COM class. COM enables one or more clients to share classes in COM components. When one client application updates an existing COM component that is not backward-compatible with the version already on the machine, the first client breaks when it tries to create a component based on the new class that is not backward-compatible.

.NET addresses the issue of DLL Hell with side-by-side execution of components via use of assemblies. .NET can perform side-by-side execution of components.

USING VERSIONING IN .NET

Versioning takes on a new meaning with .NET. With COM components, you register a component for reuse by putting several entries into the Windows Registry, a proprietary store where Windows holds application and operating system settings. The entries in the Windows Registry can end up being corrupted by bad development practices, causing applications to fail when calling the component that has corrupted Registry entries.

With .NET, the versioning has more capabilities and is easier to control. .NET uses the version number when determining which build of a class to load. Configuring what build is used is easily configured through the config file, class, for your application. See page 266 to learn about binding a component version in the `AssemblyInfo` project file.

USING ASSEMBLIES AND GAC

The .NET platform addresses the DLL Hell issue with assemblies. *Assemblies* enable you to register more than one version of the same component on the same machine. Note that the word *register* does not mean using the Windows Registry. When you register a version, the version resides in the machine's *Global Assembly Cache*, or GAC. Items in the GAC are shared assemblies that multiple clients can use. Assemblies that exist in the GAC have a version number assigned to them. When a client calls for a component, the GAC assists in matching the client component request with the correct version of the component, not just the last installed version. With the capability of Global

Assemblies, you can have two versions of the same component running on the same machine, also called *side-by-side execution*.

The .NET platform considers components not in the GAC as private assemblies and packages them in the client's application directory. You can also configure your private assemblies to exist in one of the subdirectories of the application directory. You do not have the benefit of sharing private assemblies across multiple machines, but you can deploy them very simply using xcopy, an old command-line utility that enables you to copy multiple files at the same time.

USING NAMESPACES IN THE .NET PLATFORM

In the .NET platform, you see the use of *namespaces* for identifying objects. All examples presented in this book illustrate the use of the keyword `Namespace` in the classes. When you compile a project, you use namespaces to organize the classes defined in the resulting assembly. Assemblies can contain multiple

namespaces, which can in turn contain other namespaces. Namespaces assist in providing uniqueness and simplify references when using large groups of objects such as class libraries. You can use aliases if you want to avoid fully qualifying a class nested in a namespace.

HOW WEB SERVICES FIT IN

Web Services are a big part of the distributed model for .NET. Web Services basically provide a programmable entity, such as application logic or data, via the Internet standards such as XML and HTTP. Web Services expose your systems to the Internet to yield highly distributed applications that can interact with

other systems regardless of the operating system or programming language. Web Services meet the challenge of an ultimate heterogeneous environment; it is accessible over the Internet and agnostic regarding the choice of operating system, object model, or programming language.

CREATE AN APPLICATION WITH PRIVATE ASSEMBLIES

You can share code within your application by putting it into classes within private assemblies. Organizing your code with assemblies promotes reuse of code within your application so that you do not have to write the same code in several places. To update code, change it in only one place.

When you create applications on the .NET platform, you need to choose between creating components in private or shared assemblies. Creating components in private assemblies provides the simplest deployment strategy, which consists of just copying your application files to the destination where the application is to run. You did not have the capability of Xcopy deployment with Windows development before .NET.

The classes inside your private assemblies can contain public members that your client applications can access. These members include public properties, methods, and events. With properties, you can use get and set (read and write) to control what access the client has (read, write, or read/write). The properties that you implement with get and sets use protected members of the class to store property states, thereby enabling you to validate before setting or getting a property. Also, if you remove either of the get or the set, you can make a Write-only or Read-only property respectively.

To create a private component, you first start with a Class Library project in the Visual C# Projects templates list. A Class Library Application template is similar to the Console Applications template, except that the class file is scoped as Public and contains a constructor.

CREATE AN ASSEMBLY

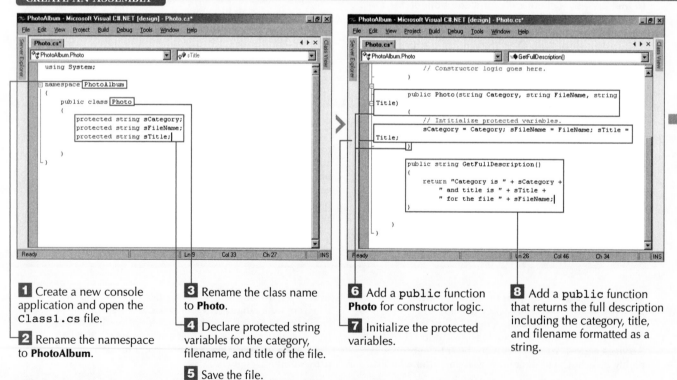

1 Create a new console application and open the `Class1.cs` file.

2 Rename the namespace to **PhotoAlbum**.

3 Rename the class name to **Photo**.

4 Declare protected string variables for the category, filename, and title of the file.

5 Save the file.

6 Add a **public** function **Photo** for constructor logic.

7 Initialize the protected variables.

8 Add a **public** function that returns the full description including the category, title, and filename formatted as a string.

Extra

You can simplify your code by using public fields for properties on your objects. Although public fields do come at a cost, you do not have any control over read/write access of the property, and validation can not be done before the property is replaced.

Example:
```
using System;

namespace PhotoAlbum
{
    public class Photo_ex{
        public Photo(){
            // Constructor logic goes here.
        }
        public string GetFullDescription() {
            return "Catergory is " + Category +
                " and title is " + Title +
                " for the file " + FileName;
        }
        public string Category;
        public string FileName;
        public string Title;
}}
```

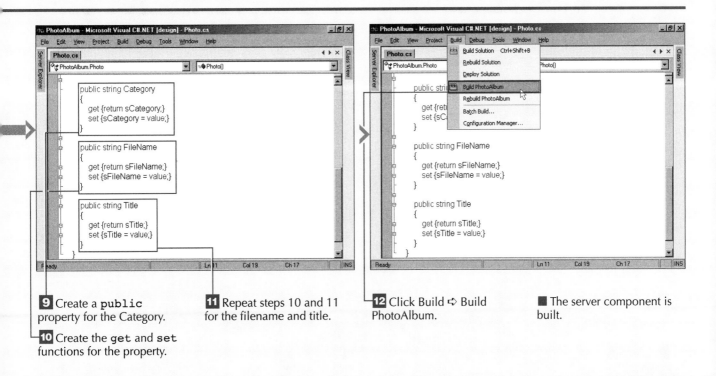

9 Create a **public** property for the Category.

10 Create the **get** and **set** functions for the property.

11 Repeat steps 10 and 11 for the filename and title.

12 Click Build ➪ Build PhotoAlbum.

■ The server component is built.

CONTINUED ▶

255

CREATE AN APPLICATION WITH PRIVATE ASSEMBLIES

You can create applications rapidly by creating clients applications that use your existing assemblies. applications. Building applications with components has been proven effective in the development community. After creating your component, you can leverage that component in a client application.

In the case of private components, you need to include the component as part of the client application. Private Assemblies is not the same concept as components with COM, in the sense that the component is not shared with other applications. You will see, however, that sharing code across applications is possible (see page 260). The benefit you get from private assemblies that was also provided with

COM is having the ability to distribute the application into separate projects, enabling a team to work on separate parts of the application and later piece it together in a build of the application.

A private assembly can be used by any client application type: Console, Windows, or ASP.NET Web application. After you create the project, you set a reference to the component DLL, which has the assembly information built in. Next you reference the component's namespace with the `using` statement. Then in code, you programmatically create an instance of the component and use its functionality.

CREATE A CLIENT

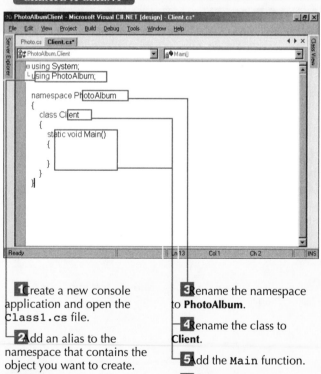

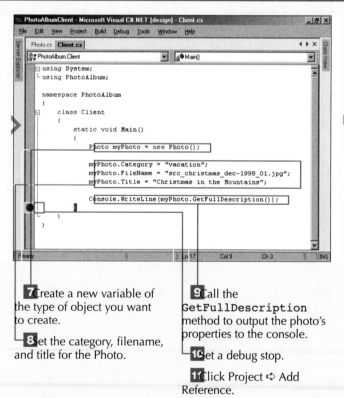

1 Create a new console application and open the `Class1.cs` file.

2 Add an alias to the namespace that contains the object you want to create.

3 Rename the namespace to **PhotoAlbum**.

4 Rename the class to **Client**.

5 Add the `Main` function.

6 Save the file.

7 Create a new variable of the type of object you want to create.

8 Set the category, filename, and title for the Photo.

9 Call the `GetFullDescription` method to output the photo's properties to the console.

10 Set a debug stop.

11 Click Project ⇨ Add Reference.

Extra

You can use collections to work with a group of the same classes. Collections are a common OOP approach to creating applications. The following code can be added to the project created in the numbered steps below to build a collection of photos. Add a new class to the project, call the class `Photos.cs` and then recompile.

Example:
```
namespace PhotoAlbum {
    using System; using System.Collections;
    public class Photos : IEnumerable {
        private ArrayList phtList;
        public Photos()
        { phtList = new ArrayList(); }
        public void Add(Photo pht)
        { phtList.Add(pht); }
        public void Remove(int phtRemove)
        { phtList.RemoveAt(phtRemove); }
        public int Count
        { get{ return phtList.Count;} }
        public IEnumerator GetEnumerator()
        { return phtList.GetEnumerator(); }
} }
```

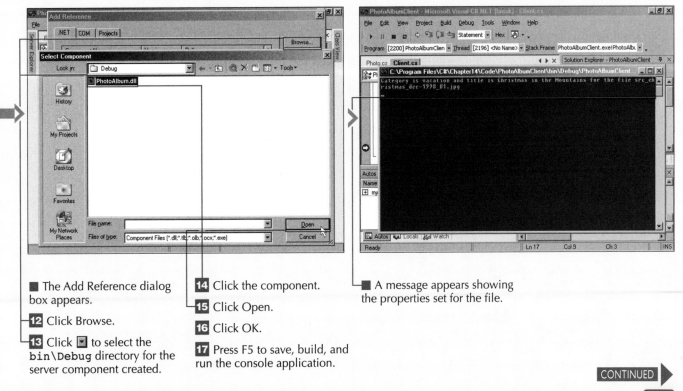

■ The Add Reference dialog box appears.

12 Click Browse.

13 Click ▣ to select the `bin\Debug` directory for the server component created.

14 Click the component.

15 Click Open.

16 Click OK.

17 Press F5 to save, build, and run the console application.

■ A message appears showing the properties set for the file.

CONTINUED ▶

CREATE AN APPLICATION WITH PRIVATE ASSEMBLIES

After creating your application with private assemblies, you can use Xcopy deployment to install the assembly. With private assemblies, you do not need to register components that the application uses. The components are discovered during the JIT compiling of the components. The issues with the Registry and DLL Hell go away. When using private assemblies for your component, the components deploy to the application directory by default and become visible only to the containing application. Because the components are discovered during JIT compiling, you can make updates on the components by just copying over the existing assemblies without unregistering and re-registering.

The process of deploying an application that only uses private assemblies is very simple. Just copy the client application and its dependencies from the output directory, which by default VS .NET builds to the bin\debug directory, and paste it to the destination client. In the case of the sample task below, you have one EXE file and one DLL to copy, and you deploy to another location on your PC's hard drive. You can modify the directions given and deploy to another PC's hard drive. In some cases, you can utilize a config file to help with locating dependencies. Because the dependent DLL is in the same directory as the client EXE, you do not need a config file.

DEPLOY AN APPLICATION

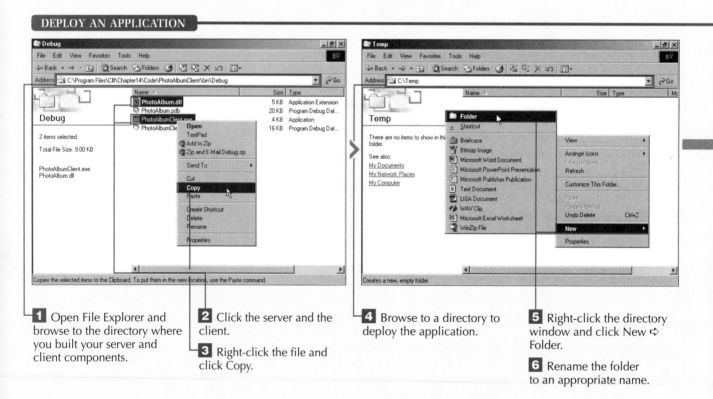

1 Open File Explorer and browse to the directory where you built your server and client components.

2 Click the server and the client.

3 Right-click the file and click Copy.

4 Browse to a directory to deploy the application.

5 Right-click the directory window and click New ⇨ Folder.

6 Rename the folder to an appropriate name.

Extra

Configuration files can provide paths that specify directories where the runtime should search for assemblies. See the `<probing>` element for an example of a redirection path. You can also redirect one assembly version to another by using the `<bindingRedirect>` element. The following example demonstrates how you can redirect to a newer version.

Example:

```
<configuration>
    <runtime>
        <assemblyBinding xmlns="urn:
        schemas-microsoft-com:asm.v1">
            probing privatePath=
            "bin;binother\sub_bin "/>
            <dependentAssembly>
                <assemblyIdentity name=
                "yourAssembly"
                    publickeytoken=
                    "23ab4ba49e0a69a1"
                    culture="en-us" />
                <bindingRedirect oldVersion=
                "1.0.0.0"
                    newVersion="2.0.0.0"/>
            </dependentAssembly>
            /assemblyBinding>
    </runtime>
</configuration>
```

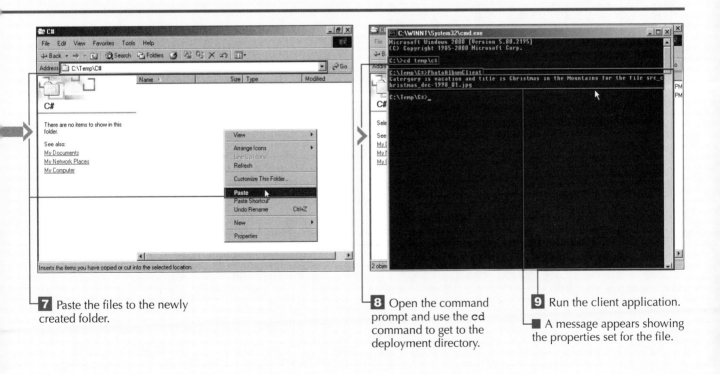

7 Paste the files to the newly created folder.

8 Open the command prompt and use the **cd** command to get to the deployment directory.

9 Run the client application.

■ A message appears showing the properties set for the file.

CREATE AN APPLICATION WITH SHARED ASSEMBLIES

You can share your code across multiple applications by using shared assemblies. Sharing components across multiple applications is the model used in COM/COM+ applications today. Shared assemblies in .NET are the closest relative to the COM+ component. Creating and deploying a shared assembly takes a few more steps than doing the same for a private assembly. See page 254 for information about creating a simple private assembly.

To create a shared assembly, first you assign a *shared name*, also known as a *strong name*. You assign a strong name through the creation of a key pair and update the

AssemblyInfo class with the key filename. The key filename assigns the path to the key in the AssemblyKeyFile assembly-level attribute that you find in the AssemblyInfo class. You can generate the key file with the strong name utility using the sn.exe tool.

After you complete the key assignment, you can compile the project. After compiling, you need to place the assembly into the GAC, or Global Assembly Cache. The easiest way to register an assembly into the GAC is to drag and drop the component into the global assembly directory C:\winnt\assembly, or your equivalent system path.

CREATE A SHARED ASSEMBLY

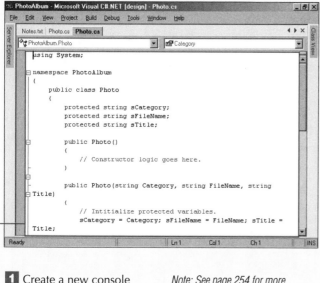

1 Create a new console application and open the `Class1.cs` file.

2 Add the implementation of the assembly.

Note: See page 254 for more information about implementing an assembly.

3 Save the file.

4 Open the command prompt.

5 Navigate to the deployment directory.

6 Type the **sn** command to create a key.

■ A key pair is created.

7 Type the **dir** command to ensure that the file exists in the deployment directory.

■ The key file is listed.

Extra

You can create and manage shared assemblies using the tools that the .NET framework provides. The `Gacutil.exe` file enables you to view and manipulate the contents of the GAC. You may not find it feasible to use the drag-and-drop method to register a component in the GAC when deploying an application to a remote machine. You can, however, use `Gacutil.exe` for deployment scripts as well as build scripts.

`Sn.exe` helps you create assemblies with strong names. `Sn.exe` provides options for key management, signature generation, and signature verification. If you have multiple keys that you want to group together into one store, you can use the `-i` switch to store them in a container, for example: `sn -i myKeyPair.snk MyContainer`.

`Ildasm.exe` takes a PE file that contains MSIL code and creates a text file suitable as input to the MSIL Assembler (`Ilasm.exe`).

A companion tool to the MSIL Assembler (`Ilasm.exe`), the MSIL Disassembler allows you to view the Manifest and the library's types.

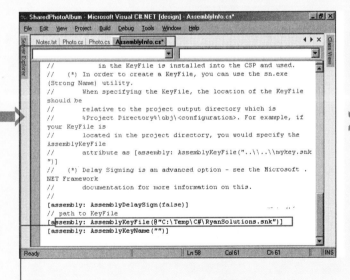

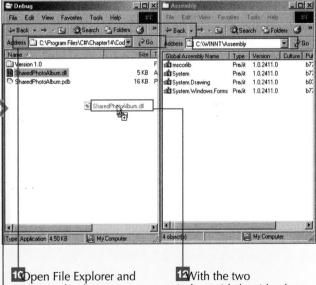

8 Open the `AssemblyInfo.cs` file for the project and update the `AssemblyKeyFile`.

9 Press Ctrl+B to build the component.

10 Open File Explorer and navigate to the directory where you built the component.

11 Open another instance of File Explorer and navigate to the `C:\WINNT\Assembly` directory.

12 With the two windows side by side, drag `SharedPhotoAlbum.dll` to `C:\WINNT\Assembly` directory.

■ The component is added to the global assembly.

CONTINUED

CREATE AN APPLICATION WITH SHARED ASSEMBLIES

You can share common classes across multiple applications by using shared assemblies with your client applications. Building clients with shared assemblies is similar to building with private assemblies. You do not need a local copy of the assembly. The client applications use the GAC (Global Assembly Cache) to determine where to find the class they need for object creation. With VS .NET you can have an option for a local copy. In most cases, you do not need a local copy. To ensure that you do not get a local copy, you can go to the properties of the reference and set the `Copy Local` property to `False`.

To use a class that resides in a shared assembly, the component must exist in the GAC. You need to set a reference to the shared component. If the shared component does not appear in the reference list, you must browse to the shared component and select the assembly file.

After you register the shared component and compile your client application, you can test your client application.

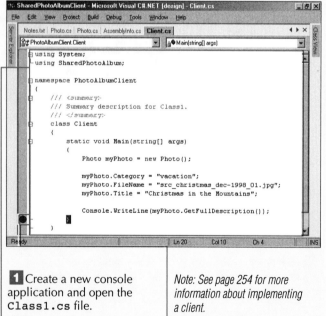

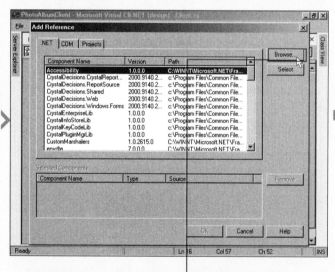

■1 Create a new console application and open the `Class1.cs` file.

■2 Add the implementation for a client application.

Note: See page 254 for more information about implementing a client.

■3 Save the file.

■4 Set a debug stop.

■5 Click Project ➪ Add Reference.

■ The Add Reference dialog box appears.

■6 Click Browse.

Apply It

You can use the constructor of the class to set initial properties on an object, which is an alternative to setting properties individually after the component is created. To run the below example, replace the `Client.cs` file in the sample task with the following code and recompile. Note the use of the overloaded constructor.

TYPE THIS:

```
using System; using SharedPhotoAlbum;
namespace PhotoAlbumClient {
    class Client{
        static void Main(string[] args){
            Photo myPhoto = new Photo(
                "Vacation",
                "src_christmas_dec-1998_01.jpg",
                "Christmas in the Mountains");

            Console.WriteLine(myPhoto.GetFullDescription());
} } }
```

RESULT:

Category is Vacation and title is Christmas in the Mountains for the file `src_christmas_dec-1998_01.jpg`

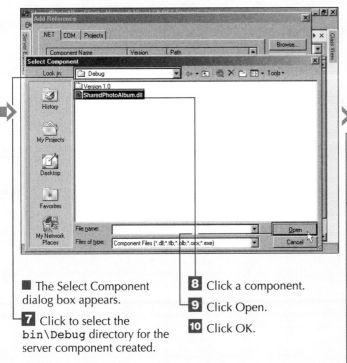

■ The Select Component dialog box appears.

7 Click to select the `bin\Debug` directory for the server component created.

8 Click a component.

9 Click Open.

10 Click OK.

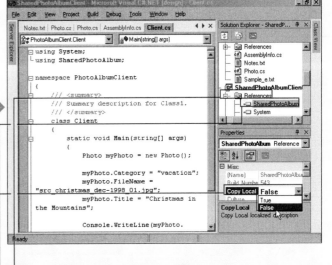

11 Expand References in the Solution Explorer for the client application.

12 Click to select the shared assembly.

13 In the Properties window, set the **Copy Local** property to **False**.

14 Press F5 to save, build, and run the console application.

■ A message appears showing the properties set for the file.

CONTINUED ▶

CREATE AN APPLICATION WITH SHARED ASSEMBLIES

You can deploy shared assemblies for code that is leveraged among several client applications. Shared assemblies can also be updated after they are deployed.

The process of deploying an application that uses shared assemblies involves copying the client application and its dependencies to the destination client machine, and placing the shared components into the GAC. GAC registration can be done by dragging and dropping assemblies into the GAC directory in Windows Explorer C:\winnt\assembly. If you want to automate the registration, you will use the Gacutil.exe utility.

After the assembly is in the GAC, you can then run your client. If you need to update the shared components, all you need to do is copy over the existing component and the client application will use that copy of the component the next time it is called. If you have a new version of the component that is not compatible with the currently deployed component, you need to version it (see page 266).

In the application deployment described here, both components and client application reside on the same machine. Remoting components, on the other hand, is much more involved and requires the use of a proxy.

DEPLOY AN APPLICATION

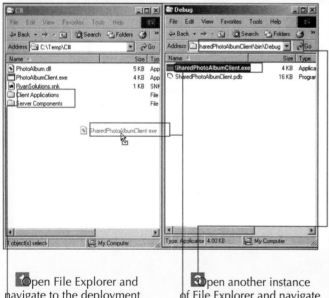

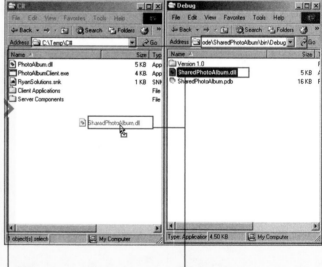

■1 Open File Explorer and navigate to the deployment directory.

■2 Create a folder for deploying the server component and another folder for deploying the client component.

■3 Open another instance of File Explorer and navigate to the directory where the **$SharedPhotoAlbum** client was built.

■4 Click the client application and drag to the appropriate directory.

■5 Navigate to where you built the server component for the shared assembly.

■6 Click the server component and drag to the appropriate directory.

Apply It

You can consume C# assemblies with a VB client. Below is a sample of a VB client application that uses the `SharedPhotoAlbum` component. To test the code, you will need to create a new VB console application project. Make sure that you reference the `SharedPhotoAlbum` component.

TYPE THIS:

```
' Equivalent to the using
Imports SharedPhotoAlbum
Module VBPhotoAlbum
    ' Main entry point into the console application (make sure that this is
    ' set in the project properties as the startup object).
    Sub Main()
        ' Creating instance of Component with the constuctor that initializes the properties.
        Dim spaTest As New SharedPhotoAlbum.Photo("vacation", "src_christmas_dec-1998_01.jpg",
        "Christmas in the Mountains")
        Console.Write(spaTest.GetFullDescription())
    End Sub
End Module
```

RESULT:

Category is Vacation and title is Christmas in the Mountains for the file `src_christmas_dec-1998_01.jpg`

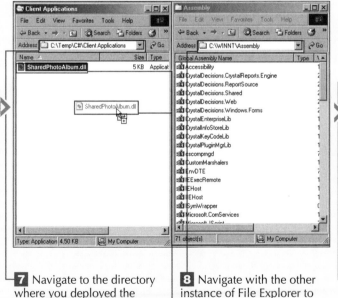

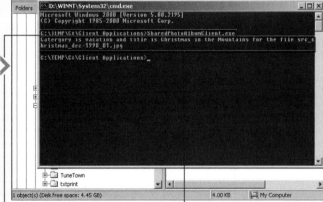

7 Navigate to the directory where you deployed the server components.

8 Navigate with the other instance of File Explorer to `C:\WINNT\Assembly`.

9 Click and drag the server component to `C:\WINNT\Assembly`.

10 Open the command prompt and go to the Client Applications deployment directory.

11 Run `SharedPhoto AlbumClient.exe`.

■ A message appears showing the properties set for the file.

VERSION A SHARED ASSEMBLY

You can version assemblies if you use shared assemblies. Versioning helps the CLR determine which physical class to load when an object request is made from a client application. Versioning of the same component enables you to manage distributing updates to applications without breaking clients.

You build version numbers from four sets of numbers that you separate by periods: Major, Minor, Revision, and Build Number. You configure the version number in the `AssemblyVersion` assembly-level attribute that you find in the `AssemblyInfo` file. To do so, you need to understand the compatibility between the two versions of the same component.

The numbered steps below enable you to create two versions of the same shared component. After you register each version, you see two rows for the component in the GAC, one for each version. Both lines look identical, except for the version number (one being 1.0.0.0 and the other being 2.0.0.0). Versioning in .NET allows for side-by-side execution of the same component, which gives the capability to have an instance of each version running at the same time on the same machine, which is a useful, new capability of the .NET platform.

VERSION A SHARED ASSEMBLY

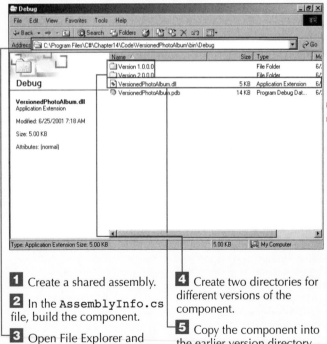

1 Create a shared assembly.

2 In the `AssemblyInfo.cs` file, build the component.

3 Open File Explorer and navigate to the `bin\Debug` directory.

4 Create two directories for different versions of the component.

5 Copy the component into the earlier version directory.

6 Open the `AssemblyInfo.cs` file.

7 Change the `AssemblyVersion` to a later version number.

Extra

You can determine different compatibility scenarios with the four sets of numbers that make up a version:

Incompatible — Change to the assembly making it incompatible with previous versions. Two versions are incompatible when the Major and Minor numbers between the two versions do not match.

Maybe Compatible — Change to the assembly that is thought to be compatible and carries less risk than an incompatible change. However, backward compatibility is not guaranteed. An example is a service pack or a release of a new daily build.

QFE (Quick Fix Engineering) — Engineering fix that customers must upgrade. An example is an emergency security fix. Does not impact compatibility.

If you install a new version of a shared component on your clients machine, the runtime determines if it can use the new version for calls from existing clients. For example, if you compile a client against a shared component with version 2.1.1.101, and then install a new version at a later date that has version 2.1.1.211, the client application uses the newer version 2.1.1.211 the next time it makes a request to load the assembly.

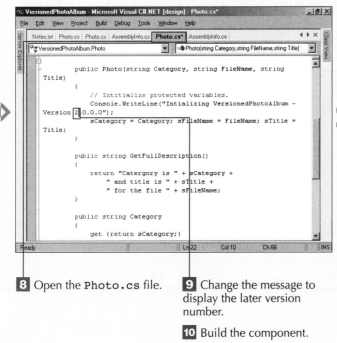

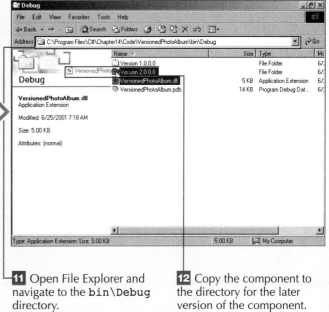

8 Open the `Photo.cs` file.

9 Change the message to display the later version number.

10 Build the component.

11 Open File Explorer and navigate to the `bin\Debug` directory.

12 Copy the component to the directory for the later version of the component.

CONFIGURE A CLIENT FOR A VERSIONED ASSEMBLY

You can utilize versioned assemblies to give your client applications an upgrade path for newer, optimized or enhanced components. With the versioning capabilities of .NET, you can use an assembly that has extended its members without the need to recompile. The *version binding policy* determines which version you need to use for a calling client to a shared assembly. The .NET runtime and/or the configuration file for the application determines what your client's version binding policy is. The configuration file can override the .NET runtime binding by setting the versioning in the `<bindingRedirect>` element of the `<runtime>` element.

The process of using a versioned assembly is not any different than what you do with an unversioned shared assembly. You just need to make sure that you select the correct version. Shared assemblies with multiple versions will have multiple entries with the same Global Assembly Name, but each entry for that Global Assembly Name will have a different number in the version column. For more information on shared assemblies, see page 260. To check that you have the right version, after you have made the reference, you can view the properties of the reference in the reference list in the project solution.

CONFIGURE A CLIENT FOR A VERSIONED ASSEMBLY

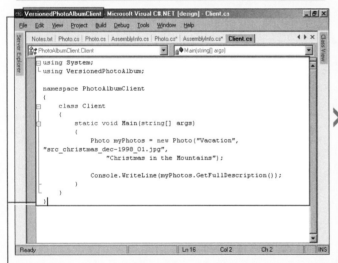

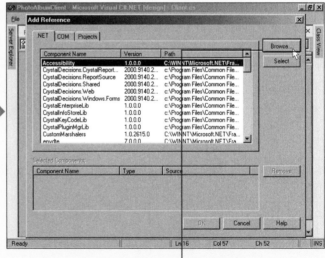

1 Create a new console application and open the `Class1.cs` file.

2 Add the implementation for a client application.

Note: See page 254 for more information about implementing a client.

3 Click Project ➪ Add Reference.

■ The Add Reference dialog box appears.

4 Click Browse.

Extra

To control the binding of a client to a versioned assembly that your client application uses, you can create a configuration file. The example shows how to use the configuration file to redirect the binding from one version to another version. For you to test the example with the code that is created in the numbered steps below, you will have to update the `publicKeyToken` to match the hash of the public key that you created on page 260.

EXAMPLE:
```
<configuration>
    <runtime>
        <assemblyBinding
            xmlns="urn:schemas-microsoft-
            com:asm.v1">
            <dependentAssembly>
                <assemblyIdentity name=
                "VersionedPhotoAlbum"
                    publicKeyToken=
                    "e79f3eb79bb2bf0a"
                    culture=""/>
                <bindingRedirect
                oldVersion= "1.0.0.0"
                    newVersion="2.0.0.0"/>
            </dependentAssembly>
        </assemblyBinding>
    </runtime>
</configuration>
```

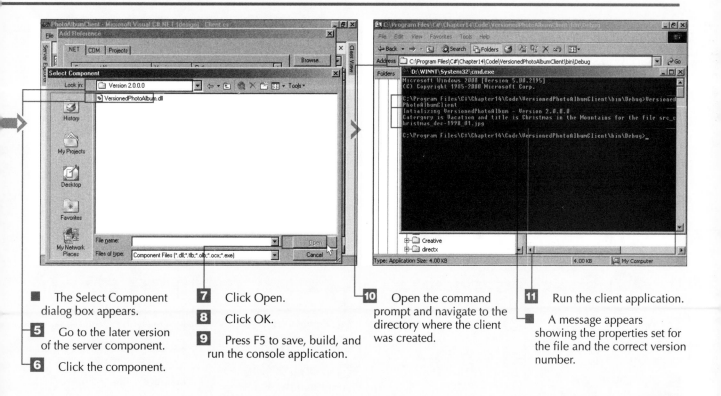

■ The Select Component dialog box appears.

5 Go to the later version of the server component.

6 Click the component.

7 Click Open.

8 Click OK.

9 Press F5 to save, build, and run the console application.

10 Open the command prompt and navigate to the directory where the client was created.

11 Run the client application.

■ A message appears showing the properties set for the file and the correct version number.

CREATE A WEB SERVICE

The next evolution of distributed programming, Web Services, allows for your applications to provide component-based services over the Internet. That is, you can call a .NET component from one machine on the Internet to another. Web Services are made available through standards like Simple Object Access Protocol (SOAP), eXtensible Markup Language (XML), and HyperText Transport Protocol (HTTP). This mechanism allows for calls to be made over known communication ports, like port 80, the standard port for HTTP. For Microsoft, Web Services are considered the basic building blocks for distributed applications.

Because Microsoft has a SOAP Toolkit that allows remote procedure calls on COM+ components over HTTP, you do

not need .NET or VS .NET for building Web services, but having VS .NET and .NET makes life much easier when you are creating or using a Web Service.

VS .NET has a project type of ASP.NET Web Service to assist in creating Web services. Creating a Web service involves the use of a few new file types, which you may not find familiar, including the `*.asmx` and `*.vsdisco`. When you first start creating Web services, you need to be primarily concerned with the `*.asmx` file. The `*.asmx` file is where you will place your Web methods. The syntax is similar to how you create methods in classes. The only major difference is the use of the attribute `WebMethod` for methods that need to be exposed by the Web service and the class must be derived from `system.Web.Services.WebService`.

CREATE A WEB SERVICE

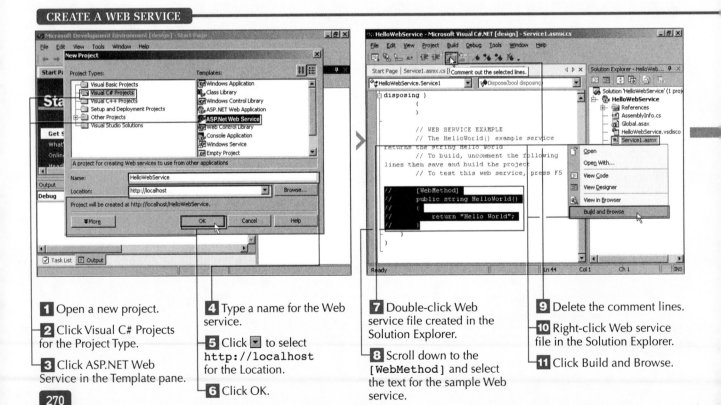

1 Open a new project.

2 Click Visual C# Projects for the Project Type.

3 Click ASP.NET Web Service in the Template pane.

4 Type a name for the Web service.

5 Click ⏷ to select `http://localhost` for the Location.

6 Click OK.

7 Double-click Web service file created in the Solution Explorer.

8 Scroll down to the [WebMethod] and select the text for the sample Web service.

9 Delete the comment lines.

10 Right-click Web service file in the Solution Explorer.

11 Click Build and Browse.

Apply It

The Web service that you created in the sample task was a simple "Hello World" for a Web service. If you want to go a step further, you can test out the below sample Web method. You will need to create a well-formed XML document, `Favorites1.xml`, in the same directory as the Web service file.

TYPE THIS:

```
using System.IO;
    [WebMethod]
    public string GetFavoritesList(int UserID) {
        string sServerPath = Server.MapPath("");
        // Here you could make a database call to get XML.
        string sFilePath = sServerPath+ "\\" + "Favorites1.xml";
        string sList = GetXMLAsString(sFilePath);
        return sList;
    }
    private string GetXMLAsString(string XMLDocumentPath) {
        FileStream fsFavorites = new FileStream
            (XMLDocumentPath,FileMode.Open,FileAccess.Read);

        StreamReader srFavorites = new
          StreamReader(fsFavorites);
        return srFavorites.ReadToEnd();
    }
```

RESULT:

The `xml` string in `favorites.xml` is returned from the `WebMethod`.

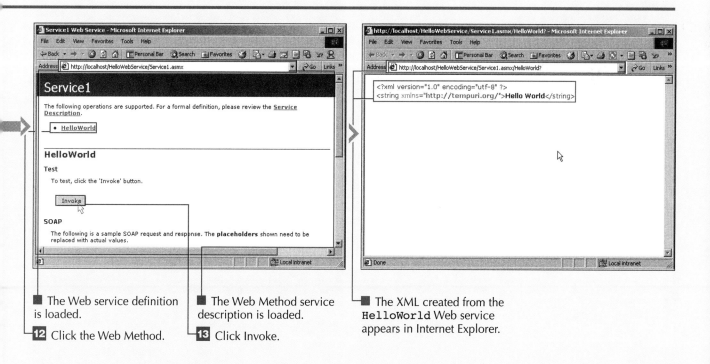

■ The Web service definition is loaded.

■ The Web Method service description is loaded.

■ The XML created from the **HelloWorld** Web service appears in Internet Explorer.

12 Click the Web Method.

13 Click Invoke.

USING A WEB SERVICE

By using a Web service in your client application or server application, you can utilize resources across the Internet and open up new possibilities of truly distributed architectures.

When you build an ASP.NET Web Service, it automatically supports clients using the SOAP, HTTP-GET, and HTTP-POST protocols to invoke Web Service methods. HTTP-GET and HTTP-POST send information via named value pairs, but do not allow for complex data types to be passed. However, SOAP, or Simple Object Access Protocol, allows for more complex data types to be passed due to SOAP's support of XML and XSD schemas.

Consuming a Web service is well supported in VS .NET, which includes a wizard-based approach to discovery and configuration of the proxy you need to make the SOAP call. The interface provided for discovering the Web service enables you to browse to the URL of the service. When you access the service, you can test the services from the interface, view WSDL (Web Services Description Language), contract, and view any documentation that exists. After you have a Web reference, you can import the namespace and then use it like a local component.

USING A WEB SERVICE

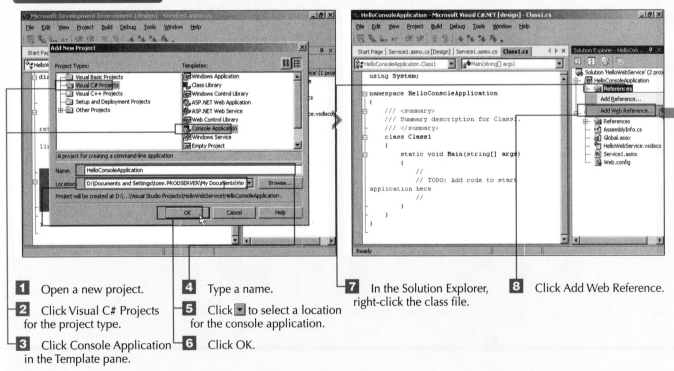

1 Open a new project.

2 Click Visual C# Projects for the project type.

3 Click Console Application in the Template pane.

4 Type a name.

5 Click ▼ to select a location for the console application.

6 Click OK.

7 In the Solution Explorer, right-click the class file.

8 Click Add Web Reference.

Extra

Heavily investing into the future of Web Services, one of Microsoft's current initiatives, HailStorm, addresses common programming needs such as personal profile information and contacts. Below is a list of some of the HailStorm Services.

HAILSTORM SERVICES	
myAddress	Electronic and geographic address for an identity
myProfile	Name, nickname, special dates, picture
myContacts	Electronic relationships/address book
myLocation	Electronic and geographical location and rendezvous
myNotifications	Notification subscription, management, and routing
myInbox	E-mail and voice mail, including existing mail systems
myCalendar	Time and task management
myDocuments	Raw document storage
myApplicationSettings	Application settings
myFavoriteWebSites	Favorite URLs and other Web identifiers
myWallet	Receipts, payment instruments, coupons, and other transaction records
myDevices	Device settings and capabilities
myServices	Services provided for an identity
myUsage	Usage report for above services

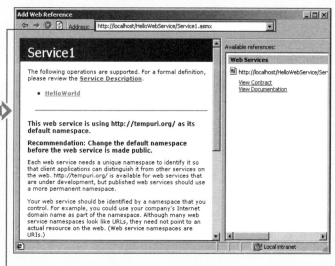

9 Type the URL to the Web Service.

Note: See page 270 for more information on creating a Web Service.

10 Click OK.

11 Open the class file.

12 Add an alias to the Web service namespace.

13 Rename the namespace to **HelloConsoleApplication**.

14 Create a new variable of type **Service1**.

15 Write the result of the call to the **WebMethod** to the console.

16 Set a debug stop.

17 Press F5.

■ The output to the console appears.

INTRODUCTION TO EXCEPTION HANDLING

All good applications have code to handle exceptions that occur during runtime. Writing applications that do not have error conditions is impossible, because you cannot always control the occurance of an exception. For example, if a user attempts to read a file off of a CD-ROM and the disc is not in the CD drive, an exception is passed back from the method used to read the file. The client code that called the object, which has the capability to perform file input/output, must respond to that exception. Responding to an exception is considered catching an exception and is done in `catch` blocks.

In your programs, you can write code to both handle and throw an exception that is handled by the calling client. It is proper to throw exceptions when the requesting client has made a request that can not be fufilled. You can decide to throw an exception because of several reasons. These can be due to, but not limited to, improper passed parameters that fail validation or if the request you make to another object throws an exception. You trust that the calling client wrote the call to your object within a `try` block and has placed the proper code to respond to the exception in a `catch` block.

Unified Exception Handling

Error handling in the .Net Platform is unified across all CLS (Common Language Specification) compliant languages. Exception handling in development efforts before .NET on the Microsoft Platform has taken different forms. Visual Basic has the `Err` Object that is used to pass error information between COM components. Visual C++ uses HRESULT's to pass error information. Also, some developers have used the method returns for error codes and come up with a custom error library that describes the meaning of each return code.

The .NET Platform unifies the approach to handling errors with structured exception handling. An exception occurs when an executing program encounters any unexpected behavior or error condition. The root of an exception can occur from the runtime (CLR) or can be raised from code in the executing program. The error/exception information that is passed within and between components is contained in a System Framework class which is System.Exception.

Exception Framework Class

The System.Exception class helps you work with errors that occur in your application. The table describes the most common members of this class.

The System.Exception class is the base class for all exceptions. The runtime handles exceptions without regard for the language that generated the exception. Each language has its own syntax for working with exceptions, but that syntax works with the same framework class. When an exception occurs, the exception is passed up the stack until it is handled. If the exception is not handled, the program terminates.

There is an exception information table for each executable supported by the runtime. Each method of that executable has an associated array of exception handling information in this table. This exception table is extremely efficient and virtually has no affect on performance. If the exception does not occur, then no performance penalty occurs. The processing overhead is only realized when the exception occurs.

THE SYSTEM.EXCEPTION CORE MEMBERS	
PROPERTY	DESCRIPTION
HelpLink	(read/write) URL to further error information
InnerException	(read) for referencing the inner exception, allow preservation of error hierarchy
Message	(read) text description of the current error
Source	(read/write) string that identifies the source that generated the error
StackTrace	(read) string that contains the sequence of events that lead to the error
TargetSite	(read) method that originated the error

Basics of Working with Exceptions

You can properly implement exception handling by understanding the basics of how exceptions are handled in the flow of your code. The basics of exception flow are the following:

When an exception occurs, the exception is passed up the stack and each catch block is given the opportunity to handle the exception. To be caught by the same catch block of the procedure, the exception must be thrown within a try block of that procedure, otherwise the exception is raise up the stack to the next catch block. The order of catch statements is important. You need to place catch blocks targeted to specific exceptions before a general exception catch block, or

the compiler will issue an error. The proper catch block is determined by matching the type of the exception to the name of the exception specified in the catch block. If there is no specific catch block, then the exception is caught by a general catch block, if one exists.

To aid the troubleshooting process of the current developer or any other developers that use your code, you can write error information that is as detailed as possible and targeted to a developer. Also, make sure that you cleanup intermediate results when throwing an exception. Your callers will assume that you threw the exception back through the stack after you resolved the error (for example, rolling back database changes).

Exception Handling Model

You can safely run code in the CLR by creating programs that handle exceptions. The runtime has an exception handling model that uses protected blocks of

code to control execution flow. The basic structure of these blocks of code for the C# syntax are in the following sample:

```
try
{
// Run code that has the potential to throw exceptions
}
catch (Exception e)
{
    // Run code that will generically handle the caught exception
}
finally
{
    // Run cleanup code (runs with or without exception occurring)
}
```

THROWING AN EXCEPTION

You can pass error information back to a calling client with exceptions. You raise exceptions by using the `throw` statement. If this thrown exception is in a `try` block, the execution passes to the appropriate `catch` block (see page 280 for details). If the exception is not in a `try` block, then exception is raised to the caller. If the caller has not made the call with `try/catch` blocks, then the exception is raised to the next caller on the stack until it is handled or leaves the application unhandled (which is not a good thing).

You can purposely throw errors programmatically in code when logical errors occur in your program. Also, you can

throw an error after an exception has been caught. When rethrowing the error, you can either insert custom error information to the exception or choose to overwrite the error information with a custom error string.

If an exception enters a `catch` block, the exception is considered to be handled and stops rising up the call stack. If you are in a `catch` block, you are able to give a `throw` statement with no expression, which will re-throw the exception that caused the entry into the `catch` block. Or, you can throw an exception that has custom information.

THROWING AN EXCEPTION

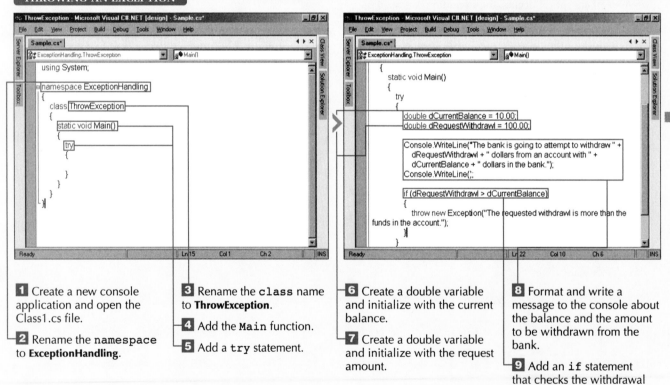

■ **1** Create a new console application and open the Class1.cs file.

■ **2** Rename the `namespace` to **ExceptionHandling**.

■ **3** Rename the `class` name to **ThrowException**.

■ **4** Add the `Main` function.

■ **5** Add a `try` statement.

■ **6** Create a double variable and initialize with the current balance.

■ **7** Create a double variable and initialize with the request amount.

■ **8** Format and write a message to the console about the balance and the amount to be withdrawn from the bank.

■ **9** Add an `if` statement that checks the withdrawal against the balance and throws an exception if the withdrawal is greater than the balance.

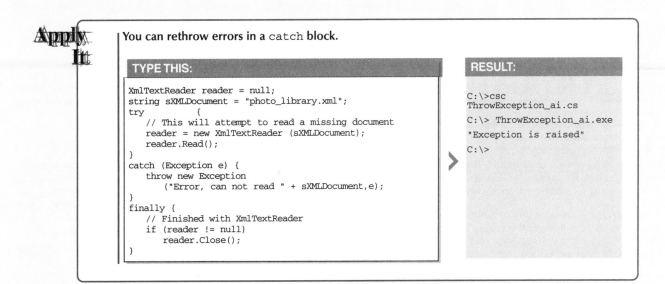

Apply It

You can rethrow errors in a `catch` block.

TYPE THIS:

```
XmlTextReader reader = null;
string sXMLDocument = "photo_library.xml";
try         {
    // This will attempt to read a missing document
    reader = new XmlTextReader (sXMLDocument);
    reader.Read();
}
catch (Exception e) {
    throw new Exception
        ("Error, can not read " + sXMLDocument,e);
}
finally {
    // Finished with XmlTextReader
    if (reader != null)
        reader.Close();
}
```

RESULT:

```
C:\>csc
ThrowException_ai.cs
C:\> ThrowException_ai.exe
"Exception is raised"
C:\>
```

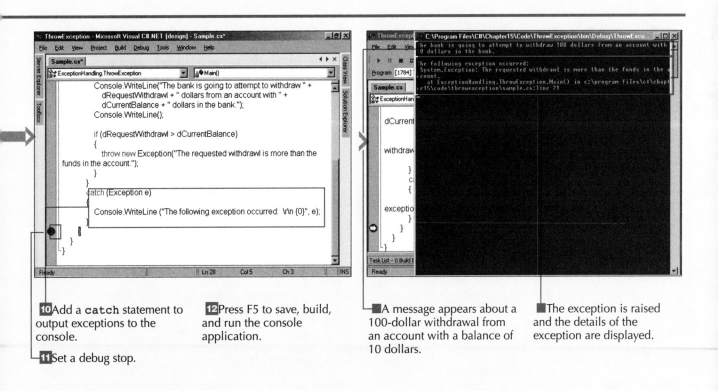

■10 Add a **catch** statement to output exceptions to the console.

■11 Set a debug stop.

■12 Press F5 to save, build, and run the console application.

■ A message appears about a 100-dollar withdrawal from an account with a balance of 10 dollars.

■ The exception is raised and the details of the exception are displayed.

EXECUTING CODE USING THE TRY/CATCH BLOCKS

You can produce production-level code by incorporating thorough exception handling. Having an unhandled error exit an application causes an application to terminate. Unhandled errors are not a user-friendly feature for an application; therefore, you should use try/catch blocks to properly handle exceptions.

Some current error-handling techniques pass back errors in the return of a method. If this is your current practice, you should instead throw exceptions and use try/catch blocks to properly manage any exceptions that occur.

Using a try/catch block is fairly simple. Inside a procedure, you can place any code that generates an exception in a try block and place any code that needs executing to handle that exception in a catch block. The catch block can consist of one or more catch clauses (see page 280 for further detail on how these catch clauses are examined). Optionally, you can have a finally block that will run after the try succeeds or the catch block finishes handling an exception (see page 282 for further details on when and how to use finally blocks).

EXECUTING CODE USING THE TRY/CATCH BLOCKS

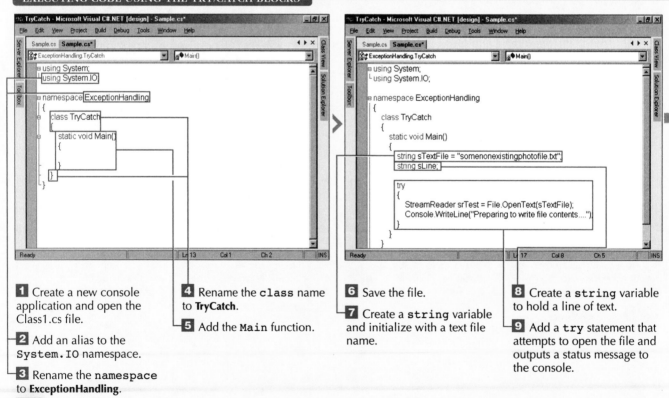

1 Create a new console application and open the Class1.cs file.

2 Add an alias to the System.IO namespace.

3 Rename the **namespace** to **ExceptionHandling**.

4 Rename the **class** name to **TryCatch**.

5 Add the **Main** function.

6 Save the file.

7 Create a **string** variable and initialize with a text file name.

8 Create a **string** variable to hold a line of text.

9 Add a **try** statement that attempts to open the file and outputs a status message to the console.

`Try/catch` **blocks are necessary for a stable application. Compile the following code and note how it responds to the missing file. There is an exception thrown by the** `StreamReader` **object and it is not handled in the below client code.**

TYPE THIS:

```
using System; using System.IO;
namespace ExceptionHandling {
    class TryCatch {
        static void Main() {
            string sTextFile = "somenonexistingtextfile.txt";
            String sLine;

            StreamReader srTest = File.OpenText(sTextFile);
            Console.WriteLine("Preparing to write file
contents....");

            while ((sLine=srTest.ReadLine()) != null)
                Console.WriteLine(sLine);
}}}
```

RESULT:

```
C:\>csc TryCatch_ai.cs

C:\> TryCatch_ai.exe

"Message for System.IO.
FileNotFoundException occurs"

C:\>
```

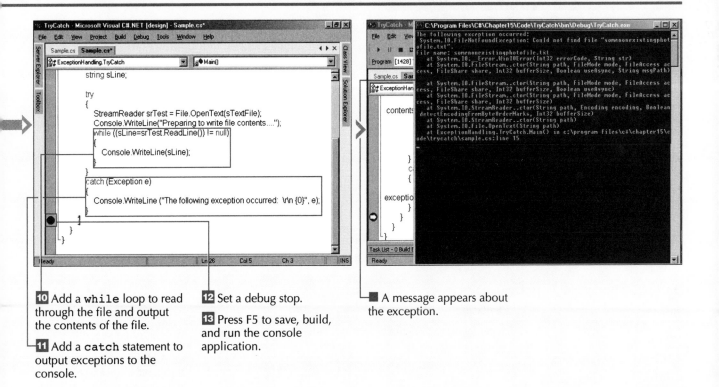

10 Add a **while** loop to read through the file and output the contents of the file.

11 Add a **catch** statement to output exceptions to the console.

12 Set a debug stop.

13 Press F5 to save, build, and run the console application.

■ A message appears about the exception.

HANDLING EXCEPTIONS WITH THE CATCH BLOCK

You can handle thrown exceptions with a `catch` block. You can insert a `try/catch` in all your procedures and just format a message to the user with the error that occurred. Just formating the current exception into a message will keep your application from terminating, but it will create a frustrated user. To keep a content application user, you want to do more that just display the current error. At a minimum you should trap for common errors and display a custom message that your user can understand.

The granularity of the exception handling determines how polished your final application is and it has a large impact on the usability of the application. Errors happen

in your application, and the way they are handled is key to a good application.

To take exception handling further, you need to handle common exceptions that you know can occur. For example, the sample task below will take you through an example that is doing file access. One of the known issues with file access is attempting to access a file that does not exist. In the case of code that does file access, you want a `catch` block that explicitly handles the exception generated from a missing file. Inside of that `catch` block you write code that will collect the relative information about the failed attempt and then log that information and/or pass the information up the call stack while throwing an exception.

HANDLING EXCEPTIONS WITH THE CATCH BLOCK

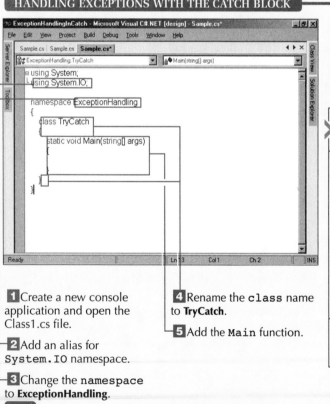

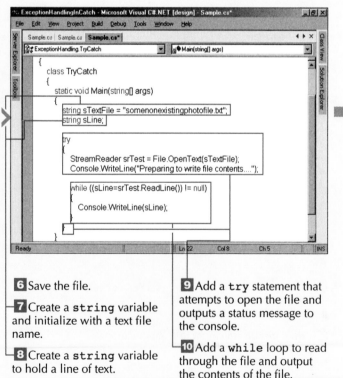

1 Create a new console application and open the Class1.cs file.

2 Add an alias for `System.IO` namespace.

3 Change the `namespace` to **ExceptionHandling**.

4 Rename the `class` name to **TryCatch**.

5 Add the `Main` function.

6 Save the file.

7 Create a `string` variable and initialize with a text file name.

8 Create a `string` variable to hold a line of text.

9 Add a `try` statement that attempts to open the file and outputs a status message to the console.

10 Add a `while` loop to read through the file and output the contents of the file.

Extra

Catch blocks can be implemented several ways. Below are several sample catch blocks and a brief explanation of what each one does.

Example:
```
// Sample 1 - Handles all
// exception, execution continues
catch
{
}
```

Example:
```
// Sample 2 - Essentially same as 1
catch (Exception e)
{
}
```

Example:
```
// Sample 3 - Rethrows exception e
catch (Exception e)
{
throw (e);
}
```

Example:
```
// Sample 4 - Handles only one
// specific error (all others
// will not be handled)
catch (StackOverflowException e)
{
}
```

Example:
```
// Sample 5 - Handles a specific
// error and all others go to the
// general catch statement
catch (StackOverflowException e)
{
}
catch (Exception e)
{
}
```

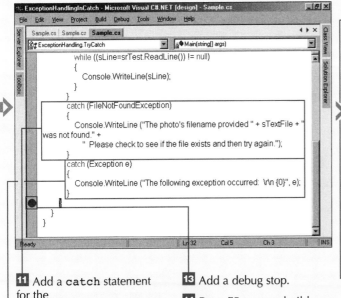

11 Add a catch statement for the **FileNotFoundException** and output an appropriate message if the exception was raised.

12 Add a catch statement to output exceptions to the console.

13 Add a debug stop.

14 Press F5 to save, build, and run the console application.

■ The **FileNotFound Exception** is raised and the message for this exception is displayed.

USING THE FINALLY BLOCK

You can run common code that needs to execute after a try/catch block by placing the code in an optional finally block. The finally block is handy for running code that cleans up object reference and any other cleanup code that needs to run after the try and/or catch blocks. The cleanup code in the finally block can be closing a file or a connection to a database.

Finally, blocks will run no matter if an exception occurs or does not occur. You will want to place the finally block after the try and catch blocks. Note that the finally block will always execute, except for unhandled errors like

exceptions outside of the try/catch blocks or a run-time error inside the catch block.

There are cases where you might release or close resources in your try block. If this is the case, you need to validate that this has happened before closing out the resource again. Checking to see if a resource is close is necessary, because you can sometimes generate an exception if you reattempt to close a resource that is already close. To check to see if the resource is already released or not, you can check to see if the object is null (if (object != null) { object.Close();}).

USING THE FINALLY BLOCK

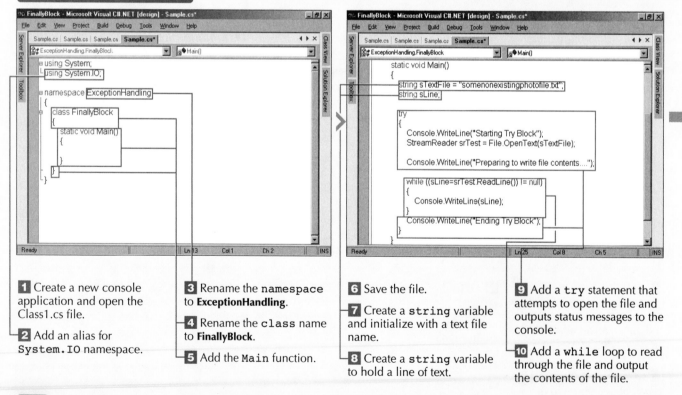

1 Create a new console application and open the Class1.cs file.

2 Add an alias for System.IO namespace.

3 Rename the **namespace** to **ExceptionHandling**.

4 Rename the **class** name to **FinallyBlock**.

5 Add the Main function.

6 Save the file.

7 Create a **string** variable and initialize with a text file name.

8 Create a **string** variable to hold a line of text.

9 Add a **try** statement that attempts to open the file and outputs status messages to the console.

10 Add a **while** loop to read through the file and output the contents of the file.

Extra

Data access code will most likely always be in `try/catch/finally` blocks. If you compile this sample and run it twice, you will generate a primary key constraint error.

Example:
```
SqlConnection cnPubs = new SqlConnection();
SqlCommand cmdTitles = new SqlCommand();
try {
    cnPubs.ConnectionString =
        "server=(local);uid=sa;pwd=;database=pubs";
    cnPubs.Open();
    String sInsertCmd =
        "INSERT INTO titles(title_id, title) " +
        "VALUES('BU2222','Book Title')";
    cmdTitles.Connection = cnPubs;
    cmdTitles.CommandText = sInsertCmd;
    cmdTitles.ExecuteNonQuery();   }
catch (Exception e){
    Console.WriteLine
        ("Exception occurred:  \r\n {0}", e);}
finally {
    cmdTitles.Connection.Close();
    Console.WriteLine("Cleanup Code Executed");
```

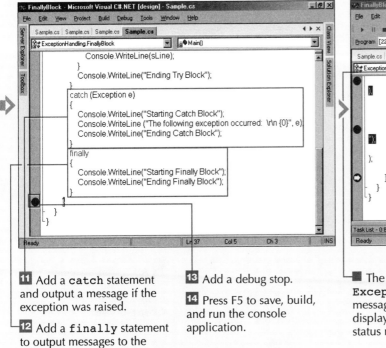

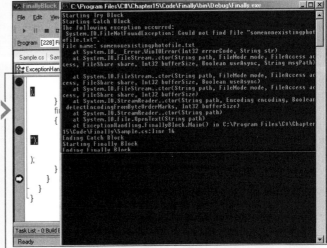

11 Add a **catch** statement and output a message if the exception was raised.

12 Add a **finally** statement to output messages to the console.

13 Add a debug stop.

14 Press F5 to save, build, and run the console application.

■ The **FileNotFound Exception** is raised and the message for this exception is displayed, along with several status messages.

WRITE ERRORS TO THE APPLICATION LOG

When working with exceptions, there are cases where you want to persist the error/exception information to a durable store. You can persist errors by using the Event Log that is built into the Windows NT and 2000 operating systems. If you log error/exception information, you can analyze a reoccurring problem and understand the sequence of events that occur to cause the problem. Logging to the Event Log allows you to perform some troubleshooting without having to run the application in a debug mode.

To access the Event Log, you will have to use the `System.Diagnostics` namespace. With this referenced,

you can create an event log source which will give context to the entries that you write to the Event Log (source name for application and which log you want to write to – Application, Security, System, or a custom event log). With that Event Log object you will call the `WriteEntry` method to put entries into the event log. When writing errors to the log, you will want to classify the severity of the error. These severities will affect what icon and type classification the error is given in the event viewer.

The task below will take you through the basic steps of setting up and logging to an Event Log.

WRITE ERRORS TO THE APPLICATION LOG

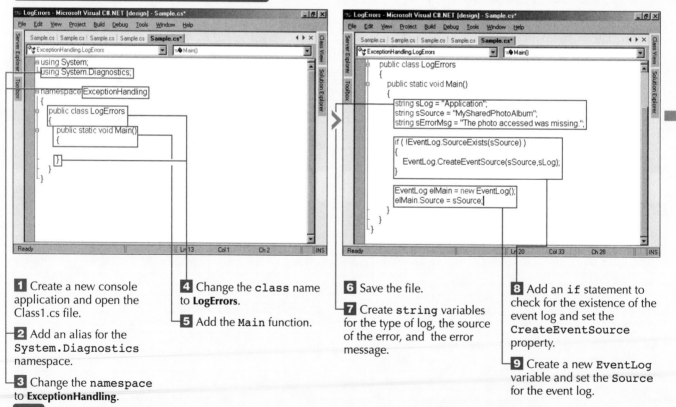

1 Create a new console application and open the Class1.cs file.

2 Add an alias for the `System.Diagnostics` namespace.

3 Change the **namespace** to **ExceptionHandling**.

4 Change the **class** name to **LogErrors**.

5 Add the **Main** function.

6 Save the file.

7 Create **string** variables for the type of log, the source of the error, and the error message.

8 Add an **if** statement to check for the existence of the event log and set the **CreateEventSource** property.

9 Create a new **EventLog** variable and set the **Source** for the event log.

Extra

You can control the severity for entries that you place in the Application Error Log. After running this sample, open the Event Viewer and note that each one has a different severity and each severity has a different icon.

Example:
```
string sLog = "Application";
string sSource = "MySharedPhotoAlbum";
string sErrorMsg1 = "Message for Information.";
string sErrorMsg2 = "Message for Error.";
string sErrorMsg3 = "Message for Warning.";

if ( !EventLog.SourceExists(sSource) ) {
    EventLog.CreateEventSource(sSource,sLog); }
EventLog elMain = new EventLog();
elMain.Source = sSource;

if ( elMain.Log.ToUpper() != sLog.ToUpper() ){
    Console.WriteLine
        ("Source is not available to use!");
    return;}
elMain.WriteEntry(sErrorMsg1,EventLogEntryType.Information);
elMain.WriteEntry(sErrorMsg2,EventLogEntryType.Error);
elMain.WriteEntry(sErrorMsg3,EventLogEntryType.Warning);
```

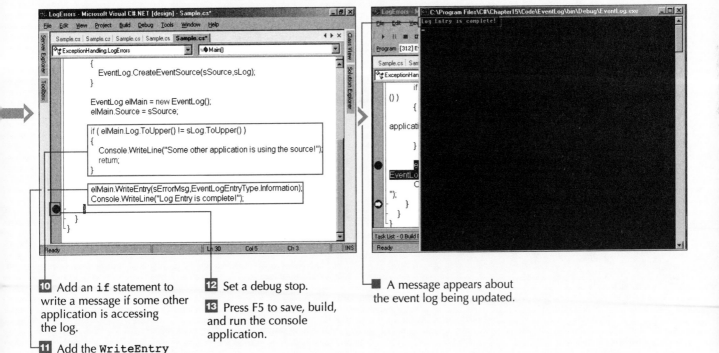

10 Add an **if** statement to write a message if some other application is accessing the log.

11 Add the **WriteEntry** function to write the details of the log entry and write a message to the console about the update being successful.

12 Set a debug stop.

13 Press F5 to save, build, and run the console application.

■ A message appears about the event log being updated.

APPENDIX

BASIC EXAMPLES

DECLARING VARIABLES

Visual Basic	C#	JScript
| ```
Dim x As Integer
Dim x As Integer = 10
``` | ```
int x;
int x = 10;
``` | ```
var x : int;
var x : int = 10;
``` |

COMMENTS

Visual Basic	C#	JScript
| ```
' comment
x = 1      ' comment
Rem comment
``` | ```
// comment
/* multiline
 comment */
``` | ```
// comment
/* multiline
 comment */
``` |

ASSIGNMENT STATEMENTS

Visual Basic	C#	JScript
| ```
nVal = 7
``` | ```
nVal = 7;
``` | ```
nVal = 7;
``` |

IF...ELSE STATEMENTS

Visual Basic
```
If nCnt <= nMax Then
    nTotal += nCnt   ' Same as nTotal = nTotal + nCnt
    nCnt += 1        ' Same as nCnt = nCnt + 1
Else
    nTotal += nCnt
    nCnt -= 1
End If
```

C#
```
if (nCnt <= nMax)
{
    nTotal += nCnt;
    nCnt++;
}
else {
    nTotal += nCnt;
    nCnt --;
 }
```

JScript
```
if(nCnt < nMax) {
    nTotal += nCnt;
    nCnt ++;
 }
else {
    nTotal += nCnt;
    nCnt --;
 };
```
```

CASE STATEMENTS

Visual Basic
```
Select Case n
    Case 0
        MsgBox ("Zero")
'       Visual Basic exits the Select at the end of a Case.
    Case 1
        MsgBox ("One")
    Case 2
        MsgBox ("Two")
    Case Else
        MsgBox ("Default")
End Select
```

C#
```
    switch(n) {
    case 0:
        MessageBox.Show("Zero");
        break;
    case 1:
        MessageBox.Show("One");
        break;
    case 2:
        MessageBox.Show("Two");
        break;
    default:
        MessageBox.Show("?");
    }
```

JScript
```
switch(n) {
    case 0 :
        MessageBox.Show("Zero");
        break;
    case 1 :
        MessageBox.Show("One");
        break;
    case 2 :
        MessageBox.Show("Two");
    default :
        MessageBox.Show("Default");
}
```

FOR LOOPS

Visual Basic
```
For n = 1 To 10
    MsgBox("The number is " & n)
Next
For Each i In iArray
    Box.Show(i)
Next i Msg
```

C#
```
for (int i = 1; i <= 10; i++)
    MessageBox.Show("The number is {0}", i);
foreach (int i in iArray)
{
    MessageBox.Show (i.ToString());
}
```

JScript
```
for (var n = 0; n < 10; n++) {
    Response.Write("The number is " + n);
}
for (prop in obj){
obj[prop] = 42;
}
```

BASIC EXAMPLES

WHILE LOOPS

Visual Basic
```
While n < 100 ' Test at start of loop
    n += 1       ' Same as n = n + 1
End While '
```

C#
```
while (n < 100)
    n++;
```

JScript
```
while (n < 100) {
    n++; }
```

PARAMETER PASSING BY VALUE

Visual Basic
```
Public Sub ABC(ByVal y As Long) ' The argument Y is
    passed by value.
' If ABC changes y, the changes do not affect x.
End Sub
ABC(x) ' Call the procedure
```

You can force parameters to be passed by value, regardless of how they are declared, by enclosing the parameters in extra parentheses.
```
ABC((x))
```

C#
```
// The method:
void ABC(int x)
{
    ...
}
// Calling the method:
ABC(i);
```

JScript
```
ABC(i,j);
```

PARAMETER PASSING BY REFERENCE

Visual Basic
```
Public Sub ABC(ByRef y As Long) ' The parameter of ABC is declared by reference:
' If ABC changes y, the changes are made to the value of x.
End Sub
ABC(x) ' Call the procedure
```

C#
```
// The method:
void ABC(ref int x)
{
    ...
}
// Calling the method:
ABC(ref i);
```

JScript

N/A (objects (including arrays) are passed by reference, but the object to which the variable refers to cannot be changed in the caller). Properties and methods changed in the callee are visible to the caller.

```
/* Reference parameters are supported for external object, but not internal JScript functions */
comPlusObject.SomeMethod(&foo);
```

STRUCTURED EXCEPTION HANDLING

Visual Basic
```
Try
    If x = 0 Then
        Throw New Exception("x equals zero")
    Else
        Throw New Exception("x does not equal zero")
    End If
Catch
    MessageBox.Show("Error: " & Err.Description)
Finally
    MessageBox.Show("Executing finally block.")
End Try
```

JScript
```
try {
    if (x == 0) {
        throw new Error(513, "x equals zero");
    }
    else {
        throw new Error(514, "x does not equal zero");
    }
}
catch(e) {
    Response.Write("Error number: " + e.number + "<BR>");
    Response.Write("Error description: " + e.message + "<BR>");
}
finally {
    Response.Write("Executing finally block.");
}
```

C#
```
// try-catch-finally
try
{
    if (x == 0)
        throw new System.Exception ("x equals zero");
    else
        throw new System.Exception ("x does not equal zero");
}
catch (System.Exception err)
{
    System.Console.WriteLine(err.Message);
}
finally
{
    System.Console.WriteLine("executing finally block");
}
```

SET AN OBJECT REFERENCE TO NOTHING

Visual Basic	**C#**	**JScript**
o = Nothing	o = null;	o = null;

WHAT'S ON THE CD-ROM

The CD-ROM disc included in this book contains many useful files and programs. Before installing any of the programs on the disc, make sure that a newer version of the program is not already installed on your computer. For information on installing different versions of the same program, contact the program's manufacturer.

SYSTEM REQUIREMENTS

To use the contents of the CD-ROM, your computer must be equipped with the following hardware and software:

- A PC with a 450-MHz Pentium II or faster processor.
- Microsoft Windows NT 4.0 or Windows 2000.
- At least 128MB of total RAM installed on your computer.
- At least 3 GB of hard drive space for OS and related software for the .NET Platform.
- A CD-ROM drive.
- A monitor capable of displaying at least 800 by 600 pixels (super VGA resolution) with 256 colors.
- A modem with a speed of at least 14,400 bps.

AUTHOR'S SOURCE CODE

For Windows 2000. These files contain all the sample code from the book. You can browse these files directly from the CD-ROM, or you can copy them to your hard drive and use them as the basis for your own projects. To find the files on the CD-ROM, open the D:\RESOURCES\CODE.EXE. To copy the files to your hard drive, just run the installation program D:\RESOURCES\CODE.EXE. The files will be placed on your hard drive at C:\ProgramFiles\CSHARP. After installation, you can access the files fromthe START menu. You will need to have the .NET framework installed on the machine in order to run the samples.

ACROBAT VERSION

The CD-ROM contains an e-version of this book that you can view and search using Adobe Acrobat Reader. You can also use the hyperlinks provided in the text to access all Web pages and Internet references in the book. You cannot print the pages or copy text from the Acrobat files. An evaluation version of Adobe Acrobat Reader is also included on the disc. If you do not currently have Adobe Acrobat Reader 5 installed, the computer will prompt you to install the software.

INSTALLING AND USING THE SOFTWARE

For your convenience, the software titles appearing on the CD-ROM are listed alphabetically.

You can download updates to the software and important links related to the source code at http://www.threewill.com/authoring/.

Program Versions

Shareware programs are fully functional, free trial versions of copyrighted programs. If you like a particular program, you can register with its author for a nominal fee and receive licenses, enhanced versions, and technical support.

Freeware programs are free, copyrighted games, applications, and utilities. You can copy them to as many computers as you like, but they have no techical support.

GNU software is governed by its own license, which is included inside the folder of the GNU software. There are no restrictions on distribution of this software. See the GNU license for more details.

Trial, demo, or evaluation versions are usually limited either by time or functionality. For example, you may not be able to save projects using these versions.

For your convenience, the software titles on the CD are listed in alphabetic order.

Acrobat Reader

Freeware. Acrobat Reader lets you view the online version of this book. For more information on using Adobe Acrobat Reader, see the following appendix. From Adobe Systems, www.adobe.com.

Antechinus C# Programming Editor

Shareware. The Antechinus C# Programming Editor from C Point Pty. Ltd. is an alternate graphic programming environment for creating and testing C# programs. You can find more information at www.c-point.com.

ASPEdit 2000

Demo version. ASPEdit is an Active Server Pages and HTML code editor so you can edit HTML and Microsoft Active Server Pages code in a graphic programming environment. From Tashcom Software, www.tashcom.com.

Internet Explorer

Freeware. Microsoft Internet Explorer is the most popular World Wide Web browser for Windows. You need Internet Explorer to access the Microsoft Web site when you need help with C#. From Microsoft, www.adobe.com.

MineC#weeper

Freeware. A sample application based on the Microsoft game Minesweeper that comes with full source code so you can see how you can use C# to program applications. You can download this application when you sign up for the Developer Express beta program. From Developer Express, www.devexpress.com.

TextPad

Shareware. TextPad is a general-purpose text editor for many different text files including C# code and HTML code. From Helios Software Solutions, www.textpad.com.

VMware Workstation

Trial version. VMWare Workstations lets you create virtual desktop environments on one computer so you can test how your C# programs run in different operating systems. From VMware, www.vmware.com.

XPressSideBar

Freeware. A sample application that emulates the look and feel of the side navigation bar popularized with Microsoft Outlook. This application comes with full source code so you can see how you can use C# to program applications. You can download this application when you sign up for the Developer Express beta program. From Developer Express, www.devexpress.com.

XtraGrid

Freeware. An application that lets you create and edit grids such as those you find in spreadsheet tables. XtraGrid lets you enter and manipulate data in grid form for integration into C# programs. From Developer Express, www.devexpress.com.

TROUBLESHOOTING

We tried our best to compile programs that work on most computers with the minimum system requirements. Your computer, however, may differ and some programs may not work properly for some reason.

The two most likely problems are that you don't have enough memory (RAM) for the programs you want to use, or you have other programs running that are affecting installation or running of a program. If you get error messages like `Not enough memory` or `Setup cannot continue`, try one or more of these methods and then try using the software again:

- Turn off any anti-virus software.
- Close all running programs.
- In Windows, close the CD-ROM interface and run demos or installations directly from Windows Explorer.
- Have your local computer store add more RAM to your computer.

If you still have trouble installing the items from the CD-ROM, please call the Hungry Minds Customer Service phone number: 800-762-2974.

USING THE E-VERSION OF THIS BOOK

You can view *C#: Your visual blueprint for building .NET applications* on your screen using the CD-ROM disc included at the back of this book. The CD-ROM disc allows you to search the contents of each chapter of the book for a specific word or phrase. The CD-ROM disc also provides a convenient way of keeping the book handy while traveling.

You must install Adobe Acrobat Reader on your computer before you can view the book on the

CD-ROM disc. This program is provided on the disc. Acrobat Reader allows you to view Portable Document Format (PDF) files, which can display books and magazines on your screen exactly as they appear in printed form.

To view the contents of the book using Acrobat Reader, display the contents of the disc. Double-click the PDFs folder to display the contents of the folder. In the window that appears, double-click the icon for the chapter of the book you want to review.

USING THE E-VERSION OF THIS BOOK

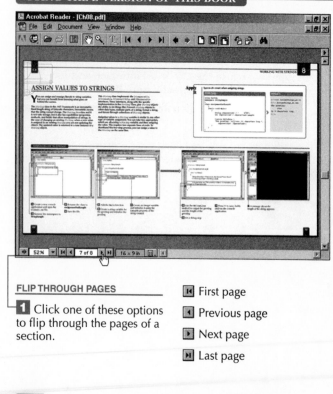

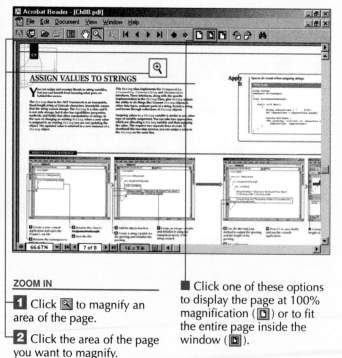

FLIP THROUGH PAGES

1 Click one of these options to flip through the pages of a section.

◄ First page

◄ Previous page

► Next page

► Last page

ZOOM IN

1 Click 🔍 to magnify an area of the page.

2 Click the area of the page you want to magnify.

■ Click one of these options to display the page at 100% magnification (🔲) or to fit the entire page inside the window (🔲).

Extra

To install Acrobat Reader, insert the CD-ROM disc into a drive. In the screen that appears, click Software. Click Acrobat Reader and then click Install at the bottom of the screen. Then follow the instructions on your screen to install the program.

You can make searching the book more convenient by copying the .pdf files to your own computer. Display the contents of the CD-ROM disc and then copy the PDFs folder from the CD to your hard drive. This allows you to easily access the contents of the book at any time.

Acrobat Reader is a popular and useful program. There are many files available on the Web that are designed to be viewed using Acrobat Reader. Look for files with the .pdf extension. For more information about Acrobat Reader, visit the Web site at www.adobe.com/products/acrobat/readermain.html.

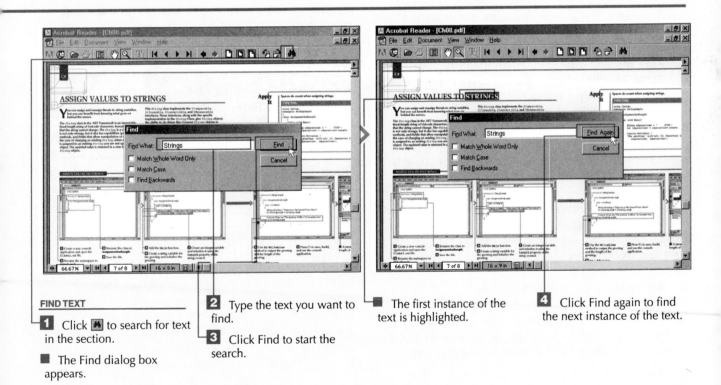

FIND TEXT

1 Click 🔍 to search for text in the section.

■ The Find dialog box appears.

2 Type the text you want to find.

3 Click Find to start the search.

■ The first instance of the text is highlighted.

4 Click Find again to find the next instance of the text.

APPENDIX

HUNGRY MINDS, INC.
END-USER LICENSE AGREEMENT

READ THIS. You should carefully read these terms and conditions before opening the software packet(s) included with this book ("Book"). This is a license agreement ("Agreement") between you and Hungry Minds, Inc. ("HMI"). By opening the accompanying software packet(s), you acknowledge that you have read and accept the following terms and conditions. If you do not agree and do not want to be bound by such terms and conditions, promptly return the Book and the unopened software packet(s) to the place you obtained them for a full refund.

1. License Grant. HMI grants to you (either an individual or entity) a nonexclusive license to use one copy of the enclosed software program(s) (collectively, the "Software") solely for your own personal or business purposes on a single computer (whether a standard computer or a workstation component of a multi-user network). The Software is in use on a computer when it is loaded into temporary memory (RAM) or installed into permanent memory (hard disk, CD-ROM, or other storage device). HMI reserves all rights not expressly granted herein.

2. Ownership. HMI is the owner of all right, title, and interest, including copyright, in and to the compilation of the Software recorded on the disk(s) or CD-ROM ("Software Media"). Copyright to the individual programs recorded on the Software Media is owned by the author or other authorized copyright owner of each program. Ownership of the Software and all proprietary rights relating thereto remain with HMI and its licensers.

3. Restrictions On Use and Transfer.

(a) You may only (i) make one copy of the Software for backup or archival purposes, or (ii) transfer the Software to a single hard disk, provided that you keep the original for backup or archival purposes. You may not (i) rent or lease the Software, (ii) copy or reproduce the Software through a LAN or other network system or through any computer subscriber system or bulletin-board system, or (iii) modify, adapt, or create derivative works based on the Software.

(b) You may not reverse engineer, decompile, or disassemble the Software. You may transfer the Software and user documentation on a permanent basis, provided that the transferee agrees to accept the terms and conditions of this Agreement and you retain no copies. If the Software is an update or has been updated, any transfer must include the most recent update and all prior versions.

4. Restrictions on Use of Individual Programs. You must follow the individual requirements and restrictions detailed for each individual program in the What's on the CD-ROM appendix of this Book. These limitations are also contained in the individual license agreements recorded on the Software Media. These limitations may include a requirement that after using the program for a specified period of time, the user must pay a registration fee or discontinue use. By opening the Software packet(s), you will be agreeing to abide by the licenses and restrictions for these individual programs that are detailed in the What's on the CD-ROM appendix and on the Software Media. None of the material on this Software Media or listed in this Book may ever be redistributed, in original or modified form, for commercial purposes.

5. Limited Warranty.

(a) HMI warrants that the Software and Software Media are free from defects in materials and workmanship under normal use for a period of sixty (60) days from the date of purchase of this Book. If HMI receives notification within the warranty period of defects in materials or workmanship, HMI will replace the defective Software Media.

(b) HMI AND THE AUTHOR OF THE BOOK DISCLAIM ALL OTHER WARRANTIES, EXPRESS OR IMPLIED, INCLUDING WITHOUT LIMITATION IMPLIED WARRANTIES OF MERCHANTABILITY AND FITNESS FOR A PARTICULAR PURPOSE, WITH RESPECT TO THE SOFTWARE, THE PROGRAMS, THE SOURCE CODE CONTAINED THEREIN, AND/OR THE TECHNIQUES DESCRIBED IN THIS BOOK. HMI DOES NOT WARRANT THAT THE FUNCTIONS CONTAINED IN THE SOFTWARE WILL MEET YOUR REQUIREMENTS OR THAT THE OPERATION OF THE SOFTWARE WILL BE ERROR FREE.

(c) This limited warranty gives you specific legal rights, and you may have other rights that vary from jurisdiction to jurisdiction.

6. Remedies.

(a) HMI's entire liability and your exclusive remedy for defects in materials and workmanship shall be limited to replacement of the Software Media, which may be returned to HMI with a copy of your receipt at the following address: Software Media Fulfillment Department, Attn.: *C#: Your visual blueprint for building .NET applications*, Hungry Minds, Inc., 10475 Crosspoint Blvd., Indianapolis, IN 46256, or call 1-800-762-2974. Please allow four to six weeks for delivery. This Limited Warranty is void if failure of the Software Media has resulted from accident, abuse, or misapplication. Any replacement Software Media will be warranted for the remainder of the original warranty period or thirty (30) days, whichever is longer.

(b) In no event shall HMI or the author be liable for any damages whatsoever (including without limitation damages for loss of business profits, business interruption, loss of business information, or any other pecuniary loss) arising from the use of or inability to use the Book or the Software, even if HMI has been advised of the possibility of such damages.

(c) Because some jurisdictions do not allow the exclusion or limitation of liability for consequential or incidental damages, the above limitation or exclusion may not apply to you.

7. U.S. Government Restricted Rights. Use, duplication, or disclosure of the Software for or on behalf of the United States of America, its agencies and/or instrumentalities (the "U.S. Government") is subject to restrictions as stated in paragraph (c)(1)(ii) of the Rights in Technical Data and Computer Software clause of DFARS 252.227-7013, or subparagraphs (c) (1) and (2) of the Commercial Computer Software - Restricted Rights clause at FAR 52.227-19, and in similar clauses in the NASA FAR supplement, as applicable.

8. General. This Agreement constitutes the entire understanding of the parties and revokes and supersedes all prior agreements, oral or written, between them and may not be modified or amended except in a writing signed by both parties hereto that specifically refers to this Agreement. This Agreement shall take precedence over any other documents that may be in conflict herewith. If any one or more provisions contained in this Agreement are held by any court or tribunal to be invalid, illegal, or otherwise unenforceable, each and every other provision shall remain in full force and effect.

INDEX

Symbols & Numbers

+, additive operator, 42
*/, asterisk-slash characters
    ending a comment, 55
    XML documentation, 59
@,at sign character, verbatim string literal, 158
\, backslash character, escape sequences, 159
>,caret mark, truncated button bar indicator, 31
{ }, curly braces
    enumerations, 156
    interface accessors, 194
=!, equal sign/exclamation point, equality operator, 42
==, equal signs character
    equality operator, 42, 99
    string comparisons, 164
!=, inequality operator, string comparisons, 99
//, slash marks
    comment indicator, 54
    XML documentation, 58
/*, slash-asterisk characters
    beginning a comment, 55
    XML documentation, 59
[ ], square brackets, arrays, 136

A

abstract
    keyword
        base class specification, 71
        properties, 192–193
    class
        described, 66
        XMLWriter, 246
    properties
        declarations, 192–193
        described, 192
        restrictions, 193
accessibility levels, classes, 52–53
accessors
    described, 184
    get, 110
    interface, 194
    set, 110
Acrobat Reader, e-version of book, 290
Active Server Pages (ASP), 10
Add Class Wizard, 50–51, 67–69
Add Interface Indexer Wizard, 154–155
Add Method Wizard
    adding
        methods, 116–119
        static methods, 123

Add Reference dialog box, 262, 268
ADO.NET
    commands, 231
    connections, 230
    data adapters, 231
    described, 230
Alt key, switching between help topics, 19
Antechinus C# Programming Editor, CD-ROM, 290
API (Application Programming Interface), 238
application log, writing errors to, 284–285
Application Programming Interface (API), 238
applications
    ASP.NET support, 10
    creating with public assemblies, 256–259
    deploying
        with private assemblies, 258–259
        with shared assemblies, 264–265
    template types, 6
arithmetic operators
    constant expressions, 88
    described, 44
Array.IndexOf method, searching arrays, 148–149
Array.LastIndexOf method, searching arrays, 149
Array.Sort method, sorting arrays, 146–147
array-of-arrays (jagged arrays)
    adding to code, 142–143
    described, 136
arrays
    array-of-arrays (jagged arrays), 136, 142–143
    Arrays Tutorial, 137
    Console.WriteLine statement, 144
    declarations, 137
    described, 136
    enumerations, 156–157
    foreach statement, 144–145
    initializing, 137
    iterate through, 144–145
    multidimensional (rectangular), 136, 140–141
    search criteria, 148–149
    single-dimensional, 136, 138–139
    sorting, 146–147
    square brackets [and], 136
    structure rules, 141
    three-dimensional, 140–141
Arrays Tutorial, accessing, 137
ASP.NET Framework
    separation of user interface/user services, 217
    tracing code, 219

Visual studio.NET integration, 10
    Web Forms, 216–217
    Web project startup, 10–11
    Web site creation, 218–219
ASPEdit 2000, CD-ROM, 291
assemblies
    described, 253
    private, 252, 254–259
    shared, 260–269
    version binding policy, 268
    versioned configuration, 268–269
assembly, 53
AssemblyInfo class
    shared assemblies, 260–261
    version number configuration, 266
assignment statements, examples, 286
assignments, C# language comparisons, 3
Attribute Usage attribute, 46, 48
attributes
    AttributeTargets class, 48–49
    AttributeUsage, 46, 48
    Conditional, 46, 48
    described, 46
    inserting, 46–50
    Obsolete, 46, 48
    reflection process, 46
    structs, 153
    union, 83

B

backups, before installing Visual studio.NET, 37
base class
    abstract keyword, 71
    described, 68
base keyword, 76
blocks
    catch, 274, 280
    try/catch, 280
books
    Contents window groupings, 16–17
    scrolling topics, 17
bool keyword, 96–97
bool type, 88
Boolean type
    conversion non-support, 97
    described, 86, 96–97
    value assignments, 96–97
boxing
    described, 104
    value type/reference type conversions, 104–105
bug reports, logging, 62–63
Build Number version, 266
building blocks, 64

INDEX

INDEX

INDEX